BOOKS BY REV. IVAN STANG

THE BOOK OF THE SUBGENIUS
(WITH MANY OTHERS)

HIGH WEIRDNESS BY MAIL

A
DIRECTORY OF THE FRINGE

—MAD PROPHETS, CRACKPOTS,

KOOKS, AND TRUE VISIONARIES

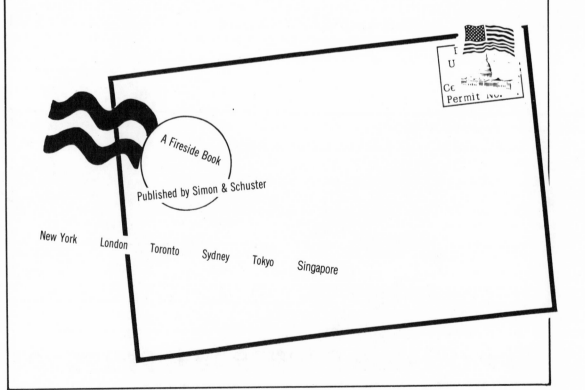

A Fireside Book

Published by Simon & Schuster

New York   London   Toronto   Sydney   Tokyo   Singapore

HIGH
WEIRDNESS
BY MAIL

REV. IVAN STANG

CHURCH OF
THE SUBGENIUS™

A FIRESIDE BOOK

PUBLISHED BY SIMON & SCHUSTER INC.

SIMON & SCHUSTER BUILDING

ROCKEFELLER CENTER

1230 AVENUE OF THE AMERICAS

NEW YORK, NEW YORK 10020

FIRESIDE AND COLOPHON ARE REGISTERED TRADEMARKS

OF SIMON & SCHUSTER INC.

DESIGNED BY BONNI LEON

MANUFACTURED IN THE UNITED STATES OF AMERICA

10 9 8 7 6

LIBRARY OF CONGRESS CATALOGING IN PUBLICATION DATA

Stang, Ivan.

  High weirdness by mail.

  "A Fireside book."

  1. Eccentrics and eccentricities—Directories—

Humor. 2. Associations, institutions, etc.—Directories—

Humor. 3. Mail order business—United States—

Directories—Humor. 4. Catalogs, Commercial—

Directories—Humor. I. Title. II. Title: Weirdness

by mail.

PN6231.E29S73   1988   016.65913'3   88-3607

ISBN 0-671-64260-X

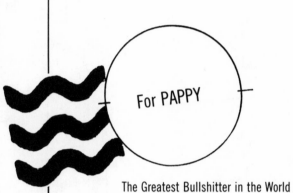

For PAPPY

The Greatest Bullshitter in the World

—Thanks for the genes!! They've come in handy.

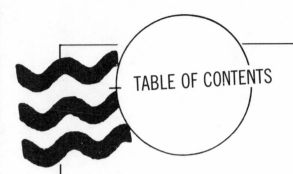

TABLE OF CONTENTS

PLACE STAMP HERE

Postal rates listed in this book were correct as we went to press. Please check with your post office for current rates. Avoid the horror and embarrassment of improper postage.

—The Publishers

Address

MAIL Today..

INSTRUCTIONS FOR USE

THE KEYS TO INSTANT SUCCESS, MYSTIC KNOWLEDGE, MIRACULOUS INVENTIONS, and CONTACT WITH THE SPACE BROTHERS ARE WITHIN YOUR GRASP!

—for only a 22¢ stamp!

Do you have "different" tastes? Intrigued by the bizarre, the kooky, the kinky—as long as it keeps its distance? Enjoy getting unsolicited, *unspeakably weird* things in the mail—for free? Love to snicker in superiority (perhaps largely imagined) at the incredible gullibility of others? Enjoy reading the headlines on sleazy tabloids, and ads for local psychic fortune-tellers? Appreciate unexpected glimpses of the strange "realities" behind religions other than your own? Entranced by the thought process of the mentally ill? Bored to tears by any music, video, and literature that *isn't* almost shockingly original?

    Painfully aware that all the great geniuses and inventors of the past appeared totally insane to everyone around them?

    Then . . .

HAVE WE GOT A HOBBY FOR YOU!!

    The Traveling Snake-Oil Medicine Show isn't dead—it just travels by mail. Simply by writing for information—*without sending money*—you can embark on a never-ending tour of the zoo of beliefs, the circus of gullibility, the freak show of faith, the arena of the utter strangeness of true genius, of that which is all-too-literally ahead of its time. (After all, sometimes the snake oil actually DID WORK!)

Your 22¢ investment will pay off geometrically as your address is sold from one mailing list to another. Soon, A MILLION CONTRADICTORY PATHS TO HAPPINESS will be vying for your *personal* attention in the mailbox, paths ranging from inadvertently hilarious delusions to the wisdom of the ages, yet—and this is the most revealing part— each one *the only TRUE PATH!!*

This book is essentially a collection of snide put-downs of hundreds of well-meaning, sincere people in all walks of extremism. Some are nice extremists. Some are *very* nasty. But, you ask, what earthly function could this book possibly serve, aside from providing a few disgusting mockers with a laugh or two, and giving their postmen hernias??

Who knows? You MIGHT just happen to stumble in these pages upon the *one religion* that will work in your life, or the clue that will lead you to the missing component of that invention to which you've devoted the last twenty years. The utter snideness in these pages may help deprogram some fence-straddling kid out of diving head-first into a soul-sapping vampire cult—or aid him in *finding* one, if that's what he needs. The broad range of belief systems and delusion styles covered (presenting, as they do, a vivid picture of the normally inconceivable *range* of human paradigms) may snap you out of a near-fatal rut of normalcy. It should also serve as a reminder of the actual freedom of superstition, degeneracy, hate, flimflam, and gullibility that we enjoy in the U.S. All that being so, *still,* this book's MAIN purpose *is indeed* to provide a bunch of mockers with a few good laughs.

If you sincerely desire a *truly* well-rounded education, you must study the extremists, the obscure and "nutty." You need the balance! Your poor brain is already being impregnated with middle-of-the-road crap, twenty-four hours a day, *no matter what*. Network TV, newspapers, radio, magazines at the supermarket...even if you never watch, read, listen, or leave your house, even if you are deaf and blind, the *telepathic pressure alone* of the uncountable Normals surrounding you will insure that you are automatically well-grounded in consensus reality. But screw consensus reality; what we all need is more of that ill-named *common sense* stuff...not really such a common commodity at all.

The great mystic J. R. "Bob" Dobbs often preached on this. "You know how dumb the average guy is?" he once asked his flock of apprentice Sales Ministers. "Well, by definition, half of them are even dumber than *that*." Sad but true, and getting worse each year. **The kooks are our future.** The average fifth-grader these days doesn't know whether Japan is a state or a city; wonders what happens when you get to the "edge" of the United States on a map; doesn't know, and *can't understand* what a glacier is; and even believes that the government is there to protect him! The years to come promise incredibly fertile fields for the sowing of superstition, cultism, and pseudoscience; they'll grow so fast we'll wonder if there had ever really been an Age of Reason. Make no mistake, it shall be a rich harvest for industrious Skull Farmers of every creed; the brains of the all-too-willings are out there, ripening, ingesting a rich loam of made-for-TV UFO movies, absurd claims for "holistic" vitamins, and radio preachers who converse with angels...millions of potential vegetables just waiting to be plucked, shucked, and hauled off to market.

But now, **you** will be ready for it.

Our Criteria For Listing

"Weird, cheap, and by mail" pretty much sums it up. "Weird," of course, is a subjective term. You may argue that some of these groups aren't weird at all, but perfectly normal, even commendable by your standards. Alright then, let's say I evaluated them in terms of how weird *my mother-in-law* might think they are. OK?

Most of the listings describe magazines, newsletters, cassettes, records, small gadgets, nostrums and remedies, catalogs—but few books or videotapes. Those aren't cheap, whereas sample magazines are often free. You can stumble upon classic crackpot paperbacks in any used bookstore, but I don't think you'll be finding any of *these magazines* in shopping malls. Few normal libraries would even allow them on premises! Also, the magazines discuss and advertise books, but not vice versa. Besides, I had to draw the line somewhere. There's a limit to how much crank literature through which even *I*, Stang, Professor Emeritus of Crackpotology, can wade before my nervous system suffers meltdown.

As will swiftly become obvious, the items listed aren't selected on any basis of "class" or even sanity—although one occasionally stumbles upon both—but a certain rare, delicate spirit of incurable psychosis. These are the uncut REAL THING—straight from the authentically diseased minds of transcendent visionaries and compulsive would-be saviors DRIVEN to communicate their CRUCIAL DISCOVERIES to a *SMIRKING* world.

The art magazines, comic books, music tapes, etc., are exceptions, in that their creators are generally quite deliberate about being weird. However, considerable pains have been taken to cull out the merely "artsy" or avant-garde. Only the borderline psychos of the art and entertainment worlds grace these pages.

And, of course, there are bound to be some people listed here who have actually made stupendous breakthroughs and who, while we sit here mocking, are accomplishing more than we in our smugness could possibly imagine.

I make not the slightest pretense of completeness. This is only a sampling, a cross section. One *can't* be truly comprehensive with something like this; for years I'll be seeing fantastic new nut tracts and tearing my hair that I didn't encounter them in time for this book. There's no end, Praise Dobbs, to the variety of *apparently senseless* human explorations into new mental territories. Whether the quests be for bucks, enlightenment, or eternal youth, there will always be people crazy enough to brazenly march right past that brink of rationality and over the cliff. And you should be damned thankful for that! Historically, it's always been the kooks and the crazies who were *dumb enough* to "fight City Hall" and stand up against the blind colossi of political oppression, status quo science, and "good taste."

The subjects have been divided into the categories of science, religion, politics, art, and so on, then broken down into vaguely related subclusters. These divisions are by necessity somewhat arbitrary; in the world of philosophical misfits, normally unconnected subject matters tend to meld into one another. UFO contacteeism, "channeling," and speaking in tongues, for instance, might as well have been lumped together. Rather than repeatedly list things that cross many categories, I've pigeonholed them for your convenience, though probably to the outrage of some of the listees. Thus, you'd be making a mistake to read only those sections you assume will interest you. You should at least *skim* the whole thing for what may be a quite *disturbing* picture of human philosophical variety.

Science explains the physical world, art explains the emotional world, politicians "explain" themselves, and religions explain the unexplainable (which may lead some to suspect those particular explanations) . . . cram all these ingredients into a brain in turmoil, set controls to "blend," scramble them all together in a big mental slurry, and, VOILA! FREE ENTERTAINMENT!

WHERE LAYETH THE BLAME

I didn't locate all of these groups and write every listing by myself. I copped quite a few descriptions from three of my fellow self-published writers: Mark "Remote Control" Johnston of *The Amazing Colossal Mindblaster* magazine, Mike Gunderloy of *Factsheet Five,* (both of which regularly feature listings like this), and Waves Forest and his *Further Connections* report. Waves's are kept separate from the others, quarantined, so to speak, because his intentions are far more benign than the rest of ours. Mike Gunderloy's original reviews, for that matter, were so maddeningly fair and objective that I altered many of them to more closely match the caustic, insensitive tone set by myself and Johnston.

Less frequently, I also cannibalized the writings of a few other crankwatchers: Tim Cridland (*Off the Deep End* magazine), Lou Minatti (*The Subjectivist League*), Johnny Marr, Candi Strecker (*Sidney Suppey's . . . Confused Pet Monthly*), and Stephen Doig (reporter for a major metropolitan newspaper that would no doubt prefer to remain nameless).

These writers are credited ((in double parentheses)) at the very end of each of their listings, and addresses/prices for their own indispensable publications are to be found in the very last section, "Sources of Sources." They represent the up-and-coming "new wave" of Crackpot-'n'-Cult Impressarios, the very "voices" of the Kook Generation.

The good Will ("O'Dobbs") Frazier performed the unenviable chore of retyping the other writers' listings—most of them originally reproduced in eyestrainingly tiny reduced print—onto computer discs.

Tim McGinnis, our editor and most valued Conspiracy infiltrator, doubled his already high sainthood status by once again convincing a major publisher that there is an audience for full-tilt strangeness.

Respected kook-spotter Ted Schultz originally got the ball rolling when he asked me to contribute reviews like these to the special issue of *Whole Earth Review* that he guest-edited (#52, the all-weirdness special). Many of these reviews come from that article. Even before that, I had printed a few of them in the official Church of the SubGenius journal, *The Stark Fist of Removal.*

Eternal thanks (but no royalty checks) are also due Jay Kinney (who started long before I did), all the speciality mags in which I found promising addresses, Popess Dominatrix Cecelia Pinson-Smith (for helping mail the 500 letters double-checking the addresses), and a whole slew of people who suggested subjects for listing: T.J. Tellier, Rev. Bag of Water, Seth Deitch, Byron Werner, G. Gordon Gordon, D. Lee Lama, Bob Lee, the original Puzzling Evidence, the original Drs. for "Bob" of Little Rock, LIES, Hal Robins, Sterno Keckhaver, Nanzi Regalia, Carl Tralla, Pat Daley, Mike Flores, Dennis Cripps, Glenn Bray, and no doubt many other associate members of the Church of the SubGenius.*

I must confess that some of the sarcastic phrases, witty one-liners, and evocative metaphors which pepper the commentary are not mine, but were borrowed from my esteemed colleague in SubGenius preaching, St. Janor Hypercleats. Too many other worthies to name have also been plagiarized, although to a lesser extent.

Finally, there is no way to overstate my debt to my lifelong friend and spiritual mentor, the great Dr. Philo Drummond—the man who not only brought me to "Bob" Dobbs, sharpened my appreciation of deranged extremism, and instigated our collecting (and subsequent exploitation) of crank literature to begin with, but whose very being exemplifies both the highest and lowest forms of SubGenius enlightenment. His philosophy, developed under "Bob" Dobbs' personal tutorship and further honed by his own dauntless pursuit of Slack Awareness, has immeasurably influenced—some would say tainted—my entire worldview and hence the style of this book. I can honestly state that without Dr. Drummond's inspiration and counseling, this project would never have seen print. If you're looking for someone besides me to punish for perpetrating this book, it's only fair that Dr. Drummond be your next target.

I JUST DON'T UNDERSTAND YOU PEOPLE! YOU ISSUE DIRECTORIES LISTING EVERYTHING FROM SOUP TO NUTS...

Someone else, as always, provided the will to go on, an excuse for existence, and two excellent reasons for charging enough for my work.

As for the reports . . .

They're short, to begin with, partly to match modern attention spans and partly so that you could afford or, indeed, even *lift* this book.

* My editor tells me that to preserve credibility, I mustn't talk too much about my own *favorite* cult, the Church of the SubGenius, simply because I happen to be president of that group's P.R. and sales arm, the SubGenius Foundation, Inc., as well as owner of the Sacred Trademark, editor of the Media Barrage radio tapes, and smiter of the "Bobbies" . . . thus creating, he suggests, a slight conflict of interest. Therefore, I'll instead refer to the soul-preserving tenets of this ONE TRUE CHURCH only obliquely, in footnotes and asides. A LOT of footnotes and asides.

And OBJECTIVITY? HA! *It is to laugh.* Don't look for your so-called objectivity here! As Sacred Scribe of the Church of the Sub-Genius, I can lay claim to being every bit as "cranky" and "kooky" as any of my victims listed herein. But at least I'm honest about it. You wonder how I got this way? From working on this book and previous projects like it, literally wading through roomfuls of crank literature for weeks on end! How can a person take *any* of it seriously, after seeing the totality in such broad perspective? Gazing upon the physical evidence of the *full range* of human folly, day after day, on this vast scale, made this one of the most mind-blowing jobs I've ever done—and I specialize in mind-blowing jobs. (A warning for youngsters who think that sounds like fun: unless you know somebody, it takes almost twenty years to build a "rep"!)

Iron-hided cynicism was clearly the only practical point of view from which to approach materials that represent their makers' most fervently cherished beliefs. To grossly insult almost everyone listed was the only way to be *fair.* Certainly, many of the listees will be furious at the way they are described, the callousness with which their entire world is held up to ridicule, and the casual manner in which matters of potentially global importance are dismissed.* However, I would think they'd be used to it by now.

You see, years of diligently studying the Word of Dobbs grants one the ability to instantly voice strong opinions on any subject even while possessing little or no real knowledge about it. That's what you're paying for, anyway ... opinions so overblown they make you laugh. After all, this book has to SELL! (And at worst, it'll probably be seen by a lot more people than most of the kook publications will, simply by virtue of mainstream distribution! Ironic, isn't it? PROOF that there's NO JUSTICE, when snide bastards like mè rake in the cash while sweet little old New Age ladies, after striving to be positive and spiritual their entire lives, can't even get *one serious newspaper story* printed about their communications with the Light Beings from Arcturus!) But, as Dr. Gene Scott said to his TV flock one night while showing off the personal wealth he had amassed with their love offerings, "Hey—you don't want a *stupid* preacher, do you?" Like Dr. Scott, I'm giving you and me, both, credit for some intelligence, if not for any sense of moral integrity, political responsibility, or sound artistic judgment.

And yet ...

Believe it or not, some of my belittling comments are for "noble" ulterior purposes. As long as I'm sarcastic as hell, implying that these people are "kooks," this book will not be suppressed; it doesn't overtly threaten the establishment knowledge conspiracies. BUT THE ADDRESSES STILL GET OUT THERE. Information is power, and the real idea here is to keep the information flowing by hook or by crook. The entertainment value of the sar-

---

* I hope this does piss you off, you DUMBASS ZEALOTS! Hell, go ahead, bring on those psychic curses! Beg your "gods" to destroy me! I fear none of your pitiful witch-doctor hexes, based as they are on patently absurd superstitions —for the Power of the Almightly "Bob" gives me Dominion over you. Begone, unclean spirit!

casm makes the difference between 50,000 copies being printed by a huge book company, or 5,000 being printed by me. Copies of this "funny book" will be floating around for years, whereas more serious studies will be so rare and/or inconvenient to locate as to be practically nonexistent . . . and easily confiscatable.

So I could claim that I've rudely trashed these well-meaning innocents only so that YOU, the UNBELIEVER, will be able to find this book, order secret wisdom from these "kooks," *and then make up your own mind as to whether they're really nuts, or unsung geniuses with the keys to planetary salvation right under our uncomprehending, nay, even MOCKING noses.*

HELPFUL HINTS

Few hobbies are simpler. Here's how it's done:

You type up a form letter, saying something ambiguous like, "I am interested in your product/services. Please send details, catalog." Xerox a few dozen copies of it. Go through this book, as well as the cheesy ads in the back of your favorite lowbrow magazines (*Soldier of Fortune,* perhaps, or the *Weekly World News,* or that great old standby, the *National Enquirer*), and mail off for anything that interests you. With the more fanatical groups, a simple request for information like this can net you several

thick volumes of priceless *bulldada* (a collectors' term meaning "that which is great because it doesn't know how bad it is"). If you take the time to ask for "complete info" in just the right way—tricking them into seeing you as a potential long-term customer—the most desperate crackpots can be gold mines. A rule of thumb seems to be that the weirder and broker they are, the more they'll send. It's supply and demand. There's no demand for the truths they so selflessly hold out to a scoffing world, so if you show even the slightest interest they'll bombard you by mail with lurid accounts of their amazing discoveries.

I have never spent a penny (aside from the initial 22¢ stamp and 4¢ Xerox) on 95 percent of these groups.*

However, not all of those listed are stupid kooks, by any means. Some are smart kooks, and the "free info request" letter does not work with them. Send them whatever meager money they require, and do it quickly. The miraculous doesn't hang around forever.

Generally, the religious, political, and fringe science groups in the first half of the book are good for freebies. The weird entertainment sources in the last half—comic publishers, bands, etc.—usually want to see some green. Prices are shown at the end of each review. If there's no price listed, it's a giveaway. And when it says to "send SASE," that means "self-addressed, stamped envelope." Even if SASE isn't required, throwing in a loose 22¢ stamp or two will always help insure that you get maximum goods.

Spirit mediums, UFO contactees, fly-by-night Mystery Schools, and self-publishing artists are notoriously short-lived, although

* I did pay for my membership in the Couch Potatoes Lodge—but that's one that I really *believe* in.

I've been amazed at how long some of the least likely ones have been located in one place, consistently churning out manifestos and come-ons. At the time of this writing, all addresses were active, but we can't guarantee how long they'll last. A few are bound to have moved by the time you write them.

Likewise, we can't be held responsible for the regularity, or lack thereof, with which subscriptions and orders may be filled. If you send for something but get no reply, don't jump to conclusions. Most of the time it's because the money, letter, or goods got lost in the postal system.

WHEN ORDERING U.S. MAGAZINES, CANADIANS SHOULD ALWAYS ADD EXTRA MONEY FOR POSTAGE, AND VICE VERSA. WHEN ORDERING FROM OVERSEAS, ADD AS MUCH EXTRA MONEY AS YOU THINK IT *SHOULD* COST FOR POSTAGE, AND THEN DOUBLE IT.

Canadians will usually accept U.S. funds, though the reverse isn't true. When ordering from other countries, you may have to get currency converted at a large bank, or obtain IRCs from the post office.

When sending checks, particularly to the more obscure, small-time outfits, look to see if there is a human's name on the address line below the name of the publication. If there is, make the check to the human. Many don't have business accounts.

Never be shy about writing back to publishers with comments, pro or con. Cranks thrive on hate mail; it reinforces the heady, delicious feeling of being a one-eyed man in the country of the blind. Try to put yourself in their shoes. Imagine how it feels to be one of the ignored, the mocked, those spurned by the "Thems" who control our minds with their small, limited concepts of "fine art" and "accepted scientific theory"—the very *scourges* of intelligence, distracting people from the essential truths at hand. . . .

Some of these gems come in sloppy packages, but don't be fooled by appearances. The old "You get what you pay for" mantra is true of machines, appliances, and printing techniques, but is often very misleading when it comes to art, ideas, writing, music, and particularly *information.*

SHOULD YOU MENTION THIS BOOK?

USE YOUR JUDGMENT. There aren't really any overpowering reasons to do so.

With artists and the more sane-appearing researcher-types, it won't hurt to tell them you found them here. With the "kooks" (go ahead and define that term for yourself—*I trust your judgment*), avoid any reference to this book, or they may decide you're a mocker out to persecute them—as they're sure to believe I am doing.

WARNINGS!

1. Don't fall into the trap of the fanatical completist collector. It must NOT become a compulsion. Be thankful that "perfection" is merely a convenient mental construct, an impossible ideal—especially in a field with horizons as infinite, and ridiculous, as human opinions. Sloppiness and incompleteness are necessary adjuncts to unrestrained, fully intuitive discernment. That's why you DON'T want to end up like me, with so much more crap coming in the mail every day than you can possibly read, that you don't want to read *any* of it. It can easily get to the point where you're hard-pressed just to keep *boxing* it, much less enjoying it.

2. Beware of "Viewpoint Shock," resulting in depression. Never kid yourself that you've seen it all. No matter how weird you think you are, sooner or later you're going to encounter someone much weirder. Overexposure to conflicting alien belief systems can leave you seeing the world as one big locked ward in which even the doctors are hopelessly insane. Kook literature has a way of creeping into your own thought processes, until you become as paranoid as they are. But never lose sight of the benefits: you get to pick from a huge choice of afterlives, second chances, reasons to feel superior, guardian angels, and, of course, scapegoats (Where would *any* religion be without scapegoats?)

3. If you're going to pursue this seriously, it might be a good idea to rent a post-office box (about $25 a year) or other type of mail drop as insurance against Klansmen and

Moonies showing up at your door. It won't stop the Feds, though! They get curious about people who subscribe to certain magazines. You can offset this by requesting mail from so many opposing groups that they realize you're just a fellow snooper, and blow you off, rather than away.

You might also use a fake name, or a contracted version of your real name, so the Saucer Nazis and Men-in-Black can't track you down. The problem there is that some mailpersons won't deliver to aliases, unless you tell them you're using the "pen name." On the other hand, I've used my home address for years, and I haven't once had any kook, psychotic, holy man, or enlightened genius appear at my door. The Secret Service, yes. But they weren't trying to sell me anything; they just wanted to know what the hell this "Bob Cult" thing was all about. (They left as ordained SubGenius ministers!) Otherwise, no one's ever bothered us. BUGGED us, perhaps, and in more ways than one.... But as for raging, axhandle-wielding fanatics, no. WAIT!! What's that noise outside the window?? It's . . . no. . . . GLEAUAAAGH!!!

4. Waves Forest adds this: "In the case of political, social, or scientific reform groups, bear in mind that the international intelligence networks have thousands of personnel just for the purpose of penetrating such groups and steering them along directions less likely to threaten the established power structures. Generally, the smaller they are, the less likely they are to be severely infil-

trated. There are also organizations actually created by the CIA or related agencies to look like they are run by concerned private citizens. These act as 'vacuum cleaners' to suck in the genuine concerned citizens, reassured that since such an organization exists they don't need to set up their own. With their reformist urges channeled along 'acceptable' paths they feel like they're making a difference without actually doing anything that might weaken the top monopolies.... The most obvious of these, such as U.S. A.I.D., the National Cancer Institute, World Watch Institute, and others have been left out, but odds are that in a list this size, a few such phony reform groups may have slipped by. Use your own intuition in deciding who to link up with."

In all of the upcoming categories, there are many other publications besides the listed samples. But they all review each other. Unlike the mainstream newstand magazine publishers, who often refuse even paid ads from their rivals, hardly any of these little publishers and ranters are in it for money. They are compelled by a desire to share. (Forget for a second that you don't really *want* what they're begging you to take.) Despite all the compulsions, delusions, bitterness, and fanaticism that mark so many fringe cause groups, the drive to share gives the worst of them a measure of dignity that the popular slick publishers can't seem to comprehend. They may be wrong, insane,

simpleminded, or whatever; but, with only a few exceptions, they mean what they say. They're sincere. In that respect, these kooks and weirdos possess truer humanity—faults and follies notwithstanding—than many of those who gave them that label. Or, I should say, who gave US that label.

I *love* the kooks and weirdos. True, I'm raking them over the coals, but I'm also putting their addresses in front of thousands of people. And, believe it or not, I can't even find it in my heart to totally hate our common foes, the Normals. Without that vast majority of complacent, unthinking Normals, life for the weirdos would be *too easy*. Without Normals, in fact, weirdos would have no reason to be weird!

One thing, then, we can know for certain: it takes all kinds.

PLACE
STAMP
HERE

HIGH
WEIRDNESS
BY
MAIL

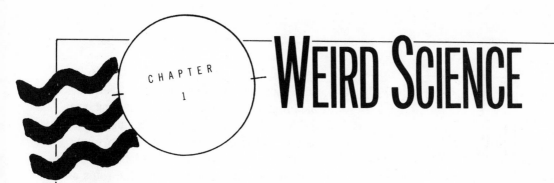

CHAPTER 1

WEIRD SCIENCE

When writing to these outfits, it's a good idea to sound as nutty as they do. You'll get faster service and a lot more loot.* But keep in mind that some may not be nearly as "nutty" as you think, lost as you are in a backwash of "conventional science" ignorance.

Of course, to you, this is all a joke, a parade of "crazy people" for you to sneer at—ha, ha—but will you be laughing quite so hard when you're shivering in a concentration camp hovel in 1993, knowing, finally, that half of what these kooks said was TRUE, but you *ignored* it; knowing that the "silly kooks" you MOCKED *could* have ushered in a new PARADISE ON EARTH had not people like you *laughed* at them? **Will it be so funny then?**

---

* As "Bob" said, "If you act like a dumb shit, they'll treat you as an equal."

THE EARTH IS THE CENTER OF THE UNIVERSE!

Bible-Science Association
2911 E. Forty-second St.
Minneapolis, MN 55406

Your headquarters for Creationism over Evolution. The booklet *Geocentricity* offers, for 35¢, biblical *and scientific* proof that the earth is standing still at the center of a revolving cosmos. I'm with them—screw those telescopes and all that astronomy stuff anyway. Humanists like Copernicus, who say this planet is nothing special, are just trying to avoid thinking about The Judgment. "It is not the Earth that is spinning, but the sky that is spinning." *Something's* spinning, that's for sure. Loaded with very sincere "scientific" babbling; their logo is an atom hovering over a Bible! Free catalog of books, audio cassettes, and videos on the *real* history of our planet, all biblically verified. Adam and Eve lived 6,000 years ago. Videos of the ruins of their home, and also of the Tower of Babel. Native Americans are ancient Hebrews. Photos of the Ark of the Covenant. "Giant Man Tracks" next to dinosaur footprints in Texas prove nine-foot-tall Covenant Men walked with the Great Reptiles. (One interesting thing they keep defiantly pointing out: if the story of Adam's fall into sin and death in the Garden of Eden is a myth, then Jesus was on the *wrong planet!!*) These people have spent a LOT of money searching for the fossil of Noah's Ark on a mountain in Turkey. 50¢ for a dozen tracts; newsletter, $12/year.

Another "demonination" of this profoundly influential movement is **THE TYCHONIAN SOCIETY**, 4527 Wetzel Ave., Cleveland, OH 44109. Send for sizable *free* bulletins packed with articles proving the Bible infallible through arcane mathematical and geological arguments! Much "higher-brow" than the Bible-Science group, which makes it all the more peculiar. Dunno why they even mess with the detailed "scientific" arguments— their bottom line is that God Said It, They Believe It, and That Settles It. And try **THE INSTITUTE FOR RESTORING ANCIENT HISTORY**, PO Drawer 495, Winfield, KS 67156—they know where to find the ruins of the Tower of Babel, and both Arks (Noah's and the Ark of the Covenant). They're also rabidly anti-Catholic. . . .

...And It's Also Flat!

Flat Earth News

International Flat Earth Research Society
$10.00 yearly to Associate Members only.

Box 2533, Lancaster, California 93539-2533
Phone: (805) 946-1595

Quarterly   **RESTORING THE WORLD TO SANITY**
Charles K. Johnson, President   **Marjory Waugh Johnson, Secretary**

International Flat Earth
Research Society
(of Covenant People's Church)
Box 2533, Lancaster, CA 93539

The unutterable stupidity and vanity of those who STILL MAINTAIN against all common sense that the world is "round" will soon learn the hard way, when they fall off the edge. Well, that's an exaggeration. There is no edge; the flat world just stretches on and on into infinity. I mean, these folks aren't *kooks* or anything! In fact, they're obviously almost the last sane humans left...just ask them! If the world were "round," they reason, then Australians would hang by their feet! They don't, so all this occult gibberish called "science" is disproven. Yet NO ONE WILL LISTEN. Look at the ocean—it is FLAT. It is a LAW of GOD that water lays flat. So where's the CURVE?? "Airplanes all fly Level on this Plane Earth." This is "...the oldest continuous Society existing on the world today. It began with the Creation of the Creation.... We are...the Elite, the Elect, who use Logic Reason are Rational [*sic*]. Summed up, we are Sane and/or have Common Sense are contrasted to the 'herd' who is unthinking and uncaring.... The Fact the Earth is Flat is not my opinion...it is a Proved Fact. Also demonstrated the Sun and Moon are about 3,000 miles away.... The Planets are 'tiny.' Sun and Moon DO Move, earth does NOT move, whirl, spin and gyrate.... Only the illogical, unreasoning "Herd" prefers the way-out occult theology of the old Greek superstition earth a spinning ball!" [Punctuation his.]

$6 for Flat Earth Map, $10/year for newsletter; beg and plead for their info. Anybody who's this cantankerous must be *pretty OLD*, so write soon before this World Class Ranter goes to his Reward in Heaven (which is *up*). Say you BELIEVE!! Send 'em a big SASE.

Miracle Device Renders Aluminum Harmless!

Ministry of Dietetic Law
Box 825, Vacaville, CA 95688

These concerned citizens sell a Polarity Pillow that negates the toxic effects of that deadly poison, aluminum (the very "Valium" of metals), which has been introduced into our environment to sap our will.

Time Cameras! Antigravity Devices! 4 Sale Cheap!

Active R&D
PO Box 323
Coeur d' Alene, ID 83814

Ask for catalog of build-it-yourself plans for Lucid Dream Machines! Antigravitics! Contacting aliens! Increased gas mileage! Aura Energizers! Focalizing Crystal Power Rods! Psychotronic ESP-amplifiers. Spaceship plans. Time cameras. *Time cameras?* The damn secrets of the universe have been for sale right under our noses all this time, and nobody's paid any attention! Although shot through with side-splittingly bizarre claims, this is nonetheless a good source for technical books on suppressed research areas like antigravity, orgone therapy, free energy systems (once called "perpetual motion machines"), psychotronics (psychic power amplifiers), and so on. Keep in mind that *if* these things are for real, companies and governments such as Mobil Oil, the AMA, and the Current Administration Corporation would *want* them to look like the ravings of acid-damaged Utopian dreamers. Free sample of newsletter *Hyperview,* or $11.95/year.

The Hollow Earth Spews Forth Demons

Shavertron
PO Box 248, Vallejo, CA 94590

In vast tunnels beneath our planet dwell quasi-physical entities called Deros, who date back to prehistory—and who still prey on humans by mind control. This discovery by the late Richard Shaver is kept alive and thrashing in this magazine, which is actually balanced by healthy doses of humor and skepticism. The editor has a great handle on the whole issue of harrassment by invisible entities. Or didn't you know that was an issue? Not entirely a kookzine, but also a forum for kook-theory *fans.* Send $3 for sample. Last I heard, they'd stopped publishing new ones, but still have plenty of great back issues.

Communist Descendants Of The Abominable Snowman

Inner Portraits by
Stanislav Szukalski
Glenn Bray, PO Box 4482
Sylmar, CA 91342

This large, fancily printed book is a real treasure on two normally conflicting counts: Szukalski's artwork is astonishing, while his bizarre discoveries in his science of Zermatism, to which his art relates, are among the most compellingly weird this writer has encountered. There are two races: true Humans, and *Yetinsyn* half-breeds, the degenerate progeny of human women raped by Yetis (i.e., Bigfoots, Pans, Abominable Snowmen). The Yetinsyny tend to be criminals, communists, and dictators. There's far more to it than that, though, and it's nearly impossible to do justice to the *style* of this book; Szukalski is an unsung Crazed Genius whose written rants, beautiful art, and tragic life story all swing between the upliftingly surreal and the psychotically paranoid. A god among kooks. $12.95 postpaid and actually well worth it! (Serious Zermatists can pursue further studies in a series of videotaped Szukalski lectures—$38.50 each.)

It Will Be 2000 A.D. Next Year!

New Beginnings Newsletter
20 Fairway Hills
Waynesville, NC 28786

Halley's Comet was a portent, warning you to report for active duty in the upcoming Final Battle. "Time has been shortened, and in 11 months it will be the year 2000.... But what must be done with those of mingled serpent seed and the seed of fallen angels?" Identity Christianity (a popular right-wing theory that says Anglo-Saxons are the true

Israel) is foretold in the dimensions of the Great Pyramid! Plus the usual Rockefeller/Zionist–hate. Monthly newsletter available "on freewill offering basis"; lots of sick racist cassettes also offered.

GENUINE HIERONYMOUS INSTRUMENTS!! NO CHEAP FAKES!!

Advanced Sciences Advisory Journal
PO Box 109, Lakemont, GA 30552

Dr. Hieronymous sells radionic beam projectors and Cosmic Pipes through this newsletter, which also runs articles on Universal Energy, psychotronics, gravity control, and the like. A small Cosmic Pipe of, say, forty acres is only $500! These are not the IMITATION Hieronymous Instruments, folks. Your soul is a gravity field; "the universe was *created* and all systems are in a state of *devolution*." Are we not men? But I shouldn't make fun; the actual scientific content of these psychotronic mags is so far over my head that for all I know, they may be entirely right! What's tough is not *knowing*. Dr. Hieronymous is one of the most respected persons in his field! $2.50 each/$15 yearly.

THE ULTIMATE SUPERBRAIN HUMAN FUNCTIONING SECRETS!

Modern Humans
Fry's, 22511 Markham
Perris, CA 92370

Incredible free tabloid catalog comes in two parts—first, ads for various rare books and folios on psychotronic technology, Crystal Levitators, time machines, Tesla space-drive inventions, pyramid power, alien aircraft on the moon, divining rods, perpetual motion machines, etc. Second half is a giant come-on for the "Modern Humans" course in Superbrain energies, much of which is devoted to explaining why they charge so much. This catalog will allow you to hold up your end of the conversation while talking to street-corner weirdos and bag people. "Our Time Camera covers from one hour to 99 million years! Just think what you could do! You'll have a blast with this gem of a unit!" We can only pray that this knowledge does not fall into the wrong hands! But don't worry; the government and the scientific establishment will make damn sure of that, because the wrong hands might be yours. Best feature is the primitive clip-art. Send $1 for more detailed catalogs.

CHARACTER ANALYSIS OF THE STARS THROUGH BIORHYTHM!

The Truth
PO Box 3893-TRU
Chatsworth, CA 91313

Much easier than astrology! Celebrity Biorhythm charts; penetrating insights into the lives of nobodies; case histories of murderers "explained" by this new science. Peppered with oddball opinions and curious jargon. Order your own in-depth analysis—or learn this art yourself! $8/twelve issues; ask for free sample.

CASSETTE TAPE LECTURES IN THE FORBIDDEN SCIENCES!

1st Church of Mr. Science
Seth Dietch, ℅ Chalfen
25 Grant St.
Cambridge, MA 02138

Extremely convoluted explanations for why everything is so...so...*so much the way it is.* Lecture Series Tape #1 describes, through narration and sound effects, a newly discovered time-warping subatomic particle —the Mutron—that is responsible for everything from Jesus to the extinction of the dinosaurs. Side two has a lecture called "Facts About the Beforelife." The Universe is now 90 percent explained! Unlike most metaphysical tapes, these are quite fast-paced and loaded with funny sound effects and momentous musical flourishes. Great for mysterious airplay on radio, you DJ's. There are at least three tapes in this series. $5 per sixty-minute stereo cassette.

UNIVERSE TWO: NOT BETTER, JUST DIFFERENT

The Quarternion Journal
Alice Hall, PO Box 315, Station 'A'
Vancouver, B.C., Canada V6C-2M7

Devotes itself to "highly abstract possibilities in science and art." Highly abstract is right! Nuttiest damn theories on logic, reality, and the universe you could hope to find. Bizarre diagrams illustrating the foundations of existence. This is what you might call "naive quantum physics." No price listed; send $2 and request sample of #1.

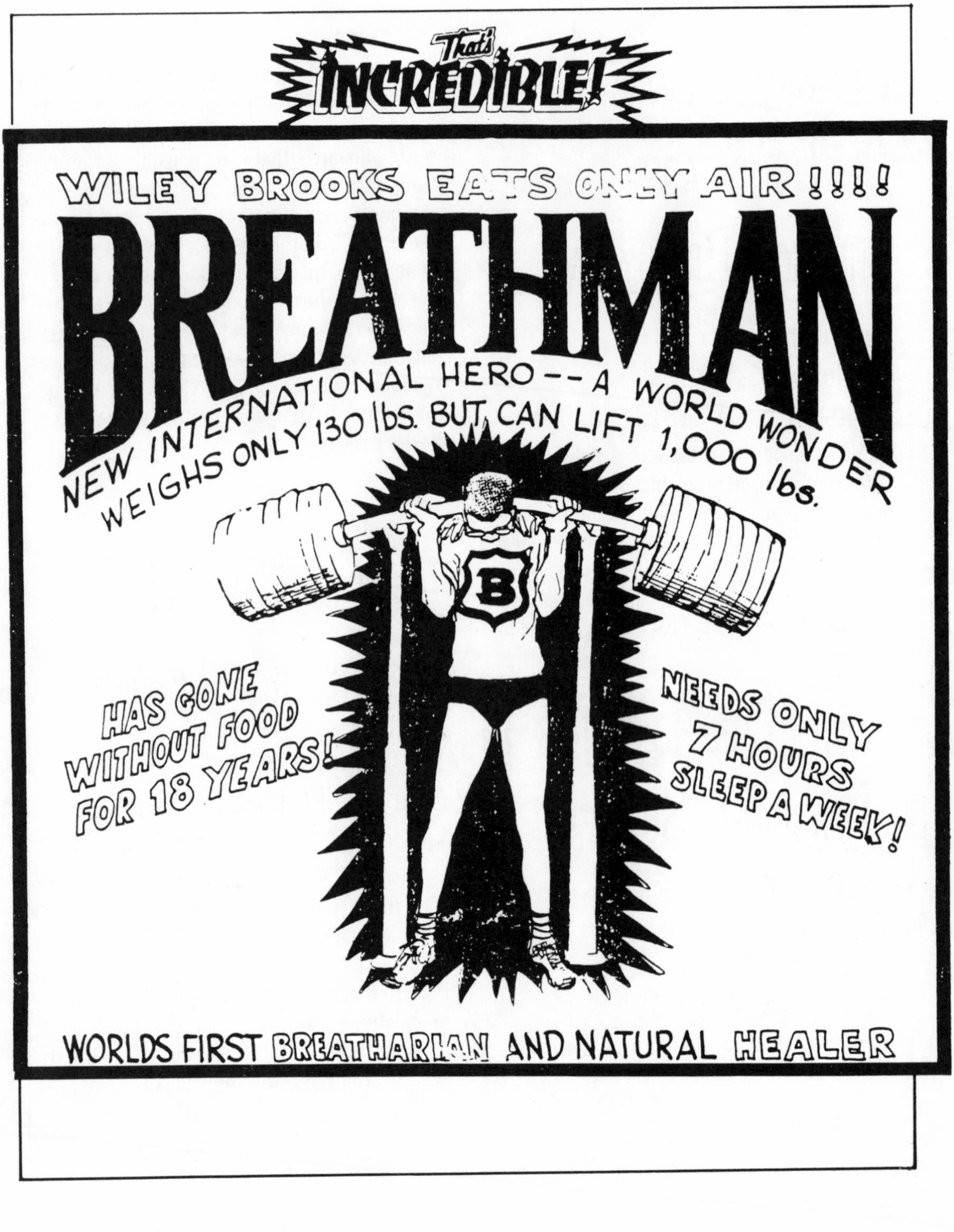

That's INCREDIBLE!
WILEY BROOKS EATS ONLY AIR !!!!
BREATHMAN
NEW INTERNATIONAL HERO -- A WORLD WONDER
WEIGHS ONLY 130 lbs. BUT CAN LIFT 1,000 lbs.
B
HAS GONE WITHOUT FOOD FOR 18 YEARS!
NEEDS ONLY 7 HOURS SLEEP A WEEK!
WORLDS FIRST BREATHARIAN AND NATURAL HEALER

HEALTHFUL LIVING BY EATING AIR!

Breatharians
PO Box 833, Larkspur, CA 94939

Eating is merely an acquired habit. Wiley Brooks, the guru of Breatharianism, espouses a system of physical vitality by which one may stop eating and drinking entirely, and live, lichenlike, off light and air. "Modern man is the degenerate descendant of the Breatharian, and has descended through five stages: Breatharianism, Liquidarianism, Fruitarianism, Vegetarianism, and Carnivorism." This health cult's faith was severely shaken when Brooks was discovered to have been sneaking out at night and buying junk food at convenience stores for all these years. Presumably, his followers have forgiven this serious backsliding, but it's left them on shaky ground so don't send money until you ascertain that they're still there.

TOLD YOU SO!

Coming Changes
937 St. Mary's St.
De Pere, WI 54115

Compilation of news concerning earthquakes, sunspots, economic disasters, etc. . . . Unseasonable weather we've been having lately, eh? Signs of the Tribulation Period

and the Last Days! Safe geological areas pinpointed! The whole idea is that these events are foretold in Christian prophecy, Edgar Cayce prophecy, and dang near every other kind of prophecy. Actually, the editor does provide a nice rundown of *patterns* of scary events, which point, of course, to some monumental social upheaval ANY MINUTE NOW. . . . The clippings are most useful to us religio-sadists as a morbid compendium of disaster news. Also provides a good sense of the hugeness of our planet and the infinite number of misfortunes that can befall us. (Which, to me, paints an odd picture of the Lord as sick humorist.) Bimonthly newsletter, $18/year; beg for free sample.

DOWSER'S SUPPLIES

Dowser's Precision Supply Co.
McCormick Bldg., Suite 11
Trinidad, CO 81082

Catalog of divining rods and other accessories for the dowser, such as "false image rejector rods," special oil and gas dowsing rods, pendulums, and other psychic tools. An experienced dowser can scan *maps* for water, mineral veins, gas pockets, hidden toxic-waste sites, etc. Another product, the little Psionic Generator, has vanes that spin when stared at. Free brochure.

Another company with more high-priced dowsing gear (plus radionics and radiesthesia equipment for diagnosing illnesses) is Bruce Copen Labs., "Highfield," Dane Hill, Haywards Heath, Sussex RH 177EX, England.

Lakeside Resort Condos Of The Gods

The Steele Group
Steele, IL 60919

"Dawn of a New Age City"—an actual New Age town where you can escape the end of the world and learn from the "ancient Brotherhood..." except that it isn't quite built yet. Based on *The Ultimate Frontier,* a techno-occult book foretelling disasters for the turn of the century. Starts off looking like a planned community built on alternate technology—fuel alcohol, wind energy, hydroponics...then you find out they're going to make you an "Initiate" of the White Brotherhood, and you have to kiss your capacity for critical thought bye-bye. Free info.

One-stop Weird Science Source

Borderland Sciences Research Foundation
PO Box 429
Garberville, CA 95440–0429

Among the granddaddies of weird science, these folks have been around since 1945—long before New Age latecomers. They publish papers on subjects like ether physics, radionics, dowsing, Nikola Tesla's mind-boggling inventions, hollow earth, UFOs, cancer cures, etc. Their bimonthly *Journal of Borderland Research* features nifty plans for all kinds of build-it-yourself devices like Jet Lag Neutralizers and Homo-Vibra Ray Machines, some of which they also sell preassembled. Also serves as a contact nexus for other Bold Surrealist Scientists. The journal is $20/year or $3.50 for a sample; write for free info.

The Living Sphere, also issued by this group, is equally diverse and intriguing, but more concerned with myth and the supernatural, especially the more bizarre legends, cults, and paranormal reports from foreign lands. Wacky at times, but deliberately so... they have fun with the occult. *BUT AT WHAT COST??* Well, at the cost of $4/sample, $20/year.

An Amazing *Upside Down* Discovery In Science!

Alphonse Pitner
1301 E. Druid Rd.
Clearwater, FL 33516

Hand-written announcements detailing a discovery sure to shake the very foundation of mathematical sciences. Almost completely by accident, this father-and-son team·stumbled upon the union of (G), the Universal Gravitational Constant, with (c/Vo), the inverse of the Electromagnetic Coupling Constant. Of "tremendously enormous importance," it says here. "Man's search for this FUSION OF CONSTANTS is AT LONG LAST over!" What a relief!! I had lost a lot of sleep over that. How did Einstein miss this *simple* calculation?? Beg them for the tellingly hand-scribbled details.

Nature's Mysteries Unlocked With Unified Natural Laws

Uni-Geo Research
Paul E. Patchin, PO Box 9471
Kansas City, MO 64133

Matter becomes *lighter* before tornadoes, but *heavier* before earthquakes! "This data cannot be refuted.... TIME is a great precision controlling force over a wild, erratic EARTH ELECTRICAL ENERGY which was by instruments found to have a controlling relationship with NATURE'S functions of MATTER, EVAPORATION, GROWTH and NATURAL DISASTERS." See? It all ties in. The government has "for 20 years of carnage" deliberately roadblocked the knowledge by which we could have predicted ALL natural disasters. This poor old dude has been totally and deliberately ignored by the so-called experts. *How can you or I be sure he's wrong?* Free info; complete data $4.

"Learning This Secret Will Help You More Than Anything Else In The World"

Superet Light Center
2516 W. Third St.
Los Angeles, CA 90057

$1 pamphlets (add 75¢ each for postage) that reveal Light Secrets of the Superet Light Atom Aura Science. Did you know that *cities* and *canyons* have auras? The Grand Canyon holds "the Blueprint of Earth Life. The future is revealed by the AURA of our Country America ... for It is the Aura Science."

LIFE-SIZE SKELETON MODELS AND MUCH MUCH MORE

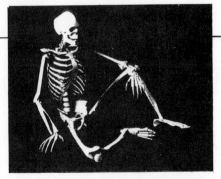

nuclear detonator with the junk in this big FREE catalog. ((With Remote Control))

Edmund Scientific
101 E. Gloucester Pike
Barrington, NJ 08007

The "Spencer's Gifts" of modern science, boon to junior-high science nerds since I was a kid, and still going strong. Every conceivable geegaw, tool, and kit for amateur science hobbyists. They have Three Mile Island and *Challenger* Space Shuttle plastic model kits (for the morbid child-at-heart)!! Remember how you could hold a cheap magnifying glass under the hot sun and scorch leaves and hapless insects? Well, today's kids can purchase three-by-four-foot giant Fresnel Lenses that will "melt asphalt in seconds." Also: enormous balloons and UFO kites for scaring the paranoid old occultist ladies in the neighborhood. Spy-o-scopes and Giant Ears for snooping on Sis when she's huffing glue with the neighbor's boy. Hologram pendants with blinking eyes and psychedelic optical illusions. Van DeGraff generators, 50,000-volt Tesla coils, Jacob's ladders. Unfortunately, it looks like they don't carry the home atom-smasher anymore. Someone's Mom probably complained. But a sharp ten-year-old could probably still assemble a small

UH, WHICH EARTH DID YOU SAY WE WERE ON?

Theistic Evolutionists' Forum
E. T. Babinski, 224 Parliament Dr.
Greenville, SC 29615

Once a Young-Earth Creationist, the editor now prints this big amateur magazine in which Evolutionist cranks and Creationist troglodytes can rant and rend and tear at each other. Compares Flat-Earth, Geocentric, Heliocentric, Young-Earth, and Old-Earth Creationist views, proving why the Bible will never allow them to agree with each other. Oozes with personality. Good-Gog-A-Mighty, I believe there are even references to the Church of the SubGenius in here!! Also publishes *Monkey's Uncle,* a *satire* of both atheist and fundamentalist foolishness. $12/year, $7.50 for sample . . . sounds high, but worth it for its potential weaponry value in psychological warfare.*

* But how come no textbooks tell where *SubGeniuses* come from?

Stone Soup "4 Sale"

Flower Essences and Gem Elixirs
Pegasus Products, Inc.
PO Box 228, Boulder, CO 80306

Hooo-Boy! Get your damn chakras straightened out, your aura degaused, and your spiritual Humgeebliophasers recastroamalgamatoned, by drinking the juice of stones and flowers. The recipe: groovy flowers or gems (depending on the elixir) are put in water under the sun for several hours, and "placed under a pyramid surrounded by quartz crystals and lodestones for increased amplification." But don't drink too much—you'll detoxify too rapidly!! Here's the blurb concerning one of dozens:

"RUBY ELIXIR: develops Divine love and spiritual inspiration, leadership abilities improve, eases disorientation, improves relation with father, opens heart chakra, and one goes from procrastination to stability. . . . Helps solve disputes." *

Blivet Upon Blivet Of Bizarreness

Health Research
Box 70, Mokelune Hill, CA 95245

These people carry so much bizarre shit it'll make your head hurt trying to figure it all out.** Books on every weird theory imaginable: hollow earth, UFOs, suppressed inventions, little green men, orgone therapy, the list just goes on and on. Thousands of reproductions of warped, out-of-print, SHUNNED TEXTS. Here are book titles from just the FIRST PAGE: *World Beyond the Poles; Great Secret of Count Saint-Germain; 4,000 Errors and Unfavorable Biblical Verses; My Water Cure; Secrets of the Flying Saucers from Khabarah Khoom.* Catalog #1 is on "Health" and #2 is "Occult," $2.50 each ((With Remote Control))

* SubGenii will probably want to stick to good old-fashioned Frop, our all-purpose, one-size-fits-all medicinal herb, grown in Tibet on the graves and droppings of holy men and Yetis. What "Bob" smokes. You may be more familiar with its botanical name, Habafropzipulops.

** But, as Dobbs stated so philosophically in his Seven Commandments, **"Too much is always better than not enough"**—although some scholars now assert that he was referring specifically to Frop. If this is true, then one of the Fundamental Laws of the Church has been horribly misapplied for more than thirty years!

DEATH RAY INSTRUCTIONS

Tesla Book Company
PO Box 1685, Ventura, CA 93002

After a hard day at the office I like to curl up with a glass of sherry, a good cigar, and a copy of "Electromagnetic Phenomena in Complex Geometrics and Non-linear Phenomena, Non-linear Waves and Magnetic Monopoles." And if you believe that.... Nevertheless, this is a good research source for the hard-core Tesla student. Death rays, cold explosions, weather modification, free energy receivers, and other fun stuff that Mr. Wizard never got around to explaining. Free catalog. ((Remote Control))

"YOU'LL PAY SOMEONE TO CHOKE YOU"

... for missing out on this one (according to them):

Lindsay Publications
PO Box 12, Bradley, IL 60915

Fascinating catalog of books on lost technology, Bronze Age techniques, how to make your own tools, melt metals, build generators, make dynamite, etc. ((Remote Control))

I can see how this might come in handy in a Nuclear Winter situation. For a while.

MOON ROCKS—OR PAPIER-MÂCHÉ MOVIE PROPS??

Future Science Research
PO Box 06392
Portland, OR 97206–0020

Send SASE for free info on "Moongate," NASA's cover-ups on the moon landings, Mars photos, and "Star Wars." They used antigrav motors on the *Apollo* lander—that's why the special effects on the "landing footage" look so fakey. No real rocket exhaust...it just sort of floated down. It's the same technology the government uses on its secret UFO terrorism experiments. And the *Viking* lander's Mars photos clearly showed Cyclopean Jesus portraits carved into mountainsides.

BEAM ME UP ... NO, ON SECOND THOUGHT ...

The L-5 Society
1060 E. Elm Street
Tucson, AZ 85719–4109

This is the Gerard K. O'Neil, Stewart Brand, Ben Bova crowd that wants to build huge orbiting "artificial planet" space stations. Yeah. Great. But first they'll have to either overthrow or join the powers that've already staked a claim on the cosmos—and not for hydroponic gardening, either. No way is "the Con" going to allow this. Civilian space stations might deliberately bump into laser war satellites in foolish attempts to subvert the secret Depopulation Experiments!! I say, go at it Ghengis Khan style—"ALL WORLDS OR NONE!" Total conquest of the universe, or we NUKE EARTH. All or nothing, baby.

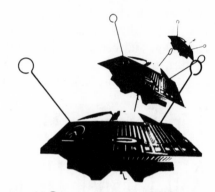

PLAY "CHICKEN" WITH REAL UFOS

Saucer Technology
Box 132, Eureka Springs, AR 72632

Specializing in research into electronic levitation, antigravity propulsion, and other "unusual" energy systems. Learn how to build your very own flying saucer! Fool your friends! Scare your neighbors! Get shot down by the Air Force and never be heard from again! Free information. ((Remote Control))

MAYBE *WE'RE* THE CRAZY ONES

All Source Digest
Byron Peck
2318 Second Ave., #12
Seattle, WA 98121

Library and bookstore of antigravity, perpetual motion, and other fuelless, free-energy literature. "HOW WOULD YOU LIKE TO NEVER HAVE TO PAY A UTILITY BILL AGAIN?" The *only way* to make that dream come true is to become a member of this group! (Says so right here!) They have seemingly bottomless archives of scientific manuals on every miracle machine imaginable. $2 for baffling catalog of forbidden knowledge; *All Source Digest* is $10! Must be big. *"The nation that controls magnetism, controls the universe."*—from *Dick Tracy.*

MAY THE VRIL ENERGY BE WITH YOU

The Final Solution
Box 85811
Seattle, WA 98145–1811

Hitler's mystical visions and occult destiny; Golden Dawn influence on Nazi occultism; the Vril or "rock destroying force" mentioned by Mme. Blavatsky in her shunned *Secret Doctrine.* When Hitler got word of a force called the *Vril-Ya* (like the Hindu *Prana,* the Cabalistic *Yesod,* the *Telesma* of Hermes, Schroedinger's Negative Entropy, or the alchemical Quintessence), he sent explorers all over the world in search of it— among other things, they discovered the South Polar entrance to the Hollow Earth.*

EARTHQUAKE PREDICTION —BIBLICALLY!

Total Health, Inc.
Richard Ruhling, Dansler Rd.
Wildwood, GA 30757

Dr. Ruhling has been dutifully alerting newspapers about upcoming earthquakes. The Bible lets him predict these things down to the week; lives could be saved if we but had eyes to see. Strangely, the forecasted earthquakes didn't occur; but you won't know *when* this guy is right until it's *too late,* will you? ((From Doig))

THEY WANT YOU TO *THINK* IT'S "SCIENCE FICTION"

Rex Research
PO Box 1258, Berkeley, CA 94704

Sells reprints of technical papers about neglected inventions of all kinds. Many old studies on bio-energetics, unusual motor designs, suppressed miracle cures, forgotten doohickeys, and energy generators that may yet turn out to be the ones that save our planet.** $2 for the comprehensive catalog.

THE FOUNTAIN OF YOUTH AND ETERNAL UPRIGHTNESS

Turn-On Products
Box 21, Olympia, WA 98507

HIGH-TECH SPANISH FLY! The amazing POLARIZER balances and aligns your ENTIRE MAGNETIC FIELD, especially when you

---

* They also discovered the Fortresses of Solitude of both Superman and Doc Savage—but it was the lost Monkery of "Bob" that they were *really* looking for. Sorry, Schickelgruber . . . wrong continent!

** By some fluke of Fate, "Rex Research" also happens to be one of the hosts of the incredible SubGenius radio show on KPFA in Berkeley! But don't let that color your judgment. However, he *does* also sell the radio tapes for $6.66 each. Try one and learn where David Byrne got his "Puzzling Evidence" stuff.

sleep north to south. Reduces weight, increases height and intelligence, lowers cholesterol and blood pressure, provides viral immunity, all through MAGNETOTHERAPY. Gray hair turns brown. Gives you pep. Makes you aggressive. Better sex. Staves off astral attacks from bad entities. Only $495!!! (There oughta be a law! Come to think of it, I believe there is.)

BUT THAT OTHER 10 PERCENT COULD HAVE SAVED THE WORLD BY NOW!!

The Mind Science Journal
PO Box 1302, Mill Valley, CA 94941

"Joining People Together in Awareness for the New Age." Speculations on whether the missing children have been kidnapped by the UFOs and classifieds which list many New Age groups; also thoughts on Mary Magdalene as the beloved disciple of Christ (and an o-so-sexy one, too! But they aren't talking about that). The production quality isn't high, but the energy level certainly is, even if 90 percent of the stuff here is crap. Vol 1 #5/6 is $1 (?). ((Factsheet Five))

BUT WE LIKE BREATHING COAL DUST!

Access to Energy
PO Box 2298, Boulder, CO 80306

"A Pro-Science, Pro-Technology, Pro-Free Enterprise Monthly Newsletter." Commits the cardinal sin of being in favor of nuclear energy. After all, the underground press is only for the "right" sorts of unpopular ideas, true? Topics have included the actual damages from Chernobyl, the miscarriage of justice in the Karen Silkwood case (her heirs got $1.3 million), and VDT radiation. "NEGOTIATION, NOT DISARMAMENT!" $1.50 each; $22, "or $1 in pre-1965 US silver coins" per year! ((With Factsheet Five))

DON'T EXPECT FREEBIES

Institute of Noetic Sciences
475 Gate Five Rd., #300
Sausalito, CA 94965

The price ($35/year minimum) will probably turn away at least half of the brilliant thinkers this program is supposed to enlist. Founded by moonwalker Edgar D. Mitchell, it partially funds research into subjects like Tibetan meditators, multiple personalities (which may reveal something about the *poltergeist phenomenon,* believe it or not), Soviet-American scientific exchanges, etc. You get their newsletter with membership, chock full of Big Names in fringe research.

There's More Than One Way To Microwave A Cat

Resonance
Judy Wall, PO Box 64
Sumterville, FL 34267

Newsletter of the MENSA Bioelectromagnetics Special Interest Group. An interesting mix, amateurishly printed; some of it is kook stuff, at least from the standpoint of conventional physics. But some refers directly to current normal research—for instance, the effect of magnetic fields on mice, reported in issue #3. There's probably lots happening when electromagnetic radiation interacts with living cells, but I'm also sure that the subject attracts those who try to square the circle. $1.50 each. ((With Factsheet Five))

The Electron Creep

USA Confidential
Alliance News Service
PO Box 9009, Denver, CO 80209

I'm none too sure about this one. Billing itself as "the last bastion of free press in our controlled world," this "courtesy copy" nonetheless contains only three articles. The first purports to be about new secret military vehicles that move via "electron-creep" and are made out of plastic: pure crap. Then a confident prediction that the bust is coming in our economy and the Yuppies will be in the soup without the paddle. Finally, "Judeo-Christian" is attacked as being a deceiving term. If anyone knows what this guy is about, clue me in. $42/year. ((With Factsheet Five))

The Shunned Secrets Of Magnetism

Cadake Industries
PO Box 1866, Clayton, GA 30525

Selling all manner of odd magnetic devices, Tesla books, manuscripts on every kind of wild energy, and a book called *The Awesome Life Force,* which must be some sort of major classic, because it's hard-sold by almost every *other* catalog in this section, too.

This Could Be The One . . .

Joseph Newman Publishing Co.
Rte. 1, Box 52
Lucedale, Mississippi 39452

That certain agencies of the government and the courts have spent thousands of dollars trying to discredit Newman suggests that *this* time, the "mad inventor" is onto something BIG. REALLY big. Joseph Newman claims to have invented a device that creates more energy than it uses. He identified the gyroscopic properties of subatomic particles, and built a unique arrangement of coils and magnets to draw energy directly from them, thus converting almost immeasurably small amounts of the machine's mass into energy. Dozens of respected physicists and engineers have tested the machine (which can, for instance, run a big car on a one-and-a-half-volt transistor battery) and, mouths agape, agreed that it really might lead to a free-energy world utopia. (Most of these scientists had laughed at him before investigating!) However, the U.S. Patent Office keeps saying Newman's device is a fraud, and various politicians have gone to extreme lengths to prevent development of this possible threat to the Establishment's high corporate echelons. Theory and device are detailed in his new book, *The Energy Machine,* $38.45 including postage, but for an SASE, Newman will send you a frightening series of documents claiming that he (and any other human being who doesn't own stock in an oil company) has been the victim of a massive governmental cover-up and smear campaign against any invention that might decentralize energy control, wreck fuel-source monopolies, and make utility companies a thing of the past. Free energy would indeed turn the basic political power structure of the world upside down; if Newman turns out to be right, the current U.S. administration will go down in future history as despicable enemies of humanity. For that matter, *I'll* look like an idiot for listing him in a book of (mostly) kooks! But let's not jump to conclusions. Newman may

be a crackpot after all; lately he seems to be doing everything he can to prove just that. New mailings from him increasingly exhibit all the tell-tale signs (as shown here): a florid, ridiculously over-embellished writing style suffused with clumsy grammatical clumsiness of grammar; laughable malapropisms and incinerations; needlessly high verbose-fullness of ludicrosities; and Random Capitalization of every other Noun; shrill, melodramatic Accusations of ENDLESS PERSECUTION by Secret Enemies in High Places who think he's Paranoid; transparently false humility regarding his own immeasurable genius, boundless humanitarianism and universe-saving discoveries. . . . All are hallmarks of the classic kook, unaware that his pathetic, overdone attempts at sophistication not only fool nobody, but make him look even crazier. (What? You say that I've just perfectly described my *own* writing style? Well, then his is even *worse.*)

Now, I don't expect someone to be a good writer just because he's a mechanical genius; and, if his inventions *are* for real, then his paranoia is more than justified. If he started out legitimately defending himself, however, he's now digging his own grave, and that grave gets deeper with each new mailing. We can only await further developments. I sincerely hope he finds someone else to be his spokesman.

Telling you how to help Joe fight City Hall is the *Energy Machine Newsletter,* $15/year, and he also sells numerous small books, Xeroxes of articles, and even videotapes on his invention. ((With Waves Forest))

A large packet of free info on Newman's

work (and the war against it by the U.S. government) can also be had from:
Evan R. Soule, Jr.
1135 Jackson Ave., Suite 305, New Orleans, LA 70130

QUICKIES

from Waves Forest's *Further Connections.**

BREAKTHROUGH, Boardroom Reports, PO Box 2908, Boulder, CO 80322: The best available survey of high-tech breakthroughs and coming products in all mainstream science and industry. $59/year/twenty-four issues.

CURRENT CONTENTS, Institute for Scientific Information, 3501 Market St., Philadelphia, PA 19104: Lists tables of contents of thousands of scientific and technical journals as they appear; a tremendous time-saver for research. Seven weeklies in different areas of science, one in arts.

CYCLES, The Foundation for the Study of Cycles, 124 S. Highland Ave., Pittsburgh, PA 15206: Documents evidence of long- and short-term cycles in economics, politics, health, social development, weather, science, and other areas. Very useful for anticipating future patterns and events. Nine issues a year.

FRENETTE'S FUELLESS FURNACE, Eugene Frenette, Box 255, Derry, NH 03038: Frenette has invented a friction-effect heater that cuts heating costs by about a factor of ten. It consists of a steel cylinder spinning inside a larger cylinder with an eighth-inch clearance, with a high-temperature oil in the space between. A small motor drives the device. The friction and molecular shearing in the oil generates temperatures up to 300 degrees, with far less energy input than would be required for conventional space heaters doing the same job. A thirty-inch diameter unit heated a sixteen-room mansion for about $30 a month.

PLANETARY ASSOCIATION FOR CLEAN ENERGY, 212–77 Metcalfe St., Ottawa, Ontario K1P 5L6, Canada: One of the most professional publications dealing with free energy options, ELF, weather war, gravity control, and subtle-energy physics. Newsletter: $20/year/four issues.

LIVING PHYSICS, 20 Nassau St., Princeton, NJ 08542: Bogdan Maglich, editor: An enthusiastic, cutting-edge alternative to the usual dry, dehumanized scientific literature. $19/year/four issues.

MARINE RESOURCES CO., 819 Ball Ave, Galveston, TX 77550: Wolf Hilbertz has developed the cleanest, most economical construction method this civilization has seen. The electroaccretion process has the potential to eliminate housng shortages worldwide, without cutting down a single tree, or in any way harming the environment.

INTERNATIONAL ASSOCIATION FOR PSYCHOTRONIC RESEARCH, Maximilianstrasse 8, Postfach 8 A-6010, Innsbruck, Austria: Studies interactions between con-

---

* In the last chapter, see info on Waves's huge listing of MANY more resources for gravity control, free energy, and other fringe sciences!

sciousness, energy, and matter, and possible applications of those interactions.

PSYCHIC RESEARCH, INC., 1725 Little Orchard St. Unit C, San Jose, CA 95125: "Scientific research and education to aid mankind." Marcel Vogel holds many basic patents on liquid crystals, was the first to demonstrate that plants respond to a variety of human thoughts, and to quantify the plants' reactions; probably understands the subtle properties and applications of quartz crystals better than anyone in the Western world. It also looks like his team will be the first to prove with hard science that psychic energy is real and measurable, and to pin down its properties, frequency ranges, and capacities for world transformation. Marcel personally exemplifies the gentle, neutral-observer viewpoint that is required for successful research in exotic sciences. Newsletter $25/two years/twelve issues.

CENTRAL PREMONITIONS REGISTRY, PO Box 482, Times Square Station, New York, NY 10036: Purpose is "scientific evaluation of premonitions and their use as an early warning system for assassinations, plane crashes, floods, fires and other catastrophes." Director is Robert D. Nelson.

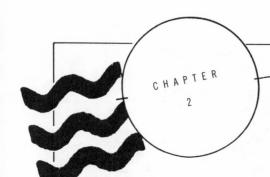

CHAPTER 2

UFO CONTACTEES

—AND THE RESEARCHERS WHO INSPIRED THEM

Of the thousands of people who have received the telepathic siren call of the space people, only a handful go public. Most aren't making any money, or even trying to—an indicator of their seriousness. They heard the voices in their heads, and took them at face value.

I'm not saying these folks are liars. They're sincere, and *that's* what's scary. Somtheing DID happen to them. They think it was good. I don't know what it was, but I *don't* think it was exactly *good*.

O High SlackMaster "Bob," and All Protecting Entities from Planet X, let it not happen to me.

You Have Been Remembered By The Superior Rational

**Rational Culture
Caixa Postal 78.019–26150
Belford Roxo, Rio de Janeiro
RJ Brasil, S. America**

Flying saucer cults have become so prevalent in South America that they might as well comprise a new religion; this is one of the biggest "denominations." It's also the funniest, partly because the translations from Portuguese into English are so badly done as to severely amplify the already psychotic tone. "Our world is a bird that fabricates other birds, that we are and that here we are in passing." See? Not only are their newsletters and "space bible," *Universe In Disenchantment,* dictated by the space brothers, but the book was actually *printed* by them! Millions of copies, imported by spaceship, imbued with healing power. Just owning one will cure any disease and even clear your home of poltergeists. The cosmic alien authors, collectively called the Superior Rational, offer a history of the universe by which we didn't evolve from monkeys, but from ash-monsters formed from primordial "resin." "The primitive bodies were little monsters and afterwards monsters. Then monsters, after big

monsters and after huge monsters . . . improving as the deformation progressed: they screamed-utter, made gestures to understand each other." This may sound, and—who knows?—may even *be,* really stupid, but in size this cult is gaining on the Mormons. Write for price list under current exchange rates; say you need lots of info because you are "with the Superior Rational." SPECIFY THAT YOU WANT IT IN ENGLISH!!

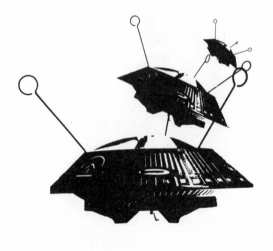

EVIL ILLUMINATI SPACE-BOLSHEVIKS SECRETLY RULE WASHINGTON!

Cosmic Awareness
PO Box 115, Olympia, WA 98507

The Lord God Almighty, using a new name, speaks through His earthly vessel, Paul Shockley, about everything from the hollow earth-saucers to the takeover of the U.S. government by Russian clones...and the takeover of Moscow by secret *Christian* clones. The *Cosmic Awareness* newsletter on current events is like a soap opera from Hell; I guess the Lord has gotten cynical. Metaphysical paranoia with a uniquely sardonic slant; much less corny and clichéd than most Space Voices of God. No second-guessing these characters. Send only $1.50 for their 100-page classic book, *Cosmic Awareness Speaks*. **A great buy.**

INTERPLANETARY NEWS!

The Planetary Center
7803 Ruanne Court
Pasadena, MD 21122

Contactee Laura Mundo, another sweet little old lady,* has been publishing saucer teachings in a newsletter for years. She is very ill, physically this time, and now her people are giving away copies of her many booklets, plus selling her autobiography, *The Mundo UFO Report,* for only $2—a steal! (Unlike many other saucerians, Mundo hasn't been doing it for the money.) Classic contactee stuff; the Space Brothers have communicated with Laura for years and she reveals the paths to becoming a Pre–Atomic Energy Being like them. (The Trinity, by the way, really means neutrons, protons, and electrons.) Published in the Interest of Humanity. Get copies while you can; they're gradually closing shop. A shame. But the newsletter's still coming out, and being written by somebody with that unmistakable "Saucer Psycho" style. Lots of George Adamski inside gossip for you heavy UFO contactee buffs. "One way societies on other planets and the people attain and remain in atomic balance is by never allowing any unnatural money systems like ours to exist. Because it does not adjust to extreme natural changes, ...it temporarily "limits" God, which then has to force Its way, as It is doing on this planet presently." They're against psychic communication with entities—face-to-face encounters ONLY.

---

* Her followers have since informed me that Laura Mundo "...isn't *always so* sweet!" They didn't elaborate. Has she become the Wrathful Hand of the Pre–Atomic Energy Beings??

HAVE YOU LIVED BEFORE ON OTHER WORLDS?

Unarius
145 S. Magnolia Ave.
El Cajon, CA 92020

This must be a huge embarrassment to the less flamboyant New Agers. Ruth Norman, aka "Uriel," by virtue of being a Great Light-Bringer Consciousness in disguise as a nutty old lady, has successfully managed to keep herself surrounded by fawning teenage boys. Her husband was Jesus incarnate—but He died a few years back, durn it! He and almost every other dead holy man *and* great deceased scientist speak through Ruth, however, and the results fill more than eighty books. As vividly illustrated by photos of Ruth's garish costumes and Temple, this is one of the most patently, brazenly, ludicrously, *and inadvertently* fake saucer cults going; because of that, it's also one of the most successful. Some choice teachings: Earth is about to become the thirty-third member of the Interplanetary Confederation. Satan has learned his lesson and is now a good guy. (If he can change, so can you!) The aliens, guided by Ruth, will arrive in a huge "city" made of thirty-three saucers stacked in a pyramid. Newsletter, $8/year, or $1 for wonderful *Introduction to Unarius* booklet, well worth it for the shock you'll receive when you fully comprehend that people BELIEVE this stuff.

SURVIVE DOOMSDAY WITH THE SPACE BROS!

New Changes (Blue Rose Ministry)
Robert Short, PO Box 332
Cornville, AZ 86325

If you are "ready," you can become one of the Chosen Ones who will be rescued—by saucer—from our doomed planet. These folks are the select trance mediums for space reps from dozens of worlds. Many booklets and cassette tapes offered, including guided tours of the Outer Planets by astral beings. For instance, "Ankar 22" of Jupiter describes all social and technical aspects of his home planet. This information is available telepathically, for NOTHING; yet NASA spends MILLIONS on crude rockets, and hasn't even been able to detect the huge cities on Uranus!! This one uses a lot of revealing, lowbrow punctuation techniques: *"You can 'learn' the 'mystic connection' between the Hopi's, the Pope's and the UFO's!"* Often, just the unschooled grammar, fractured sentence structure, and homemade pseudoscience jargon make these publications worthy of detailed study, independent of the actual content. Large selection of cassettes called "Planetary Tours." Visit Space Channel Robert Short in person, or call 602-634-6269 and he'll tell you (for $50) what his space buddy "Korton" suggests for your prosperity in the future. But what if "Korton" instructs that you shouldn't spend your money on fortunetellers—would Rev. Short pass it on to you? He probably would! (Many New Agers have reported visible saucers appearing in the sky when he speaks at outdoor UFO conventions; if he were to lie, the saucers might disintegrate him.) The *Solar Space Letter* is $8/year; beg for sample.

THE UFO DID IT

Nina Hagen—various albums, Columbia Records

No list of contactees would be complete without mentioning the rock 'n' roll albums of this East German–born singer. You can't write her, but her albums on the Columbia label are available in any large record store, and if you live in Hollywood, you can attend her meditation services. The best (weirdest) is *Nunsexmonkrock;* others are *Ekstacy* and *Fearless.* Each has a couple of UFO songs, recorded multi-multitrack with dozens of Nina-voices singing at once. Since she sounds alternately like an angelic yodeler and a demon-possessed growler, the effect is quite psychedelic. The saucers have led her to believe she is the Fifth Buddha, the New Christ. Watch for interviews with her in the rock press. She's a superstar in South America; with her spooky/sexy charisma and large following, she has the potential for spreading pop UFOism on an international scale.

WAR ON SKEPTICS

Secrets newsletter
Rte. 4, Box 156
Marshall, AR 72650

It will be "too late for all but a handful to escape the pulverizing, the fire and deadly smoke that will come raining down from out of the strange craft we call Flying Saucers, totally obliterating cities, towns and the countryside (fear of this invasion is the real reason for Mr. Reagan's 'Star Wars' program)." $1 for sample; $8/year.*

BE NOT ASHAMED OF YOUR ALIEN HERITAGE!!

Starnet
RD 1, Box 176, Addison, PA 15411

Networking Central for the Star People. Some folks, such as this newsletter editor, are really displaced or reborn extraterrestrials; this is an attempt to trigger the ignorant ones to remember their heritage, come out of the closet, and unite into a force of Good.

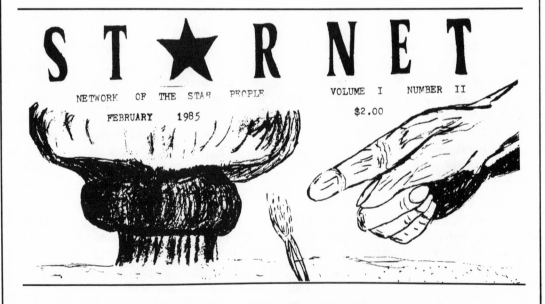

STARNET

NETWORK OF THE STAR PEOPLE

FEBRUARY 1985

VOLUME I   NUMBER II

$2.00

* Little do these people know, but that "handful to escape" will be those bearing SubGenius Church Membership/ High Priest(ess) ID cards! They also neglect the exact time and date for this event (properly called **X-DAY**): 7:00 A.M., July 5, 1998. Remember that.

Eventually, they'll openly declare themselves and "invite diplomatic relations with the nations of Earth." Judging from the self-inflating rants in the last issue I saw, they just seem like ordinary airheads. Clever! Ascended beings disguising themselves as saucer kooks with delusions of grandeur, in order to throw off suspicion!* But then, a new editor is taking over who promises to be a much more humble sort, as transplanted Advanced Evolutionary Souls go. $2/issue, or $15/year.

MARS NEEDS ACID

**Canadian Raelian Movement
PO Box 86, Youville Station
Montreal, Quebec H2P 2V2, Canada**

Meet Rael, Space Hippie and New Age Messiah. Just as you suspected that first time you took too much, all atoms are entire universes, and our universe is just an atom in a larger universe. PRETTY COSMIC, HUH? We were created by the Space-ELOHIM; Rael will help us build an Embassy in which to greet them. Ask for free into, or go the distance and order *Space Aliens Took Me to Their Planet—The Book That Tells the Truth* for $10. Specify English, because they have many translations.

GAS MUSIC FROM JUPITER

**International Space Science
Foundation
2035 E. 3300 South
Salt Lake City, UT 84109**

I didn't send for this one but somehow wound up on their mailing list anyway. Boy, am I lucky! These Chosen Ones have actual recordings of aliens from space! And for only twenty bucks they're willing to set me up in a distributorship whereby I can help spread this urgent message from our Space Brothers and make TONS of money at the same time! What a deal! If you ask nicely, I'll bet they'll send information on how you too can get in on this once-in-a-lifetime opportunity. ((Remote Control))

UNCLE SAM'S SAUCER

**Blue Book Publishers
64 Prospect St.
White Plains, NY 10606**

Books discussing UFOs as secret U.S./Russian disinformation efforts; conspiracy and mind-control literature, such as on how the Dow Jones average is controlled to manipulate public psychology in the stock market; and some new assassination conspiracy literature. Write for current info. Ask for a copy

---

* "Bob" Dobbs uses almost *exactly* the same ploy, yet people recognize him as Space Messiah anyway!

of *The CIA and the Saucer* by Dr. Leon Davidson. According to Dr. Davidson, the CIA under Allen Dulles was builder and operator of the flying saucers seen in close encounters, specifically the 1964 Socorro, New Mexico, sightings. His "proof" is pretty tenuous, but what the hell, it makes for interesting reading, and it's free. ((With Remote Control))

NAZI SAUCERS CONTROLLED BY HITLER'S BRAIN

Samisdat
Ernst Zundel, 206 Carlton Street
Toronto, Ontario, M5A 2L1, Canada

Catalog of historical Nazi books and tapes plus rants by the apparently brain-damaged,

and the ultimate bookshop for info on secret UFO bases at the polar opening to the Hollow Earth—an extension of the occult religion to which Adolf Hitler subscribed, concerning an advanced race of Hollow Earth Aryans who who would bring "Order" to our planet. SCARY. So scary the Canadian government has gone after him, and it's turned into a big freedom-of-speech court mess whereby the "liberal" authorities are proving themselves bigger Nazis than Mr. Zundel, if such a thing is possible. (Only in America can any old deranged nobody print books about how much they hate them Jews.) Secret Nazi Weapons of WW II; videotapes, posters; Holocaust revisionist diatribes.

Excerpts from Zundel's "trial" can even be had, from his Zionist-hating revisionist pals at Truth Missions, PO Box 3849, Manhattan Beach, CA 90266. Even the local Jewish community was appalled by the Canadian courts' ironically Nazi-like handling of the case!

Paperbacks Of The Gods

A newer Von Daniken type would be Zecharia Sitchin, author of The Wars Of Gods And Men *and* The 12th Planet
($4.50 each from Avon Books, The Hearst Corp., 1790 Broadway, New York, NY 10019)

Astronauts from The 12th Planet settled the earth and implanted the genetic seed of *Homo sapiens.* Planet Earth was battleground for a conflict that began on another world. Gods destroyed the first civilizations. Hell, Edgar Cayce got all this info with a lot less research.

Dress For Transmigration

Starliner Connection
North Star Rte. 588
Corrales, NM 87048

UFO jewelry. Winged sphere pendants, cosmic lightning–zapped UFO necklaces, $20 to $50 range. Be "KNOWN" when "THEY" arrive.

An Ancient Astronaut Rants

L/L Research
PO Box 5195, Louisville, KY 40205

Ask for a free copy of their 229-page book, *The Ra Material.* Sort of a cross between *Seth Speaks* and *Chariots of the Gods;* the "Ra" beings attempted to pass on *The Law of One* series to the Egyptians 11,000 years ago, but didn't succeed until today, with L/L Research. Spiritualism never died, it's just changed with the times. Ouija boards are out and Cosmic Consciousness is in. Frankly, I prefer the old-timers with their ectoplasm and spirit horns. At least they knew how to put on a show. No set prices for books and tapes; they have a message, so make an offer. A low one. ((With Remote Control))

What Gall

Guardian Action Publications
PO Box 186, Aztec, NM 87410

Here we go again. You'll be left behind without *Project: World Evacuation* by the Ashtar Command, compiled by Tuella, speaker for the Intergalactic Space Confederation. More "saved at the last minute by the UFOs" bullshit. Don't these people know that the ONLY ones who'll be saved when the Xists land in 1998 are true SubGeniuses? Everyone else will be cast into the lake of burning fire while we party our asses off on the escape saucers. By the way, "Tuella" bears a striking resemblance to your mama. Free information, suckers. ((Remote Control))

It Came From Mount Shasta

Search
Palmer Publications, PO Box 296
Amherst, WI 54406

Following Ray Palmer's death, his wife, Marjorie, managed Palmer Publications until a few years ago, when she sold the business. The new owners carry on, still publishing *Search* and *Space World* magazines, as well as books about the Shaver Mystery, UFOs, and the paranormal. ((Remote Control))

Starting To Sound All Too Familiar

Mark-Age
PO Box 290368
Ft. Lauderdale, FL 33329

We are living in the Mark-Age, brothers and sisters. The time of Purification is at hand. It is time for all Higher Beings to declare themselves citizens of the I-Am Nation and join the White Brotherhood in paving the way for the Second Coming of Sananda, Prince of Earth. At least that's the story according to spirit channels Pauline Sharpe and Charles Gentzel. Gentzel transferred to the etheric realms (i.e., croaked) back in '81, but Pauline, who calls herself Nada/Yolanda, is still cranking it out. Carries a whole bunch of books on how to be the very best person you can possibly be and what to do when "Dad" finally shows up. To paraphrase Barnum, there's a higher being born every minute. Free catalog. ((Remote Control))

You Must Be Told

Saucerian Publications
Box 2228, Clarksburg, WV 26301

Ask about *The Story of the Mitchell Sisters.*

Yeah, But Can They Hex The IRS For Me?

Inner Light
Box 753, New Brunswick, NJ 08903

Cheap books on everything ultraterrestrial. Magic, Kel books(??), Tim Beckley's classic occult UFO books, Evil Eye Curses, intense contactee tales, magic seals, space gods . . . many books I wish I could possess. Free catalog.

Hang On To That Dollar

Mikkel Dahl
Shepherdsfield, RR 4, Box 399
Fulton, MO 65251

Beg for information from this mystic seer/contactee. He's BEEN there! Send SASE, not $.

While They Last

Autographed copies of the famed, yet somehow little-known *Extraterrestrials Among Us* by George Andrews is available for $11.45 from FLAME, 1004 Live Oak, Arlington, TX 76012.

The Sequel

Aliens
PO Box 62692
Phoenix, AZ 85062-2692

Buried beneath the mundane programming of our brains lay hidden memories of the alien powers granted us by Star People of antiquity. The methods of accelerated awakening have been kept alive by a "certain" Native American sect! $12/year for the newsletter, *Avatar,* by "Avram." Avram must be the etheric host this time. But you have to be a $10 member, too. Nice scam—it works for "Bob"!

Stang's Fave

Focus *and far more*
William L. Moore Publications
4219 W. Olive, Suite 247
Burbank, CA 91505

Focus is a small but frequent newsletter on UFO cover-ups, mysteries, abductions, cults, etc. That's just the beginning, though —here you can also acquire secret research reports about everything from Hitler's flying discs to UFO-crash-site guides, and books on everything else abnormal. A mother lode of the coolest UFO esoterica. *Focus* is $20/year.

More Quickies

from Waves Forest

UFO/CONTACT NEWS California UFO, 1536 S. Robertson Blvd., Second Floor, Los Angeles, CA 90035: 213-273-9409; 213-466-2631; Vicki Cooper.

UFO/CONTACT NEWSLINE: 213-976-UFOS; three-minute computer bulletin board, changes daily.

Fund for UFO Research, PO Box 277, Mount Ranier, MD 20712: Reports on current sightings and FOIA-released government UFO documents.

JESUS CONTACTEES AND OTHER "CHANNELS"

"My people are destroyed for lack of knowledge." Hosea 4:6

The good news is, Jesus Christ has come again. The bad news is, He keeps coming and coming, again and again, under dozens of different names. It's getting hard to keep track of just how many Jesii are running around out there. For some reason, He often chooses not to contact any mainstream Christians, but works within strict New Age guidelines, speaking through mediums and Neo-Theosophists like the ghost of your dead grandma or any other common earthbound spirit. Other times, perhaps out of a sense of irony, He uses the very members of His fan club that one would expect Him to avoid—the hate-filled fanatics who want to persecute minorities in His name. How are Jesus contactees any different from UFO contactees? **You got Me.**

What follows is but a smattering of the multiple Jesii one can now choose from . . . look for more as the year 2000 approaches. If you suffer from that nagging Gnostic feeling that "He" is back, check these out. You may change your mind.

Incidentally, this writer has nothing against Jesus per se. Jesus is one of "Bob's" oldest drinking buddies. It's just that certain of His fans—people who gloat when abortion clinics are bombed, who celebrate when AIDS strikes homosexuals—have made Him look like an embittered, jealous, bigoted hypocrite. Yeah, I bet JESUS is REAL PROUD of these characters.

Jesus loves you, dear friend . . . all the Jesuses love you . . . they want you . . . they want your ESSENCE. . . .

ANY MINUTE NOW . . .

Tara Center
Box 6001, N. Hollywood, CA 91603

This well-funded group of New Agers keeps promising that the new God Junior is about to reveal Himself; He has bodily materialized as a Pakistani living among the poor in London, but "cannot" reveal Himself until the world press starts to give Him some credence. This "Mexican standoff" has been going on for seven years now; meanwhile, the faithful keep subscribing to the newsletter, forming "Transmission Groups" to send out good vibes, and . . . waiting. This "Slowpoke Jesus"—well, actually Maitreya the Christ, the New Age number-one hit version of Jesus —sends out occasional antihunger messages by overpowering the mind of Benjamine Creme, a charismatic medium from the Alice Bailey school of the occult. Express solidarity, and you'll get their cliffhanger-style mailings. The latest newsletter says Maitreya is about to start miraculously effecting AIDS cures in London. Watch the newspapers! Free info.

THE ROCK-VOMITING MESSIAH

Aquarian Foundation
315 Fifteenth Ave. E.
Seattle, WA 98112

Write for info on Rev. Keith Rhinehart, aka "The Master Kumara," another new Jesus who holds public seances at which he "apports" precious gems out of his mouth and emits ectoplasms that occasionally materialize into the Ascended Masters who secretly rule this Plane. The A.M.'s look like guys wearing sheets and fake beards. Old-time Spiritualism complete with disembodied voices of deceased relatives. Rev. Keith is actually pretty damned talented as a mentalist, and he may *be* psychic; the sleazy showbiz aspects of his live act make it hard to tell, though.

"Spiritual Healing From The Planets."
Sunday, April 12, 1987:
SEE INSIDE OF PROGRAM FOR DETAILS

"TOMORROW'S RELIGION HERE TODAY"
SPIRITUAL TRANCE WORLD PROPHECIES
OPEN TO THE PUBLIC
Sunday, January 18, 1987
SEE NEXT PAGE FOR DETAILS
YOU ARE INVITED, BUT NOT URGED, TO ATTEND

Move Over, Rev. Moon

Church of New Birth, Inc.
PO Box 996, Benjamin Franklin
Station, Washington, DC 20044

Until 1923, lawyer James Padgett was Jesus' instrument on earth. Volumes 1–4 of *The True Gospel Revealed Anew by Jesus* are only $7.95 each. Hey, look—Joseph Smith started out this way, and look how well the Mormons did! They own whole states and Indian tribes.

Yup, Ah Remembers Creation Jes Lak It Wuz Yesterdee

Search & Prove
Box K, St. Paul Park, MN 55071

God Almighty calls Himself "Mora" when addressing this particular down-home cult. He definitely "talks down" for this one, sounding like a friendly old hick codger. (Wondrous, isn't it, how He can change styles depending on the financial standing and social class of the potential follower?) Cassettes are available of the Spirit Teachers talking through reg'lar folks. Lessons in Astral Projection. It's easy! In fact, these worthies hold weekly out-of-body meetings, leaving their gross physical vessels at home instead of driving miles to get together. Must be convenient. I'll bet you could psychically eavesdrop on these astral meetings without paying any dues, and they'd never notice you were there.

Lourdes Of The New Church

Roses
Our Lady of the Roses Shrine
Box 52, Bayside, NY 11361-0052

At Bayside, "The Lourdes of America," the Virgin Mary speaks through housewife Veronica Lueken and unveils a series of blood-soaked warnings about cults, commies, and child molesters. Flying saucers are demons that kidnap children. A real tear-jerker, written in flabbergastingly florid zombo-Catholic style. "Discover Heaven's point of view." Ask for info on cassettes, back issues. They send loads of goodies if they think you're a live one.

Big B.V.M. Flap Continues

Diamond Star Research
Rte. 2, Box 608, Necedah, WI 54646

Apparitions of the Blessed Virgin Mary "and other Celestials" appear to these worthies, bearing messages of peace/hate for the innocent/guilty. Newsletters, $3 each, go into great detail about Her secret warnings to mankind. Some UFO connections. In 1950 the B.V.M. appeared to Mrs. Fred Van Hoof, and has been in regular contact ever since. The Van Hoofs erected a huge shrine in Her honor that includes life-size sculptures of Jesus, the Apostles, St. Francis, and The Virgin Herself —all your favorite superheroes. But what about Santa Claus? Throw him in and they'd have one hell of a Christmas display. Oddly, they also distribute *The Protocols of Zion*, famous but fraudulent document of Zionist subversion (actually written by some now-deservedly-dead anti-Semitic hate-monger). Intro booklet is $1.50, but try asking for the free color brochure first. ((With Remote Control))

San Diego Medium
Mark Probert
In deep trance

E-Yada-Yada-Yada

Inner Circle Teachers of Light
Universal Life Church
152 Thompson Ave.
Mountain View, CA 94043

The ancient, funny-named Master Entity, "E-Yada-di-Shiite," speaks through the late trance-befogged medium Mark Probert in a series of primitive, hand-lettered pamphlets and cheap tapes. Their book *The Magic Bag* is dictated by twenty-one different "teachers"! "The world is an immense sleight of hand . . . Lose Your Entanglement with Matter . . . Streamline Your Mind." The tapes are amazing—"E-Yada" actually has some very sharp routines,* although, like most channeled entities, he occasionally has trouble maintaining his holy-man accent. Send SASE.

THESE SEANCES, RECORDED ON TAPE WHILE MARK PROBERT WAS IN TRANCE, ARE JUST AS SPOKEN.

THE DRAMATIC IMPACT OF THESE LECTURES NOW ON CASSETTES ARE AWSOME AND THRILLING.

THE ENTITIES WHO SPOKE THROUGH MARK (THE MEMBERS OF MARK'S "INNER CIRCLE") DEDICATED THESE TEACHINGS TO ALL THOSE WHO EARNESTLY SEEK THE LIGHT WITHIN

---

* The tape includes rants against being a "follower" of anybody or anything, even E-Yada! A Slackful philosophy, approved by Dobbs—of whom it was said, " 'Bob' is not *the* answer, but neither is anything else."

Mighty Cayce Has Struck Out

A.R.E.
PO Box 595
Virginia Beach, VA 23451

Although the great trance medium Edgar Cayce has been dead for years, this fixture on the New Age scene has been dutifully reprinting and recategorizing every sentence he ever uttered while asleep. The bewildering thing about Cayce is that while his trance diagnoses and cures did indeed work miraculously, he also spewed forth endless accounts of life in Atlantis before the Flood and other somewhat improbable chunks of surreal ancient history—plus quite a few prophecies for the modern world that weren't exactly on target. On the other hand, has mainstream university-style history really proven itself to be any more accurate? Ask for free catalog of books and tapes.

A Devil In Every Woodpile

Jack Van Impe Ministries
Box J, Royal Oak, MI 48068

Like the more successful megabuck Christian "outreaches," this truth manufacturer is hard to fool. No amount of hard-luck whining will get you their big books for free, but they will send the *Exorcism* and *Spirit World* booklets about how demons lurk at every turn, ready to hook you on astrology, rock music, and worse. These characters rant a lot about how New Age Satanists are sacrificing babies . . . but, you know, a lot more psycho Moms have scalded their children to death "to get the Devil out of them" than have done so to get Jesus out, or for any other New Age reasons. Or maybe it's just that the newspapers are controlled by Satanists.

Rapture . . . Or Rupture? It's Up To You!

Universal Kingdom newsletter
Oregon Vortex of Light, Box 938
Roseburg, OR 97470

From the White Star Illuminator. We CAN avert catastrophe if we all join the right club —namely, this one. "No denial is valid!" We are all feeling "the Quickening" whether we believe it or not. It is essential that the earth's magnetic poles switch polarities . . . and then the foolish "experts" will all die; only "the lowly" will survive. ARE YOU READY FOR THE FOURTH FREQUENCY?? O Ye Bipeds! You can purchase Polarity Pillows here, too.

Now, Could You Run That Part About "Twitching Thighs" By Me Again?

Battle Cry of Aggressive
Christianity
Free Love Ministries
PO Box 161212
Sacramento, CA 95816

Ah ... bulldada treasures like this are what make a kook-hunter's labors worthwhile! Even with countless fanatics to choose from, rarely do we discover ranters so proud and forthright about their vindictive intolerance, so utterly uncompromising and disdainful of any and all ideas not their own. To first witness such unadulterated, limitless, psychotic hatred blithely justified by declarations of pure Christian love, reinforced by *total* disregard for reason, human compassion, or common sense, and bolstered by unshakeable faith that they *cannot* be wrong ... yes, these are what we live for.

This newsletter flawlessly epitomizes "that Ol' Time Religion"—the classic pulpit-smashing, hellfire-and-damnation brand of rural rogue Christianity. A sample quote says it all: "GOD DOES NOT WANT LIBERATED GODDESSES WHOSE THIGHS TWITCH WITH THEIR FORNICATIONS WHILE THEIR WOMBS GUSH THE BLOOD OF THEIR MURDERED CHILDREN. GOD DOES NOT NEED PAINTED HARLOTS WHO SMEAR THEIR FACES WITH THE BLOOD OF CHILDREN." (They're refering to cosmetics containing human placenta as an ingredient. I'd no idea that not just fetuses, but even placentas possess souls!) These patriots don't mince words —they'd love nothing more than to die fighting for Jesus, taking as many sinners with them as possible. Okay, sure—they *are* dangerous, hopelessly ignorant, inbred, retarded borderline lunatics with an insatiable lust for the blood of sinners—but at least they're HONEST about it, which somehow lends them a little more dignity than wimpy mainstreamers who hide the same feelings behind *polite* hatred. Free, and well worth the price.

Tribulation Money Will Fall From The Sky

Peter Popoff Association
PO Box 641, Upland, CA 91785

Similar to the above; fanatical "little Hitler" Peter Popoff can be heard on Christian radio just about anywhere, but the written material also belongs on the shelf of any devoted collector of institutionalized psychosis. Like the infamous Rev. Ewing, Popoff sells paper prayer rugs and Anointing Oils to the depressingly gullible—complete with fake handwritten notes to "YOU" PERSONALLY.

WHEN IT RAINS, IT POURS

Showers of Blessing
House of Prayer for All People
PO Box 837, Denver, CO 80201

Offers dozens of essays and monographs on **all** subjects—ask for the ones about Outer Space Demons and so on; throw in a couple of stamps for return postage. Angels surround us, and they'll feed us if we let them. Their Biblical Manna dough tastes like fudge, and you can get boxes of it in Iraq—it's supplied to churches there "by some inexplicable natural phenomenon." Some Hollow Earth and UFO references. Visionary William L. Blessing is The Voice of the Seventh Angel. Hey, uh, Rev. Blessing—don't pour out that Seventh Vial or blow that Seventh Trumpet quite yet, OK?? Give us a little more time—we still got us a bit more sinnin' to do!

. . . CAST BEFORE US SNICKERING SWINE!

Pearls of Wisdom
Summit University, Box A
Livingston, MT 59047

A magazine "dictated by the Ascended Masters to their Messenger Elizabeth Claire Prophet." Cleanse your past Karma, resolve the psychology of your past and present lives, expand your Light in the alchemy of the Seven Rays, and study the Nine Steps of Precipitation with the help of the Great White Brotherhood. Little did you know, the heroes of the American Revolution evolved after death into Ascended Masters, just like the Virgin Mary did. They and others (like St. Germain and the Archangel Raphael) speak through the Prophet Prophet, who also runs a "college" at this address. (I think *Hustler* ought to work on getting her and other New Age Priestesses to pose.) Free info if you can convince 'em you're not a mocker. Otherwise, the mag is $40/year. Or you can hit up Summit University Press for their catalog of books on the Lost Teachings of Jesus and other universe-shaking pronouncements.

REAGAN—TRILATERALIST TRAITOR AGAINST THE WHITE MAN!

Off the Cuff
Nord Davis Letters, PO Box 129
Topton, NC 28781

These Christian Patriot pamphleteers have evidence that Reagan is a tool of the Roosevelts, and actually helped the communists infiltrate Hollywood. Nancy Davis Reagan is the insidious she-devil who "coaches" her actor-husband. (I find this hard to believe; Reagan isn't a bad actor, but Nancy is awful. Compare any of Ron's classics with a Nancy movie like *Donovan's Brain,* in which her character appears not to mind in the least that her husband's mind is being controlled by a bodiless evil brain. Hey, wait a minute! Hmmmm....) Also, more Identity stuff here: the white race is the Adamic Race. When you hear generic Christians at health food stores talking about the "Adamic diet," you'll know they secretly subscribe to Identity lore about the "Anglo and Scandinavian Israelites." Guess what that makes nonwhites? Members of the Serpentine race. "Love thy brother . . . " uh-huh, sure. Author Nord Davis doesn't want money for his *Off the Cuff* rant collections, but you do have to write a personal letter or he won't send anything. You ought to hear him gloat about "sodomite Rock Hudson."

INVASION OF THE SPACE JESII

Foundation Church of Divine Truth
PO Box 66003
Washington, DC 20035-6003

Sort of like primitive Swedenborgianism, with very detailed descriptions of the "soul life" after death. Ask about the book *Messages from Jesus and the Celestials.* Gnostic/ Cabalistic mishmash.

GOD'S FLOWCHARTS

Bible Believers' Evangelistic Assoc. Rte. 3, Box 92, Sherman, TX 75090

For $2 you can get a ton of samples of those "Bible Map" brochures you may've once been handed by grim young evangelical nerds. Nifty charts show the *scaaaary* Tribulations Period that we've been "entering" for forty years now. Included is that amazing popular painting of The Rapture, showing Christian ghosts floating up out of graveyards and moving vehicles (which are crashing into other cars that *haven't* been "unmann'd"), ascending in Glory toward the Skyscraper Jesus in the clouds. The ghosts wear white sheets, of course; angelic spirits wouldn't run around *nekkid!* The Book of Revelation would make one *hell* of a monster movie. High concept.* They also offer a huge catalog of evangelical teaching supplies—slides, tapes, posters.

---

* Is it dead or alive?? Will The Rapture be more like *Night of the Living Dead,* with freshly "arisen" Christians shambling and rotting, lusting for the flesh of the living??

If You're Reading This, You Missed The Rapture *

Santos Olabarrieta
PO Box 24472
Ft. Lauderdale, FL 33307

Beg for "The Kingdom of Christ Is in Sight"—an essay that first slams many other cults and denominations, and then goes into heavy end-o'-the-world prophecy. The Rapture was scheduled for May–June 1987—by the time you read this, sinner, it'll already have happened. *And you're still here!* Tough luck, huh? But the Second Coming will occur in March 1995 . . . *before taxes are due!* No price listed . . . they do it for God.

And You Don't Even Have To Play It Backwards

Aryan Nations
Church of Jesus Christ Christian
Box 362, Hayden Lake, ID 83835

Aryan Nations #64 is a long, unbelievably detailed rant proving that the innocuous pop song "Bye, Bye, Miss American Pie" is actually a monumental piece of biblical prophecy. Its lyrics, which auther Roy Taylor picks apart literally word by word, symbolize the same things as The Song of Moses, except that it's Satan's version. In fact, there are *thirteen cassettes* on how this one song reveals the "decisive struggle between Christian America and the heathen armies of the world who are now being gathered on our door step, in Central America." Whatever you say, Roy. Proof that certain forms of fanaticism have exactly the same effect as methamphetamine. Free. ((With Remote Control))

* But stay tuned for The Rupture, on January 21, 2078.

SAVE ME! SAVE ME! I'M LOST!

Children of God
Cx Postal 1140, 20.001
Rio de Janeiro, Brasil

I'm not *positive* that this is a new address of the much-persecuted Children of God cult, but the text and pictures sure look like their stuff. Ask for the "poster," *The Comet Comes* —one side is a priceless comic book–like drawing of God, Jesus, and the Holy Spirit (a cute girl in a robe with an atom for a halo) watching Halley's Comet pass earth on their magic TV pond. The backside is a long rant about the comet being a harbinger of famine, war, and a new Depression. If this IS the new Children of God HQ, it should be a cornucopia of insanely weird booklets. This horniest-of-all-cults has been run out of several countries due to their effective use of sex as a recruitment technique—attractive street-prosyletizers screw you for God, see. For some reason their "sex is fun" stance didn't sit well with established religions, which preach the opposite. When writing, always ask for their booklets on sexuality.

GIVING HOMOSEXUALITY TO JESUS IN THE VERY "NICK" OF TIME

True Hope Church of God in Christ
950 Gilman Ave.
San Francisco, CA 94124

Great homemade pamphlet on how "Jesus Can Change the Transsexual Through His Love." You mean surgery isn't necessary?? This is a bizarre testimonial from a transsexual who ALMOST amputated his penis to become a woman, but the Lord saved him in time, and now he's male again. *Whew.*

THE MAGAZINES MICHAEL JACKSON USED TO READ

The Watchtower *and* Awake!
Jehovah's Witnesses
117 Adams St.
Brooklyn, NY 11202

At 10¢ a copy, at least the price is right. The Jehovah's Witnesses have had a tough time of it lately, because their founder predicted several very wrong dates for the end of the world. Try giving away all worldly goods, and then getting them *back* when the Judgment doesn't happen as scheduled! No wonder they have a severe "backsliding" problem.

E.T., PHONE HOME— COLLECT, TO HELL ITSELF!!

Entertaining Demons Unawares
Southwest Radio Church
PO Box 1144
Oklahoma City, OK 73101

"Your Watchman on the Wall." Another flagellating, genuflecting fundamentalist outfit. Their booklet *Entertaining Demons Unawares* exposes the *Star Wars/E.T./*Dungeons & Dragons/Saturday morning cartoon/ Satanic connection in horrifying detail. Left out *Smurfs*, though! I especially liked the bit about Wonder Woman's Antichrist origins. Keep in mind that once you send for anything from these people, you'll be on their mailing list for life. ((Remote Control))

CLONED HOMO PUNK NAZIS IN YOUR FUTURE!

Lighthouse Publications LTD.
2402 E. Denmar Avenue
Lufkin, TX 75901

Good source of religious paranoia on cassette. Learn more about the coming U.S. concentration camps, cloning for homosexual reproduction, the Mark of the Beast, the horrors of rock music, and so forth. Free catalog. ((Remote Control))

UOY SEVOL SUSEJ*

Renew
PO Box 11672
Jacksonville, FL 32239

Religious brainwashing meets the twenty-first century. Now with the help of your Walkman and these subliminal tapes you too can become one with the Big Guy. Relax to soothing ocean sounds while tiny voices (think of them as angels) whisper commands into your subconscious. Commands like "You are the righteousness of God in Christ Jesus," "I can do all things through Christ who strengthens

me," and "Buy more tapes." Of special interest are the tapes "Salvation" (for unsaved loved ones) and "From Rebellion to Obedience" (for children). Restraining straps not included. Free information. ((Remote Control))

AND SOME NEVER COME BACK DOWN . . . THEY ARE THE LUCKY ONES

The Jumping For Jesus Club
International
PO Box 381018
Duncanville, TX 75138-1018

Coach Dennis Clark forms ministry clubs of little kids who jump rope for Jesus, traveling the country spreading the good word. Teams have cute names like The Popping Preachers, The Hallelujah Hoppers, and The Faith Movers. Pretty sick, huh? Seriously, though, combining repetitive physical activity with religious teachings sounds like an extremely effective brainwashing technique, especially when applied to children. Send for info on starting your own club. Suggestions: Bouncers for "Bob" and Dobbs's Dervishes. ((Remote Control))

* The mad Professor Mark Von Mothersbaugh discovered that if a tape of the spoken phrase, "Jesus loves you," is played backward, it sounds like "We smell sausage." That in itself is cause enough for suspicion, but Mothersbaugh then found that the backmasked version of " 'Bob' loves you" sounds like, "We smell 'Bob.'" No matter how you look at it or hear it, "Bob" is the same yesterday, today, and tomorrow. THE ETERNAL "Bob."

HOLIER THAN THOU, AND A LOT UGLIER ON THE SIDE

Campus Ministry
Jed Smock, 173 Woodland Avenue
Lexington, KY 40502

Jed (his real name's George) and his wife, Cindy, travel around the country bringing their message of fundamentalist religion to heathen college students everywhere. Be sure and catch their act when they're in town. In case you miss them, write for free copies of their leaflets "The Jed Smock Story —From Professor to Preacher," "The Sister Cindy Story—From Disco Queen to Gospel Preacher," and their new ones, "South Africa —the Shocking Facts" and "Mission to South Africa." ((Remote Control))

SLOUCHING TOWARD BETHLEHEM

Free Tract Society
PO Box 42544
Los Angeles, CA 90050

Ever wonder where all those stupid little religious tracts come from? This is the place.

My favorites are "There Will Be No Fire Escape in Hell," "Urgent Space News—Message from Jesus," and "What Shape Is Your God?" Too bad they don't carry any of Jack Chick's stuff. Send them a letter and you'll get a half pound of tracts in return. ((Remote Control))

THEY REALLY KNOW HOW TO "SPEAK THE KIDS' LANGUAGE"

Youth '86
300 W. Green St.
Pasadena, CA 91123

Aimed at the college and high school crowd, this one has articles on avoiding stress, avoiding sex, the necessity of learning, the dangers of steroids, and a biblical advice column. Look at the title page and, sure enough, this is another wing of the Worldwide Church of God. Should be on your shelf, right next to *The Plain Truth*. ((Factsheet Five))

Big "Brother" Is Watching You

Catholic Eye
NCCL, 150 E. Thirty-fifth St.
New York, NY 10016

That's the National Committee of Catholic Laymen, Inc., and this is simply a four-page Roman Catholic gossip column. They talk about the dreadful trends in modern society, and deal heavily with all the latest news of the church, particularly those horrid liberal bishops flouting the pope's authority. $25/year. ((Factsheet Five))

GENERIC CHRISTIANS

Many of you who live in big cities and run mainly with fellow humanists might consider what we call "Generic Christians" just as weird as the other extremists . . . but they aren't. There are as many of them as there are of you; they're "average Americans," and you probably aren't. A book or ten could easily be filled with lists of these bland middle-of-the-road religious publications; but they just aren't as funny as the harder core fundamentalists—no funnier than, say, washing machines or toasters. They are Normal. They worship the Nice Jesus, and think evangelicals are as nutty as you! But here's a few samples of the mainstream for you sheltered beatniks.

Pink

Moody Monthly
The Christian Family Magazine
2101 W. Howard St.
Chicago, IL 60645

Ask for a sample and you'll get 'em for life. Dull, dull, dull. But not dull enough to be funny. Smugness, as usual, is the main culprit.

HAVE YOU ESCAPED THE GOOD NEWS?

Evangelism Literature for America
1445 Boonville Ave.
Springfield, MO 65802

Heavenly Gift Certificates (good for Eternal Life upon Repentance), Secrets of Stain Removal (like how to remove the Stain of Sin), and other sneaky evangelistic come-ons in pamphlet form. Not much hate here—these are funny primarily because the "clever" gags are hopelessly corny to the average sinner. A crippled sense of humor is probably the biggest stumbling block for Christian groups in general. If this is salvation, even an eternity of prime-time network TV would be better. Hey, it's *their* problem if they've lost their frontmost braincells. Ask for the sample pack.

YOU PROBABLY THINK HELL IS FUNNY, TOO

Jimmy Swaggart Gift Catalog
Jimmy Swaggart Ministries
Box 2550
Baton Rouge, LA 70821-2550

No more indecision or shopping at Christmastime. Loads of goods for people you don't really like, from the Mick Jagger of TV evangelism. Records, Bibles, tapes, books. The free catalog has paintings of starving Third World kids on every page—I guess you're supposed to feel that NOT ordering these items will perpetuate starvation. If you've never seen Swaggart preach, you've missed something. He's on TV everywhere, and well worth one view at least ("The first hit's free!") . . . the guy is *good*. He can have the most sarcastic mockers down on their knees in no time. My favorite Swaggart riff is when he whirls around and addresses Camera 2 in close-up: "And you there by television, suckin' on that JOINT!! Oh, you think Jimmy Swaggart's real FUNNY! But will you be laughing on that Day of Judgment??" WHAT A MAN! Oh, HELL is a POPULAR JOKE these days . . . a "funny" "joke!"

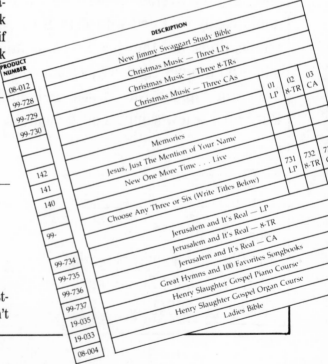

Need We Say More?

Pat Robertson for President
Box 17488, Washington, DC 20041

You know what to do.

Plain Is Right

The Plain Truth
300 W. Green St.
Pasadena, CA 91123

A slick magazine full of good old-fashioned, Bible-thumping, black-eyed-pea-eating commentary on current events, mailed out free to anyone who wants it, and anyone who doesn't. A staple in airports. Editor Herbert W. Armstrong passed away recently, but doubtless the spirit of his rants will survive in reprints for many issues to come. Sign up all your friends!

Don't look for the Moral Majority in this section; they're listed under HATE GROUPS.

JIMMY SWAGGART CHRISTMAS GIFT CATALOG
Guaranteed Delivery by Christmas!

For years we have been able to offer you the finest ministry gifts at very reasonable ministry prices. However, like you, we've been at the mercy of the Postal Service's normal 6-8 week delivery. Thus, no matter how quickly we processed your order, it took weeks, even months, for it to arrive at your home.

We are pleased to announce that for the first time in our history we are able to offer you GUARANTEED DELIVERY BY CHRISTMAS. For just a few dollars more, you can request dependable UPS shipping and have your order delivered right to your door in just 4 to 5 days. The slight charge is nothing when you consider how quickly you can now receive your order. No matter how large your order . . . no matter how far your order is shipped, you pay one small fixed amount.

As an extra bonus for those of you who request UPS shipping, we'll send you one of our beautiful Cross and Dove logo pins absolutely free!

_____ Yes, I would like GUARANTEED DELIVERY BY CHRISTMAS $3.00

Yours Free For Requesting Fast UPS Shipping

Total of Items Ordered   _____
Total Enclosed (U.S.)   _____

Guaranteed delivery by Christmas is subject to orders being received and processed prior to UPS deliver/
U.S. destinations only.

Use peel-off address label from back cover whether or not address is correct. If incorrect or if you are moving, fill in below. If you receive duplicate magazines, please attach all extra labels.

When placing your order, it is important that you doub'
you write down against the actual printed produc
shipped product by product number, NOT DESCR
product number means we can serve you faster. T'

43-61-0050-

PLEASE PRINT CLEARLY AND COMPLETE ALL APPLICABLE INFORMATION

FIRST NAME   M.I.   LAST NAME

ADDRESS

CITY   STATE   ZIP

ACCOUNT NUMBER   TELEPHONE NUMBER

Olive Wood Counselor's New Testament
Cruden's Concordance and Smith's Bible Dictionary
New Prayer Manual
Matthew Henry Commentary
Four-Volume Desk Reference Set
Expository Dictionary Set
Great Men of The Bible Set
Nelson Handbook Series
Sermons — Choose Any Three or Six

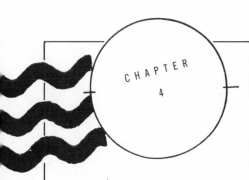

CHAPTER 4

MORE WEIRD RELIGION

O f course, "weirdness" is relative; what makes these weird is that they mostly all think that *they're* the only *normal* ones.

DOCTORS FOR WOTAN

The Runestone
Asatru Free Assembly
PO Box 1754
Breckenridge, TX 76024–1754

Dedicated to resurrecting the ancient Norse gods and the religion of Odinism. The Hoar-Frost Giants LIVE!! Ragnarok is around the corner, but most people don't even know what it is. (It's sort of like Armageddon, but with Older Gods.) A background in the Marvel Comics series "Thor" helps here. $9/year; ask for sample. You sinner there—you think you're gonna be hidin' in a liquor bottle come Ragnarok?? Eh?

END O' THE WORLD II

Psychic Prophecy News Bulletin
Burchette Bros., PO Box 1363
Spring Valley, CA 92077

Startling predictions about: the coming supercomputers that can talk to God...approaching worldwide plagues...World War Three and the Secret Ark of Deliverance... a cure for old age...Armageddon and much, MUCH, *MUCH MORE!!* Prophet Will Loy doesn't have a bad record—but then, neither would you if you tossed out the most unlikely possible predictions, month after month—a few of the nuttiest ones will inevitably end up as news headlines. Ask for free sample. Three monthly issues for $15.

You Will Meet A Tall, Dark Stranger

Astrology and Psychic News
California Astrology Association
PO Box 810
N. Hollywood, CA 91603

Black Hole exists in small town! Einstein's formula can predict your future! Dead wife conveys message through husband's calculator! Psychic suggestion brings dead girl back to life! DANGERS OF ASTRAL TRAVEL—Woman's Spirit Cannot Find Its Way Back to Her Body! Has someone put a curse on you? This tabloid beats the *Weekly World News* for "high concept," and their catalog of trinkets, tapes, palmistry services, etc., is even better. Somewhat New Age, but with a strong dose of blue-collar voodoo. Ask for sample and catalog; $20/year.

Wife Conveys Message Through Husband's Calculator

Practice For Hell

Look for classes in FIREWALKING in your town . . . the latest craze among those more affluent seekers who can spend $500 on a weekend seminar that will give them enough gumption to walk on hot coals without being burned. The reasoning is that if you can do that, you'll certainly be able to strike it rich in the business world. Only stands to reason! Don't take the course—just show up at the ceremony and watch the others hope against hope that their faith is strong.

Wait'll You See The "Home Temple" Props

A.M.O.R.C. (The Rosicrucians)
San Jose, CA 95191
(Yes, that's the full address.)

The oldest established mail order Mystery School. Once the most subversive organization in Europe, now the "Muzak" of the New Age—bubblegum cosmic wisdom and E-Z-2-Read mystic knowledge for the middle-of-the-road businessman. For that reason, A.M.O.R.C. is fairly popular and can afford to mail out impressive four-color booklets and catalogs. Watered-down occultism for people who would be turned off by the real thing. (At least, that's true of the lower Orders. Who knows what sinister Initiation awaits the diligent seeker??) Write for full set of free catalogs. You can outfit your bedroom like an Egyptian temple.

REMEMBER YOUR PAST LIFE AS PRIEST OF THE SUN ALTAR?

The Mayans
PO Box 2710
San Antonio, TX 78299

An A.M.O.R.C.–clone aimed at Hispanics; almost a word-for-word rip-off. Archetypal commercial copy of the original old occult "Mystery Schools." In a way, though, it's all the more "pure" because of that. Many packs of free booklets will follow your request for info. Tell 'em you seem to have vague memories of another life, in which you lived in a jungle pyramid as a high priest. DON'T say you still feel an urge to offer up still-beating human hearts to Quetzalcoatl—that might be laying it on a bit thick.

WITCHCRAFT FOR YUPPIES

Dromenon
Box 3300, Pomona, NY 10970

This commune epitomizes the boring, namby-pamby Aquarian approach to world takeover through "positive" grooviness and lightweight spirituality. Guru Jean Houston is a genius at mixing every overworked cliché into a great synthesis of unbearable corniness, and Dromenon is where well-to-do intellectuals can be told the sort of wimpy sweetness-and-light drivel they want to hear. The worlds *consciousness* and *transformation* crop up seven or eight times per page. For moneyed, college-graduate New Age suckers only. Write a "sincere" letter asking for information.

THE ULTIMATE "DUH"

Eckankar™
PO Box 3100
Menlo Park, CA 94025

The Stupidest Cult. A coloring-book occult/ oriental philosophy in which daydreaming and wishful thinking become "the ancient science of soul travel." Learn to project your astral body *while driving!!* Strange astral-world cosmology reminiscent of 1940s pulp science fiction. Proof that you can't go broke underestimating the intelligence of the American seeker. Ask for every free brochure they can spare, and they'll probably send you a book by the current Living Eck Master, Sri Darwin Gross. And boy, is he.

The One Sane Anchor In This Raging Sea Of False Belief

The Church of the SubGenius
PO Box 140306, Dallas, TX 75214

All of the above and below, everything mentioned in this book, and worse, combined, plus art design of an entirely alien nature. The End Times church for mutants.

THE STARK FIST is the ONLY newsletter for self-educated, common-sensed Good Ol' Boys of both sexes who just happen to believe that the Xist beings will arrive in their Pleasure Saucers at 7 A.M., July 5, 1998, and that only the Saint of Sales, J. R. "Bob" Dobbs, can save the SubGenii (and get us good tickets for the trip away from the then-doomed planet). $11 postpaid for *The Book of the SubGenius,* the two-hundred-page synthesis of all weird truths into the one ultimate weird truth . . . of

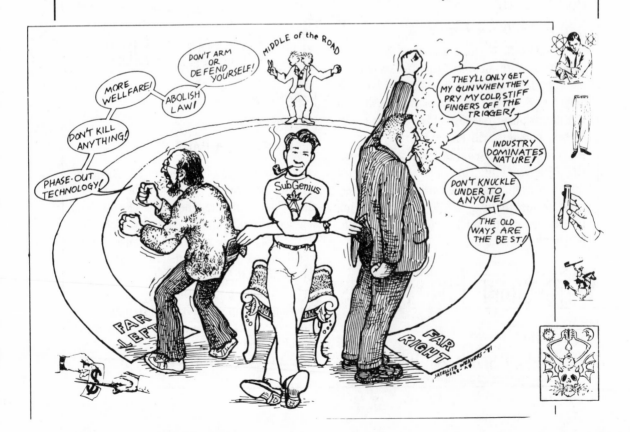

Are you worried over **money problems**, suffering from **poor health**, are you nervous and upset **over family or love problems.**

The Church of the SubGenius

P.O. Box 140306, Dallas, TX 75214

The Church of the SubGenius

P.O. Box 140306
Dallas, Texas 75214

BULK RATE

FORWARDING AND RETURN POSTAGE GUARANTEED.

AAIIIEEEEE!

Warlords of Satan
PO Box 3085, St. Paul, MN 55165

This address isn't *their* HQ—that's a well-kept secret—but that of a concerned citizen out to alert the rest of us by distributing reprints of what are probably the most disturbing religious/political tracts around. Frightening propaganda from a modern secret group of Black Magicians intent on world conquest. Essays not only rationalizing but glorifying slavery, piracy, "Black Fascism," sexual torture, unpunished killing. These people worship sheer power and advocate total disregard for human rights; the Nazis look like Christian Martyrs compared to this growing hell-cult. Also available from the same address: writings from the similar devil-cults of Baal and Belarion-the-Antichrist. $3 for Xeroxes of original "Warlords" propaganda. Should go over big with the skinheads and S&M punk types.

ABRACADABRA, YABA-DABA-DOO

Magical Blend
PO Box 11303
San Francisco, CA 94101

Slick magazine of "magickal" edge mysticism. Covers a lot of ground, what with Carlos Castaneda, R. A. Wilson, Yoko Ono, and New Age impresario Marilyn Ferguson all in one issue (#15). Great psychedelic "visionary"

color paintings, and some of the dopiest ads and come-ons a nut-gatherer could hope to find. $12/year, $3.75 each.

DON'T LOOK IN THE INNER CORE!

The Rainbow Earth Dwelling Society
L. Christine Hayes
330 Laddie Place
San Antonio, TX 78201

Ms. Hayes is in mental contact with the inner-earthers. She publishes her communications in a newsletter called the *Source,* and also has a book proving that Elvis is from "the Blue Star." ((Off the Deep End))

THE MOST HUMAN OF ALL HUMAN HUMANS

Sovereign Press
326 Harris Rd.
Rochester, WA 98579

Can't quite figure which "genre" to put this odd publisher into. Books include: Thomas Jefferson's translation of the Bible, *The Pagan Bible,* and some intriguing stuff with titles like *World Controlled Humans* and *Human Culture of Humans.*

STARRING CASPER THE FRIENDLY GHOST

ESP Laboratory
Al G. Manning
7559 Santa Monica Blvd.
Los Angeles, CA 90046

Ask for free catalog and literature. A very quirky, "jolly" psychic/researcher with a twinkle in his eye, a card up his sleeve, and the most primitive cartooning style ever.

SUBGENIUS BY ACCIDENT

Arise
S. S. Johnson, 48 N. Main St.
Sheridan, WY 82801

"Arisians think for themselves." When the rest of us clip ad blurbs out of old magazines to incorporate into pamphlets for our homemade religions, we're being "funny." Mr. Johnson, who looks to be elderly from his pictures, probably doesn't realize that pure thrift has accidentally given him a "hip" layout style. Ask for his "brochure" . . . odd . . . I think he's trying to start a new Masons.

BUT DON'T *EVER* LOOK INSIDE THE MOJO BAG!

Coven Gardens
PO Box 1064, Boulder, CO 80306

Jumbo catalog of all sorts of magickal crap. Incense, talismans, ritual daggers, tarot decks, crystal balls, voodoo dolls, and, yes, even graveyard dust ($1.25 per oz.). Catalog $2.00. ((Remote Control))

THE FILTHY BOTTOM MADE ME DO IT

Schizophrenics International
PO Box 50456, Ft. Worth, TX 76105

Definitely lives up to its name. Has that certain "something" that only comes with true psychosis. Ask for a copy of the **free** booklet *The Psychology of Purity and Chastity* by Ed Mood. "Even after we become children of the Creator we are still emotionally carnal and are in need of conversion to a human vegetable. That is what schizophrenia is all about." He says that mental illness allowed him to "purify" himself. "Sex is spiritual dirt and insanity, since it stinks worse to the tree, it is spiritual manure. . . . The emotionally carnal person eats his dirt and having eaten, proceeds to manufacture his flesh after the manner of barnyard animals by using his dirty bottom. The human vegetable converts his dirt and manure by keeping his face to the light and manufactures his flesh by using the top half of his body, as a tree, up in the air, where it is clean." Don't miss this one. ((With Remote Control))

THE CONSPIRACY BEHIND THE CONSPIRACY

Cosmic Awareness Communications
PO Box 115
Olympia, Washington 98507

Are you ready for Cosmic Awareness and the New Age? God speaks to YOU through trance-medium Ralph Duby, university lecturer, ex–army officer, and survivor of the Bataan Death March. God and Ralph answer all those nagging questions about how to tell the good UFOs from the bad ones, fluoride in our water supply, how Jehovah kept the clones confused, and more, more, more! Absolutely incredible. Plus, they carry *dozens* of other great titles, like "Is Rock & Roll Perverting Your Children?", "How You Can Help Prevent Nuclear Holocaust," and "A Cosmic History of the Illuminati." Ask for the booklet *Cosmic Awareness Speaks*. It says $3.00 but they'll send it to you free if you ask nice. A real bargain. ((Remote Control))

BURN THE HILL OF FORESKINS!

Ansaaru Allah Community Inc.
719 Bushwick Ave.
Brooklyn, NY 11221

If you've always had a burning desire to become a Nubian Islamic Hebrew and devote your life to Allah, then this is for you. Act now and you can also make big money selling "the most dynamic pamphlets in history," like "Why the Nosering?" and "Arabic Made Easy." The ranting achieves orbit at times. Free brochure. ((Remote Control))

$1,416. NINETEEN??

Vector Associates
PO Box 6215, Bellevue, WA 98007

Publishes *The True Authorship of the New Testament*, which claims the entire New Testament was written by the Pisos, a wealthy Roman family. They even offer a $1,416.19 reward to anyone who can disprove the book's thesis. Free information. ((Remote Control))

THE SECRET OF ETERNAL HAPPINESS REVEALED HERE, ON THIS DUMB PAGE OF THIS OBSCURE BOOK

While we're at it—we have been told by *reliable sources* that if you chant the phrase "Nam-Myo-Ho-Ren-Ge-Kyo" all day long, every day, you will be given power to overcome all obstacles.

AND ON A MORE CHEERFUL NOTE . . .

Relics of the Catholic Church
The Vatican, Earth

Fantastic source of holy relics. Some of the divine fossils offered for exhibit by various members of this rather large mystic fellowship include: the Virgin Mary's undergarments; Jesus' circumcised foreskin; the skeleton of Mary Magdalene; John the Baptist's hair shirt; milk from the Virgin's breasts; straw from Christ's manger; fragments of bone from the children massacred by Herod; hairs from Jesus' beard; the Shroud of Turin; the Spear of Longinus; the right arm of St. Xavier; the heads of St. Nabor and St. Felix; and a splinter of the cross. Write for details.

RATED "U" FOR UNHOLY

Satan's Hope
PO Box 353, Victoria Station
Montreal H3Z 2V8, Canada

Yep. Mail-order devil worshippers. You, too, can learn to venture past the gates of Hell and party with the Prince of Darkness. These folks are pretty slick. Their full name is the "Continental Association of Satan's Hope," so make all checks payable to "CASH." How much does their course cost? Are you ready for this? Twenty-three dollars. Free information complete with dragons, inverted pentacles, and 666s. Check it out, IF YOU DARE. ((Remote Control))

BUT WATCH OUT FOR FALLING KANSAS FARMHOUSES

Church and School of Wicca
PO Box 1502, New Bern, NC 28560

Gavin and Yvonne Frost, founders of America's first mail-order school of witchcraft, invite you to join them. Study to become a

Doctor of Celtic Witchcraft and start your own coven. Sign up now and receive a free miniature scale model of Cheops's Pyramid tuned to *your* birth sign and color. Free information. ((Remote Control))

But wait—how can this be? *These* people *also* claim to be the world's first public Witchcraft Correspondence Course:

Our Lady of Enchantment
Church of the Old Religion and
School of Wicca, PO Box 1366
Nashua, NH 03061

Maybe it's the same coven, forced by the law to move on and change names?? The **only** valid publishers of "the Craft" secrets.

BE AN ANCIENT GREEK PHYSICIAN/PHILOSOPHER FOR ONLY A FEW THOUSAND DOLLARS!!

Ancient Hermetic Order of
Asclepiads
Heirophant, Dr. David De Loera
Box 95, Calumet City, IL 60409

"The Most Ancient Order of Healers in the Western World." Oh, another one of *those*.

Borrows a lot from the Gnostics and the Theraputae (household words, right?) and mixes that with the modern techniques of "MORPHIC RESONANCE." From what I've seen, this looks like a stuffy, intellectualized mutation of your straight old-time "laying on of hands" method of healing, all gussied up with pseudoscience, Freud, Jung, and a pompous attitude. Unfortunately, it costs $5 for anything beyond the vague one-page intro letter, and the prices for medallions, robes, etc., are so outrageously high as to be downright laughable. But you *cannot* be a healer without that all-important medallion!

RA RA RA

Kaieteur Marketing
Champlain Blvd.
Ville La Salle PO Box 371
Montreal, Quebec
H8P 3V3, Canada

I think we're on a roll here. Offers courses in "Ancient Egyptian Philosophy—The Secret Knowledge." Learn how to: make yourself invisible, see in the dark, change the color of animals (?), grow hair on any part of your body (!), understand the songs of birds, cause evil spirits to leave your dwelling, cause a cow to become pregnant, stop fights in the home, and—the most closely guarded Egyptian secret of all—how to prevent bees from flying away! They have testimonials from as far away as Singapore, Nigeria, and Detroit, so IT MUST BE TRUE. Send for free information if you don't believe me. ((Remote Control))

ALL-ONE-FAITH, ALL-ONE-SOAP, OK OK!

Dr. Bronner's Pure-Castille-Soap
Labels
All-One-God-Faith, PO Box 28
Escondido, CA 92025

Go to any natural-foods store and pick up some of Dr. Bronner's liquid soap. Now take a magnifying glass and study the teeny-tiny print that fills every available square millimeter of the label. The inimitable soapmaker Bronner's label-rants are in some ways the standard next to which all other crazy, blathering religious fanatics can be measured. None can match the breathless, period-less exhortations of this Living Master of word-diarrhea; no bathroom is complete without this soap! "Love, poetry, ecstacy, uniting All-One! All-brave! All life! Exceptions? None!" If worst comes to worst, you can write the Bronnerfolks for equally mind-slamming catalogs, and a big poster-size rant-scroll. And the soap smells GREAT, incidentally.

THE SCI FI JESUS

Philip K. Dick Society
Box 611, Glen Ellen, CA 95442

If you don't know who Philip K. Dick is, you don't deserve to live! Sorry about that. After all, he was only America's greatest mentally disturbed science-fiction writer. Read *Valis*, *The Divine Invasion*, *Ubik*, or *The Penultimate Truth* and see for yourself. While you're at it, send these people $6 for four issues of their newsletter or $2.50 for a sample copy. Eventually, they'll dissect every teeny detail of this intriguing speedfreak genius's life. Also listed here are as many posthumous Dick books as he saw printed in his engrossingly baffling lifetime. He's great, I tell you! GREAT! Free info. ((With Remote Control))

THE MORAL ABC: "1st: Unless constructive-selfish, like Arctic Owl, athlete-pilot-beaver-bee, I train first me, what can save or respect me? Absolute nothing! Exceptions eternally? Absolute none! 2nd: If I'm only for me? I'm nobody! 3rd: If not now? Never! 4th: Only hard work can save us, but if we save only our clan? We're all hated then!" So we must teach friend & enemy the Moral ABC Hillel taught Jesus & overnight we're All-One! Evolving-united by full-truth, God's Law, hard work, Free Speech-Press & profitsharing Socialaction in our Eternal Father's great All-One-Faith! All-One! Then, these are the days my friend, we know they'll never end! We'll work-sing-dance-love marching on! We live God's Law today! We'll fight for it OK! We're young because we're All-One! All-One! All-One!

9th: replace half-true Socialist fluoride-poison & tax-slavery with full-truth, work-speech-press & profitsharing Socialaction! All-One! So, help build 4 billion Hannibal wind-power plants, charging 96 billion battery-banks, powering every car-factory-farm-home-monorail & pump, watering Babylon-roof-gardens & 800 billion Israel-Milorganite fruit trees, guarded by Swiss 6000 year Universal Military Training (UMT), Essene Birth-Control & Moral ABC: "1st: Train thyself & unite brave, to teach all, every slave, the Moral ABC, 6 billion strong & overnight we're All-One! All-One! Hunzas for 2000 years got it done! We're All-One! All-One!

The Second Cuming, Or, Are You One Of The "Assigned Creatures?"

Truth Missionaries of Positive Accord
PO Box 42772
Evergreen Park, IL 60642

It's tough to get a handle on this group; they have few precedents, and their material is thick with that hard-to-read verbosity that characterizes ambulatory schizophrenics. Offers biblical proof of a "Goddess Eve"—part of it involves cosmic fellatio between consenting male and female "tachyon deities." The original male tachyon deity "spurted" into the mouth of the female tachyon deity, who in turn injected it into the womb of the Virgin Mary. Repetitive but highly original and complex ravings about Holy Sperm, Yahweh's ejaculation, Pure Milk Rays, etc. Where some faiths count the angels on a pinhead, this one counts the chromosomes in Jehovah's sperm and nitpicks unto infinity about other Triple-X-rated theological details. But what about God's POOP? What about the Goddess's BOOGERS?? All materials are free; I imagine it's hard to *give* this stuff away, unheeding Earth-fools being what they are. . . .*

* After this review appeared in *Whole Earth Review,* Vice Bishop H. Jacobsen of TMC + A wrote the magazine to clarify a few things:

Not necessarily "counting the chromosomes in Jehovah's sperm" but carefully regarding the scientific fact that all females, including Mary, have ONLY X chromosomes, and the Y chromosome for Jesus' sex designation had to come from a male, and the Father (Yahweh) could not morally cause issuance of His own sperm (masturbate, etc.). Only the real Goddess could morally cause the ejaculation of His sperm. Also, the Greek word translated "begotten" in "only begotten son of God" is better translated "genetic" (it is pronounced almost the same as "gene") referring to the genes in Yahweh's sperm.

You say we have a "Triple-X theology." Maybe so, but we consider it the theological DAWN of NEW AGE RELIGION. You forgot to mention our Biblical proofs of Jesus' own sex activity before and after His resurrection (Sex with Mary Magdalene and the Goddess).

I neglected to answer your question about "God's poop" and the "Goddess's boogers" in my Aug. 25th letter to you. I'm not sure whether you ask these because of a scatological fetish or an ecological concern. Nobody asked these things before during the 16 years we've had this theology, and I hadn't thought about them. Deity DO have corresponding anatomical parts, and anal parts are not merely ornamental in Them, any more than any parts. I guess the poop would be biodegradable in Heaven. However, I don't think there are any "Goddess's boogers." What She breathes would not make any. Her nostrils always stay clean. Their poop might be the "manna," called "angels' food" in the Bible. Whatever, I'm sure They are efficient.

Yours truly,
Vice Bishop H. Jacobsen
of TMC + A

None Of Those Damn "Body-Tainted" Spirits Here

Guidance Associates
PO Box 32261, Tucson, AZ 85751

Sets up "nationwide group channeling of the *Light Beings*," disembodied entities who speak of universal laws, earth changes, man's real purpose on earth. Tapes of these channelings available for $6. "Channels abound nowadays," they say, "but to our knowledge, no one with our qualifications channels pure spirit entities *who have never been in the body,* whose outlook on humanity is undistorted by ever having been human. This is *clear stuff.* No lamenting about how they miss getting drunk on the mountaintop with the other cavemen—you know what I mean." They also offer a $4.95 *Directory of America's Best Psychics,* which tends to blow their credibility out the window, since it's very short and almost half the psychics, astrologers, and channels listed are in their home state of Arizona.

Limited Time Only

Ruth Fish
948 Maxwell Ave.
Nashville, TN 37206

Mails out reprints of flyers and articles like "The Truth About Evil Spirits," "Why Clerics Censored the Bible," and "How to Die," dealing with life after death and spiritualism. Ruth's pushing ninety so she has a vested interest in this stuff. They're all free, but give the lady a break: send stamps. She also advises you to put your return address on the envelope—as she might be gone, if you get her drift. ((Remote Control))

Gaze Deep Into The Magic Screen

Jane Jacobson
Box 44785, Phoenix, AZ 85064

Sells a $49.95 videotape crash-course in Tarot readings and a $6 Tarot book. Also a "trained healer, numerologist, and astrologist." To tell the truth, the only reason I mention this rather bland tape is as an excuse to state that, in general, New Age priestesses in their forties are better looking than Christian "tonguers" in their twenties. It must be the hairdos—New Agers wear their hair in 1960s and 1970s styles, whereas the evangelicals are straight from 1950 Alabama. You can probably tell where my metaphysical leanings point. I guess I'm just not enlightened, self-trapped as I am down here in this mundane sphere with its reproductive organs and base instincts. Shucks.

"THE HURTLESS LIFE"

Huna Research, Inc.
Dr. E. Otha Wingo
126 Camellia Dr.
Cape Girardeau, MO 63701

Has various resources available for those interested in the ancient Hawaiian Kahuna system of magic. SASE for info. IT WILL WORK FOR YOU! *If* you spend $20 for membership, that is. ((With Factsheet Five))

HONKY INJUNS OF THE NEW AGE

Thunderbow
Church of Seven Arrows
4385 Hoyt St., #201
Wheatridge, CO 80033

A neo-pagan publication aimed mainly at neophytes, shamans, medicine men. And women. Not that most self-respecting, super-macho AmerInd cultures would've allowed women in the sweat lodge! Not in the old days. . . . Drawing on numerous traditions, it provides almost a survey course in such diverse topics as astrology, runecasting, elemental magic, the I Ching, and Chinese medicine. 75¢ each, $8/year. ((With Factsheet Five))

I WAS A PSYCHIC FOR THE FBI

Psychic Guide
PO Box 701, Providence, RI 02901

This is sort of like a *Whole Life Times* for the spiritualist lunatic fringe. Inside we find channeling (including the inevitable interview with the "new" Seth, a superstar among Channeling Entities), subliminal persuasion, a nationwide guide to psychics, schools, pyramid sellers, and a shitload of ads. $2.95 each. ((With Factsheet Five))

BUNCHA WEENIES

Phallos
St. Priapus Church, 583 Grove St.
San Francisco, CA 94102

Newsletter of "The ORGAN-ized Religion," espousing the Dionysian rites of phallic worship. They're quite serious about the religious aspects—they even run a Rescue Mission for homeless homos—but they're also out for a *good time*. Worship includes "free glory hole service" and "phallic adoration circle jack-off sessions." One might assume, given their geographic location, that they have strong beliefs in life after death. The pastor walks around with his privates hanging out of his pants.* "Classified ads" in the back are AMAZING! $5/year.

* The only SubGenius ministers who dress this way *regularly* are the members of the Dallas C + W gospel band, Rev. Buck Naked and the Jaybirds.

Gods Working . . .

Mystic Press
John Kurluk, PO Box 6186
Baltimore, MD 21231

I don't know what brought it on, but the lead article in this pagan 'zine is "Diabetics are more Psychic and Mystical!" Inside, the strange coverage continues, with stories of haunted houses, Rocky Mountain Winged Men, and female spirituality. $6/year. ((With Factsheet Five))

. . . In Mysterious Ways . . .

Beyond Avalon
93 Jackson Ave.
Bridgeport, CT 06606

A new psychic journal that packs a lot into its pages. There's an article on the use of psi in the stock market, more from the Seth energies (the NEW, IMPROVED Seth, that is), psi warfare, and another piece on lucid dreaming. Also features an editorial from a channeled entity. Oddly enough, this one isn't dumb at all. But still plenty weird. $2. ((With Factsheet Five))

. . . But Not As Mysterious As Their Mortal Followers!

The Living Sphere
BSRF, PO Box 549, Vista, CA 92083

An odd combination of mysticism and deep ecology, aboriginal shamanism, Shinto, astrology, Hollow Earth, occult healing, Hopi Indian myths, Shaver-stuff, and more—forty-eight pages of fringe wisdom. Check out the article "Living Water" on the theories of Viktor Schauberger, who helped Hitler build flying saucers. $4.44. ((With Factsheet Five))

Your Favorite Kind

The American Sunbeam
PO Box 107, Seligman, MO 65745

I have no idea what this is about and I'm not sure the author, Delamer Duverus, does either. Full of unconnected ravings about the dangers of genetic engineering, the "alien Pharisees" who run our government, the KAL 007 incident, and the millennial utterances of one "JeSus Immanuel." ((With Factsheet Five))

AND IN THIS CORNER . . .

Red Buddha
N.B. Shifferly, Mind-Way Church
PO Box 664, Mansfield, OH 44901

(Also known as Zendokan Budokai of America) Journal of spiritual martial arts meditation. "Cultivate the mind and make savage the body," runs their motto, and they bring different gods into the fray each issue. Lord Krishna led the fun in one, for instance, with excerpts from the Bhagavad-Gita. The samurai tradition also puts in an appearance. If you get serious and join up, though, you're not allowed to cut your hair or shave. $1 each, $9/year. ((With Factsheet Five))

SKULL CANDLES!!!

International Imports
8050 Webb Ave.
N. Hollywood, CA 91605

Sells "Goddess Spell Kits" for putting hexes and jinxes on unwanted neighbors, etc. Lots of herbs, oils, incense, candles, powders, every range of nostrums and remedies. You can also get "Vice Spice Imitation Spanish Fly" and SKULL CANDLES!!

SHOE POLISH WEEK??

Sacred Journal of the Jihad of Our Lady of Perpetual Chaos
195 Garfield Place, #2-L
Brooklyn, NY 11215

Actually one of the funnier humor magazines around. No kidding! $1 + SASE.

YOU GO YAHWEH, I'LL GO MINE

Yahweh Kingdom City, Inc.
PO Box 2078
Sun City, AZ 85372

Sun City is a huge retirement community in Arizona, and it's common knowledge among nearby residents that a lot of the folks there are walking around without all of their neurons firing. This guy claims he talked FDR into putting the Eye in the Pyramid on the dollar bill (Who knows? Maybe he did.), LBJ and Truman speak to him from the "other side," he wants you to send him money so he can make his mortgage payment because that's what Yahweh wants, and on and on and on. A dollar will get you a bill envelope filled with more weirdness than you can shake a pacemaker at. ((Remote Control))

CROWLEY CULTS

MORE FUN THAN A BARREL O' DEMONS

Ordo Templi Orientis (OTO)
PO Box 2303, Berkeley, CA 94702

The OTO (Ordo Templi Orientis), a modern occult fan club of that spiritual bad-boy and all-around Antichrist Aleister Crowley, has been growing swiftly ever since it was popularized in the satirical metaphysical novels of Robert Anton Wilson. With its newfound pop status, "The Order" now takes itself too seriously. Lacking Crowley's all-important sense of humor, what was originally his greatest put-on is now a rallying point for antisocial rejects, vindictive pseudo-Satanists, resentful nerds who consider themselves "enlightened," and insecure intellectuals eager to freak out Mom by establishing contact with their own guardian elemental.* If you fit into any of the above categories, write for info on the chapter in your area. They also have copies of Crowley's insane books for sale. A hint—his best works by far are his dirty poems and limericks, which are so disgustingly funny they almost make up for the bullshit he spawned.

THEY WISH HE'D BEEN THE ANTICHRIST

The Magickal Link
GSG, JAF Box 7884
New York, NY 10116

One of several "official" monthly bulletins of "the" OTO (depending on which of the many bitterly feuding splinter groups you like). Crowley was an interesting fellow, but it's a damn good thing he died before this army of potential zombies started swarming. Theoretically, this is *supposed* to be the ultimate religion of the individual, so the nerdy zealousness of the Crowley fans is pretty ironic. On the other hand, these followers may really be the "punchline" of his greatest joke.**

* This may sound like a description of the typical "Bobbie" or overzealous SubGenius, but that's only because you haven't made it up to Hierarchy status yet, where reign the cool Doktor people, hip, studly saints, and buxotic Nunsnake Dominatrixes.

** If so, then "Bob" is a plagiarist!

CROWLEY SAID IT, I BELIEVE IT, AND THAT SETTLES IT

Stellar Visions
808 Post St., #93
San Francisco, CA 94109

Publishes rare books by Aleister Crowley. They also blend natural ritual oils—*no synthetics!*—and offer Abramelin Oil plus personalized Planetary and Astrological oils using your natal chart! Finest available! How'd I ever live without 'em??

FUNNY SLAVES OF THE DARK SIDE

The Aurea Flamma
OTB, Box 1219
Corpus Christi, TX 78403

Free sample for SASE. An interesting OTO local newsletter packed with elaborate mumbo jumbo from this "Gnostic-Thelemic occult fraternal order (Ophite-Cainite)." They dare to sell Occult Secrets on *cassette tapes!!* Articles and news of current occult happenings by people with names like "Fra. Ashtaroth-Arnuphis, Knight of the Star $6° = 5\square$." This one's pretty unofficial looking, but much funnier than the slicker OTO pubs. I still don't understand why anybody would want to mess with long, embarrassing rituals just to raise up demons; according to the Christians, all you have to do is listen to Led Zeppelin or even the Mr. Ed theme song backwards.* Beats me.... These "Adepts" will teach you how to get in touch with your Guardian Angel (your soul's most illuminated previous incarnation). $7.50/twelve.

LET *HIM* FINISH THIS HERCULEAN LABOR

There are dozens and dozens, probably hundreds of other "channels"; I could list more, but they're all so generically "New Age" that the repeated gushings of "light" and "love" get monotonous after a while. If you want the most complete possible list of odd groups, try J. Gordon Melton's books:

THE ENCYCLOPEDIA OF AMERICAN RELIGIONS (only $165, but it has EVERYTHING)

Gale Research Company, Book Tower, Detroit, MI 48226

or, also by Rev. Melton:

BIOGRAPHICAL DICTIONARY OF AMERICAN CULT AND SECT LEADERS ($39.95)

and

ENCYCLOPEDIC HANDBOOK OF CULTS IN AMERICA ($24.95)

* Have you *ever* gone to the trouble of playing a record or tape *backwards?* Most home audio technology makes it a big pain in the ass.

Both from Garland Publishing, 136 Madison Ave., New York, NY 10016

Your local library *should* have these, but probably doesn't. The summaries are about as fair as one could ask—the opposite of this book.

What is the one TRUE religion? Mine, of course. I asked "Bob," and he didn't *disagree*. I'm actually a . . . a *religious* kind of guy, for someone who doesn't believe *any* of that crap, but I give the Lord a lot more credit than most Church- or Temple-goers do. A LOT more. So much more that I don't feel obliged to check in with It. (Besides, that's what we pay "Bob" for!) Once I ended up in a place where there was only It and me; I learned the hard way that the only aspect of "the Lord" I'd ever begin to understand was the part from my own skin inwards. You can *enjoy* or *fear* the rest—you can fall in love with parts of it, eat other parts of it as food, drive around in another chunk of it, etc.— but to start claiming you have It's rulebook is an insult to the Itness of It All, and, for

that matter, most people's intelligence. Even SubGeniuses'.

I suspect, however—very tentatively— that there may indeed *be* other intelligences, bodiless by our standards, that do have the limited, anthropomorphic attributes commonly ascribed by some idiots to "God," but which others see as devils, others as Ascended Masters, and so on. I also suspect that everyone has a "sixth sense" (left over only vestigially from caveman days), but that it is generally so vague and unpredictable that it's useless to most people unless they've managed to keep their intuition honed—not an easy trick in this version of civilization.

My psychic abilities have certainly been dulled, no doubt by overuse of the wrong side of my brain. I know I *had* a smidgen, though; when I was a kid, I always knew a week ahead of the *TV Guide* if one of my favorite monster movies would be on TV, and as an alcoholic teenager I had a "Spidey Sense" that would alert me before anyone could catch me drinking or smoking.* Honest.

---

* The only remnant of my alcoholism is a wrecked bladder and a prescription for Antabuse, a pill that makes it impossible to drink. Antabuse sits in your blood, totally inert unless you backslide off the wagon and glag down some firewater; then it turns the alcohol into formaldehyde. You become a telltale bright red and VERY uncomfortable. If you keep drinking, you die. A cheap replacement for willpower, you say? And you intimate that if "Bob" Dobbs was really such a hot guru, I wouldn't need these pills? Well, if, for instance, Jesus were all He's cracked up to be, then theoretically you wouldn't *need Jesus* either! And a true SubGenius does not *need* "Bob." In fact, the vast majority of true Subs have never even heard of him, nor of their own Destiny. We *use* "Bob," and he uses us: a mutual exploitation. I *use* these pills because it frees my willpower for other things—like, for instance, breaking free of "Bob's" insidious Svengali-like influence (unwitting though it may be). Look, Alcoholism is Forever; I'd much rather my crutch be some inanimate pills and keep the gods or gurus as *friends*. They already have enough jerks leaning on Them. Just as newly famous celebrities are embarrassed by the unnecessary adulation of fawning fans (until they finally start believing the fans' assertion that they are *special* and become assholes), deities and prophets are always relieved to find mortals who treat them as *equals*. It's lonely at the top, you see. The sole intention of the best Messiahs is simply to trick people into giving themselves more credit. But it always seems to backfire! Even Dobbs, who is obviously far less "intelligent" than most people—indeed, he's practically retarded by normal standards— cannot seem to escape the pathetic self-hating "Bobbies" who want to believe he is a super being. He is, but not the way they think. He didn't *earn* saviorhood. He is only . . . *lucky*. Meditate upon this. What good is intelligence, prowess, courage, money, or even Truth, without LUCK? With enough Luck, is *anything* else needed? An understanding of this will take you many steps closer to *gut* knowledge, to Slack Awareness, and finally to Slack itself.

YOU JUST WAIT UNTIL PAT ROBERTSON IS PRESIDENT!!

Temple of Set
PO Box 29271
San Francisco, CA 94129

Devil worshippers! A schism from Anton LaVey's Church of Satan*, but also borrowing from the ever-fragmenting OTO. This is a "movement" dedicated to the Prince of Darkness, and they're into glorification of the ego —INDULGENCE, all-out SLACK, etc. I don't think you can get their materials without being a member; you'd almost have to live in San Francisco. The introduction materials are pretentious in the extreme; frankly, I don't think the various God clubs have much to fear from these particular minions of Old Split-Foot.

GET REAL

Temple of Nepthys
PO Box 4603
San Francisco, CA 94101

Another "authentic evolutionary successor to the Church of Satan..." identifying with a "Hecatic" current emerging from a "Satanic" tradition. Well, wouldn't want to get 'em mixed up, would we? A bit more "feminist" and "compassionate" in this case of "the Red Arts"... a "positive filtering system" for potential negative Satanism, trying to catch them kids before they get into the hard-core stuff like Temple of Set! Certainly a "hell" of a lot better written than Set's boys do it. You get all kinds of nifty Satanic membership documents for $25.

Not much money for an *eternal soul*, is it, MOCKER??

EVEN HERESIES HAVE THEIR OWN HERETICS

But then, all of the above are DEGENERATES and PRETENDERS!!! The only TRUE OTO (just ask them!) is:

Society Ordo Templi Orientis International
Caixa Postal 1163
14100 Ribeirao Preto SP, Brasil

They had to leave the U.S. when the courts ruled they *weren't* the owners of the original Crowley work, and owed all their assets to their rivals. (Don't ask me.) This is your ONLY source for UNTAINTED Crowley books.

* "Bob" is an enemy of Satan; however, this is not particularly because he is drinking buddies with the Fightin' Jesus, but because Satan owes both of them a great deal of "money." (There is gambling in Hell; during Dobbs's most recent death (1984–1986), he won his freedom from Hell in an infernal billiards game—by *cheating!*) I should mention that the Church of the SubGenius grants you just as many rights to full-tilt hedonism as these guys do, but you don't have to kiss any demons' asses, your fellow SubGeniuses are way less pompous, and it only costs $20.

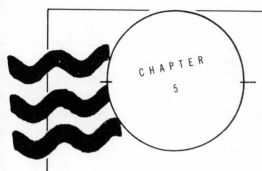

CHAPTER 5

HEALTH/SELF-IMPROVEMENT AND $CHEMES/$CAMS

LEARN NOT TO BLEED OR HURT

Conscious Living Foundation
Box 520, Manhattan, KS 66502

Dr. Tim Lowenstein sticks needles in his arm and wiggles them around to demonstrate that humans can mentally control pain and bleeding, and also to get you to send for his free magazine on stress management. What a way to get attention! Geeks at the State Fair Freak Show charge 50¢ to poke themselves for audiences. It's for real, though—yogis have been gouging themselves with nails for centuries, and, via biofeedback, you can learn it much faster than they did. Now, that's what I call *relaxed.*

SNIFF YOUR WAY TO HEALTH? GOSH, HOW ... SIMPLE

White Light Unlimited
40 W. Twenty-second St.
New York, NY 10010

Did you know you can "tune" your body into health through colors, sounds, and odors? This company sells a COLOR, SOUND, AND FRAGRANCE KIT with "7 primal es-

sences plus 2 sealing scents, 9 corresponding color plates, a beautiful quartz crystal and an audio cassette with corresponding musical notes." Right. Now put a pyramid on your car, wear your underwear on your head, and count backwards from 273 by threes. YOU HAVE ACHIEVED WHOLENESS.

HYPNOTISM BY MAIL

Path Foundation
PO Box 2001, Wichita, KS 67201

No, she won't hypnotize you by mail; this is a correspondence course in hypnotherapy. THE POSTMAN HIMSELF WILL DO YOUR BIDDING. Why not learn how to hypnotize your TV *back?*

WHY EAT ANY LONGER??

Puritan's Pride
105 Orville Dr., Bohemia, NY 11716

Typical example of the thousands of vitamin catalogs that have cropped up to feed stressed-out Americans' insatiable appetite for miracle pills. Vitamins for hair growth, sleep, energy, pain, colds, beauty, "legal highs," impotency.

LET 'EM KEEP THE MEAT THEY WERE BORN WITH

A Small Voice Crying Out in the Wilderness
The Remain Intact "ORGAN"ization, Box 86, Larchwood, IA 51241

A lone crusader trying to halt "Routine Circumcision." The tiny victims of this "HEINOUS CRIME of SEXUAL MOLESTATION . . . are strapped to a restraining board, then TORTURED in the most BRUTAL, bloody manner as their very sensitive sex organ is partially amputated without even the benefit of anesthetic!" Points out that there are no real medical reasons for circumcision, and—more importantly—it's not biblical. "The Christian TRUTH against this form of mayhem." I agree with the guy about "leaving a tip" for the doctors—they get upwards of $150 extra for this snippet of work—but doesn't he know how inadvertently hilarious his brochure must be? You'll receive a fat envelope of scare literature every couple of weeks. Lately, this obsessed fanatic has become increasingly shrill about the "Jewish connection"; also, he's noticed that his fellow Christians are shying away from his cause rather than taking up arms, and he's getting PISSED. It's bound to reach a fever pitch soon. The return address on the envelope alone is worth writing him for: "The Remain Intact 'ORGAN'ization." Now look at the name of his newsletter again. Free.

FLASH!! LAST MINUTE UPDATE! Just before going to press we learned that, sure enough, a fever pitch was indeed reached, and an ironic one at that. The local cops BUSTED our lone crusader—for CHILD PORNOGRAPHY yet! For, in their infinite discernment, they judged one single photo—a sickening close-up of a baby's dick in the process of hospital circumcision that graced a newsletter—to be erotic porn. Now our hero is dealing with the stigma and harassment that inevitably follows even a false arrest such as this. Only the most depraved and ignorant of redneck cop minds could see the snapshot in question as pornographic; it's such an extreme close-up, showing mainly the foreskin-clipping device, that you'd never in a million years recognize the tiny patch of pink as a baby's dick without being *told* what the picture was ahead of time. I cannot hazard a guess what the moral of this story is; maybe it proves that there really *has* been a fanatical and highly organized pro-circumcision conspiracy all along, and that these harmless anti-circumcision people were, if anything, *grossly understating* the situation! One shudders at what the future may bring. Roving bands of mad foreskin-amputating Circumcision Terrorists? A furtive underground movement, a People's Penis Sheath Liberation Front? Assaults on maternity wards? Compulsory Federal Penis Inspections at job interviews? Surprise raids? "Police! Everybody freeze and drop your drawers!" Grim prospects, folks. . . .

Brain-Dead, But What Great Teeth!

Safe Water Foundation
6439 Taggart Rd.
Delaware, OH 43015

Issues broadsides against fluoridation of water supplies. Some antifluoride groups are freakish cranks; this one has a lot of scary figures to back them up. Did you know that 50,000 people were poisoned when too much fluoride was accidentally dumped into the Annapolis water supply? Neither did they, until two weeks after the cover-up. It's happened more than once. Unfortunately, for the American Dental Association and the U.S. Public Health Service to admit *this late* that they were wrong about fluoride would make them look bad, so . . . *

Somehow I Don't Think Blue Cross Is Gonna Cover This

Aquarian Center of Universology
1935 Beneva Ct., #300
Sarasota, FL 33582

"Universology . . ." Hmmmm. Classes, lectures, healing, even ETHERIC SURGERY (no knives!)!! These people will bring deceased physicians back from the spirit world to perform psychic surgery and offer medical opinion; Dr. Vernon acts as medium and secretary to a large staff of dead doctor guys. You can't beat having those normally nerve-racking operations performed by ghostly entities. (But just try to sue for malpractice!) Through numerology and other advanced sciences, they'll tell you EVERYTHING about your past lives. ((With Remote Control))

---

* According to biographer Philo Drummond, it was J.R. "Bob" Dobbs himself who sold the idea (+ supplies) of fluoride to the U.S. government. His real motive for this Divine Sale: fluoride stimulates growth of the holy, Slack-sensing "Foot Gland."

DOCTORS FOR SLACK (AND WHO DON'T CHARGE ENOUGH)

Townsend Letter for Doctors
911 Tyler St.
Port Townsend, WA 98368

Newsletter for professionals in the Alternative Medicine field, who are continually under attack from the AMA-approved medical establishment, often for no good reason except that it eats away at "Their" conspiratorially inflated profits. Holistic medicine, like holistic-everything-else, is a field peppered with fruitcakes, but it also utilizes otherwise ignored techniques that work wonders. And no matter how nutty it gets, it can't get much worse than Establishment medicine. $2/sample; $20/year.

PUTTING ROVER TO SLEEP—NATURALLY!

Holistic Animal News
Box 9384, Seattle, WA 98109

Now I've seen everything! Get this (an actual quote from their promo blurbs): " 'Holistic' means treating the 'whole' animal on all levels: physical, mental, emotional, behavioral and spiritual. " That's what my old guard dog, Beast, needs—more spiritual counseling. Maybe if he examined a Kirlian photo of his aura, he'd be able to resolve his aggressive tendencies. Here's another piercing fact, certain to turn the medical establishment on its ear, from an article about healing your pup's heart condition with crystals: "Crystals are simply fossilized water." Veterinary homeopathy . . . a new age dawns indeed. Is humanism now regressing to animism?? $2.50 sample or $10/four.

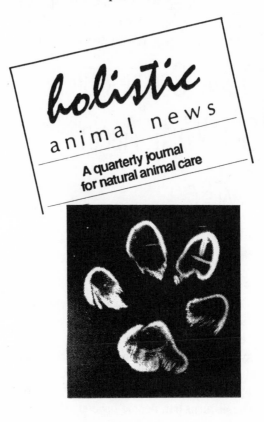

holistic animal news
A quarterly journal for natural animal care

WHY DO YOU THINK THEY CALL IT "BOO"?

Listen America
Box 100, Riverside, CA 92502

Publisher *Drug Abuse Tragedies,* a gory book purportedly documenting birth defects caused by marijuana and designed to scare the living crap out of school kids. Bet it works, too. Not funny. Sick. Warning: This absolutely disgusting full color brochure is NOT for the weak of heart or stomach. Free if you really want it. ((Remote Control))

DEATH CONQUERED!! BUT WHAT ABOUT TAXES?

Bible of the Undead
Chemung Books, 338 Deaton St.
Statesville, NC 28677

When Dr. D.C. Barrie was returned to life after being clinically dead for several minutes, he brought back with him "...a KEY UNDERSTANDING of the SCIENCE OF RELIGION..." which can enable YOU to escape aging and even death itself! All this time, it turns out, people have grown old and died not because God compelled them to, but because they *chose* to. Gosh...what chumps we've been! *The Bible of the Undead* spells out simple "...FACTS and TECHNIQUES... by which THE LEAST INTELLIGENT MAY AVAIL HIMSELF OF THIS EXCEEDINGLY PRECIOUS KNOWLEDGE, RIGHT NOW!!" I guess the *more* intelligent are plumb out of luck. Serves 'em right. For those of us who do qualify, though, $10.95 is certainly a *cheap price to pay* for a book that guarantees nothing less than bodily immortality, eternal youth, PLUS an end to all worldly problems! I wonder why more people haven't taken him up on it! If you can't yet afford outright immortality, maybe you can scrounge at least a few *days* of eternal youth out of his free promo brochure and instructions for holding SECRET DIVINE LOVE RADIATION SERVICES. Send SASE.

WAVES FOREST'S HEALTH TIPS

MRC UNIT OF REPRODUCTIVE BIOLOGY 37 Chalmers St., Edinburgh EH3 9EW, Scotland; Robert J. Aitken, M.D.: Developing a male contraceptive "vaccine" of monoclonal antibodies, based on naturally occurring antibodies found in some sterile men, that destroy their own spermatozoa. Reversible, with no apparent harmful side effects. Perhaps this will fulfill the long-unkept promise of the pharmaceutical industry to come up with a safe male contraceptive that would finally allow men to assume their fair share of reproductive responsibility.

PROJECT CURE Robert De Bragga, Director, 2020 K St. NW, Washington, DC 20069: Pushing for investigation of the medical industry's resistance to nutritional cancer therapies that have proven effective (e.g., Max Gerson's).

PSIONIC MEDICINE Dr. Aubrey T. Westlake, Psionic Medicine Society, Hindhead, Surrey, England. $20/year/two issues.

RADIONIC QUARTERLY: AN APPROACH TO HEALTH AND HARMONY Radionic Assn. Ltd., 16a North Bar Banbury, Oxon OX16 OTF, England. $15/year.

THE WILHELM REICH MUSEUM PO Box 687, Rangely, ME 04970: Orgonomy info.

THE CLEAN YIELD Fried and Fleer Investment Services, PO Box 1880, Greensboro Bend, VT 05842: A newsletter for stock market players who want to invest only in companies that appear to have clean hands. To be recommended here, a company can't be visibly involved in South Africa, nuclear power, environmental destruction, weapons production, tobacco, etc. This should weed out the worst of them. $75/year.

COMMITTEE FOR FREEDOM OF CHOICE IN MEDICINE 111 Ellis St. #300, San Francisco, CA 94192: Points out unused cures, and the artificial origins of certain new diseases, notably AIDS.

HYPER-OZONE THERAPY

Hyper-ozone therapy destroys the AIDS virus in blood, according to reports of the work of Dr. Horst Kief in Germany. It can apparently also eliminate all other disease organisms present.

The ozone is produced by forcing oxygen through a metal tube carrying a 300-volt charge. A pint of blood is drawn from the patient and placed in an infusion bottle. The ozone is then forced into the bottle and thoroughly mixed in by shaking. As the ozone molecules dissolve into the blood they give up their third oxygen atom, releasing considerable energy that kills all virus and bacteria while leaving blood cells unharmed. The treated blood is then given back to the patient. This treatment is given twice a week. The strengthened blood confers virucidal properties to the rest of the patient's blood as it disperses.

(Reported by Albert Zock in the July–August '86 *Journal of Borderland Research*, Borderland Sciences Research Foundation, PO Box 429, Garberville, CA 95440-0429; see listing in Chapter 1.)

OXIDATIVE MEDICINE NEWSLETTER Box 61767, Dallas, Tx 75261: Updates on the controversial but promising oxygen therapies.

ECHO Walter Grotz, Box 126, Delano, MN 55328: References and case histories of successful treatment of cancer, AIDS, etc. through oxygen therapy.

INTERNATIONAL OZONE ASSOCIATION 83 Oakwood Ave., Norwalk, CT 06850: Extensive archives on medical uses of ozone against supposedly incurable or terminal illness.

MONEY SCHEMES/SCAMS

This is another potentially endless section. I'll spare you by presenting just a few examples of the genre. For each one of these, there are dozens of variations . . . and I'm not even touching on the big multilevel marketing schemes. You already get their toll-free numbers crammed into your head subliminally, through TV commercials.

HELLO, SUCKER!

J.A. Keel
PO BOX 20024
New York, NY 10025-9992

You've seen all those little ads that start, "MAKE BIG MONEY IN MAIL ORDER! Send $1 for details." The mischievous John Keel (coincidentally the author of ground-breaking books of UFO paranoia like *Operation Trojan Horse* and *The Mothman Prophecies,* which he sells) puts out those little ads, too. Only his approach is entirely different. Here's how one starts off: "HELLO, SUCKER! Something's wrong here. You jumped into mail order to get rich, and instead you're getting poorer slowly. You paid a fortune to send out thousands of circulars and what did you get back? Hundreds of circulars from other mail order suckers, that's what! . . . You've tried multi-level and your 'programs' have died at the second level. What happened to the $50,000 you were supposed to collect? FED UP?" . . . and so on. Of course, he does offer the *straight* poop, the *real* way to set up a mail-order biz that works—in a $2 booklet. He also mails out a funny rant-ad sheet called BIG APPLE NEWS. Add a buck and he'll include a genuine INTERPLANETARY PASSPORT good on every planet except Neptune. (The Neptunians pissed him off.)

DREAM ON

Ernest Vandenken
7014 Thirteenth Ave.
Brooklyn, NY 11228

For ONLY $20 this "greatest psychic on earth" will tell you the three lottery numbers he saw in a dream about YOU PERSONALLY —and you'll win a fortune in ANY lottery. If you don't win in two months, he'll refund your $20. *If* he hasn't moved on to another address. You can tell he's sincere because his letter is "handwritten" to you (by machine), and the only reason he wants the $20 is as a guarantee that you won't spend your upcoming fortune *unwisely.* Gee, what a nice guy. He really cares. Just ask for info; his letter is a priceless document of scamdom.

"LADY LUCK" REALLY WORKS LIKE MAGIC! NO MUSS NO FUSS!

Good Luck Research Project
Comprehension, 1169 Summit Rd.
Santa Barbara, Ca 93108

Well, I be damn—another lucky lottery scheme! Even with just the free info, you get a Registered Lady Luck Symbol created more than 500 years ago and discovered on the walls of a sacred Aztec temple! When you order your Lady Luck pendant within five days, you get a FREE copy of "How YOU Can Make Other People Do Exactly What YOU Want Them To Do!"—now you can "force" people to love you, give you a raise, etc. How can you lose??

YOURS FREE!

Yes! When you order your Lady Luck pendant or key chain within the next 5 days you get a powerful FREE extra bonus — a copy of "How YOU Can Make Other People Do Exactly What YOU Want Them To Do!" Haven't you often wished that you possessed the RARE POWER to COMMAND OBEDIENCE from others with just a casual word, a brief glance? Haven't you wished you could DOMINATE other people with your inner force? NOW, YOU CAN!

Just imagine what it would be like to have it within your personal power to "force" your boss to give you a big raise — to "force" some YOU love to love YOU — to "force" your friends, family and business associates to give you admiration and respect. What a wonderful power to have.

The ONLY way to get your FREE copy of "How YOU Can Make Other People Do Exactly What You Want Them To Do" is to complete and mail the order form on the other side!

INSTANT $$$ THROUGH HANDWRITING ANALYSIS!!

Institute of Graphology
412 S. Lyon St.
Santa Ana, CA 92701

The art and science of Graphology will allow you—as a trained Graphologist—to INSTANTLY "KNOW" the personality traits (and weaknesses!) of business rivals, lovers, and customers, simply by glimpsing samples of their penmanship. Earn easy money as an in-demand Graphology consultant for giant firms! Impress and astonish friends with your miraculous powers of GRAPHO-THERAPY!! Write for info . . . send NO MONEY.

As a skilled GRAPHOLOGIST you can –

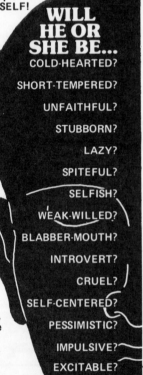

WILL HE OR SHE BE...
COLD-HEARTED?
SHORT-TEMPERED?
UNFAITHFUL?
STUBBORN?
LAZY?
SPITEFUL?
SELFISH?
WEAK-WILLED?
BLABBER-MOUTH?
INTROVERT?
CRUEL?
SELF-CENTERED?
PESSIMISTIC?
IMPULSIVE?
EXCITABLE?
MOODY?

✳ Pull off the "mask" of personality that people project — expose the character of the REAL SELF!

✳ Know IMMEDIATELY if the writer is a person you can like and trust — instead of discovering after it's too late!

✳ IMPROVE SELF-ESTEEM, DEVELOP GREATER SELF-CONFIDENCE, OVERCOME DEPRESSION, BUILD POSITIVE THINKING, INCREASE SELF-CONTROL. Change undesirable character traits in yourself and others through GRAPHO-THERAPY! It works! And it stays with you!

✳ Help your children locate and OVERCOME personality or learning problems through their handwriting — help insure good mental growth into adulthood.

✳ Analyze the handwriting of potential marrieds, business partners, roommates, employees and clients — determine if they'll be compatible, reveal if they can be trusted!

✳ Consult (on a fee basis) with Psychologists, Psychiatrists, Lawyers, Detention and Parole Officers, Family Counselors. Give them invaluable aid in personality analysis!

✳ ENTERTAIN, IMPRESS and ASTONISH at social gatherings, club meetings, business conferences — attract press attention and the ENVY of all!

WHAT'S THE WORD?

Universal Life Church, Inc.
601 Third St., Modesto, CA 95351*

Most famous (and harassed) of the Scam Churches that set you up as a "minister" for tax-avoidance purposes. For $3 you'll be legally ordained, and they sell books on how to handle your taxes ... you can write off your home as a "church," for instance. The IRS has really cracked down on this sort of thing, though, and on the Universal Life Church particularly. I'm ordained by these guys, and have performed marriages, but I chose not to play the tax game with it. Founded by a feisty fellow who got tired of subsidizing religions he didn't believe in.

If you'd prefer to obtain your ministerial status from a lower-profile "denomination" than the notorious Universal Life Church, 14 others are listed and entertainingly described in the *Directory of Mail-Order Ministries,* a free booklet available for SASE from Mike Marinacci, 1629 Brockton Ave. #4, Los Angeles, CA 90025.

THE INADVERTENT DICTIONARY OF PSYCHOBABBLE

Ken Keyes College
The Vision Foundation
790 Commercial Ave.
Coos Bay, OR 97420

These courses in "relationship consciousness," "methods for awakening," and so on aren't necessary; just get the free catalog, which is itself a crash course in all the trendy psychobabble you'll ever need to know. Win vacuum-brained friends and influence idiots.

---

* Modesto is the home of another well-known cult—**Thunderbird Wine,** which is used as a sacrament in some street religions, particularly the Maltafari of Boston (see "Billygoons" under "Horror."). The Church of the SubGenius, by the way, is the ONLY religion that is NOT tax exempt. Our prophets want profits, and we don't expect heathen unbelievers to subsidize us. Besides, we couldn't get nonprofit status anyway. The IRS thought it was *too funny* to be of actual HELP to humanity. Odd how their criteria work.

SPURIOUS™ BRAND BAD-LUCK JUJU REMOVER

Professor Matiha

PO Box 6542, Jackson, MS 39212

Puts out a giant tabloid ad for his Bad Luck negating services. This is your basic Americanized Voodoo, though they never use that name. According to the Prof, Bad Luck is contagious—you can catch it by shaking hands with someone afflicted with it, by drinking from the same cup, even by walking in that person's footprints (much like AIDS as seen by homophobics). He charges $20 to send you the details of his foolproof "method" for getting rid of Bad Luck . . . but write him a good sob story in broken English and he'll send the amazing ad.

A Word About Professor Matiha ...

Professor Matiha has been living in the United States for the past 14 years. His native country is India. He is the only known Professor who studies the art of destroying evil and bad luck. His research has led him to different parts of the world. But most of his research and findings have come from the West Indies and South Africa. Professor Matiha has no super natural powers, he only uses modern technology with historic background to defeat all forms of bad luck. His research and findings have led him to the natural names of bad luck — Tormo, Kousa, Booka No. 1 and Booka No. 2.

Professor Matiha did not advertise his method to defeat bad luck until all tests proved to be positive and showed a definite defeat against all evil and bad luck.

BIGGEST MONEY DISCOVERY SINCE THE INDUSTRIAL REVOLUTION

Neo-Tech
PO Box 906, Boulder City, NV 89005

An up-and-coming new "Instant Riches through Self Help" scam. It's fun to read the free info and imagine the kind of gullible, sad wish-they-were-Yuppies who fall for it. "Scientific Method" for prosperity makes every situation a *winnable* situation.

FACTS CONCERNING YOUR MISSION

RI Research
949 Broadway, New York, NY 10010

"You Are a Beyonder." And you have been "CHOSEN" for success, happiness, prosperity, because you "UNDERSTAND" that your fate isn't governed *only* by the stars. New Age motivational garbage.

Dr. Wallace's Chart #1
CONTRASTING CHARACTERISTICS

The Traditional Cheater	The Neo-Tech Man
Stiff, Nervous	Relaxed, Confident
Controlled by surroundings	Controls surroundings
"When should I do it" feeling — cheats at every opportunity	Knows exactly when to apply Neo-Tech — applies it selectively
Keeps people from watching him closely. Uses distractions and concealments	Lets people watch him. Needs no distractions or concealments
Causes suspicion with cheating moves — fears all opponents	Eliminates suspicion with Neo-Tech moves — fears no one
Makes victims unhappy while creating tense, traumatic atmospheres	Makes competition happy while creating friendly, easy-going atmospheres
Worries that his cheating will be seen	Knows that Neo-Tech cannot be seen
Fears his telltale characteristics	Works in relaxed harmony with his natural characteristics
Worries about the consequences of being caught in the act	Knows he cannot be caught in any act
Is negative in every way	Appears beneficial in every way

Everything Made Easy

Melvin Powers
12015 Sherman Rd.
N. Hollywood, Ca 91605

Free catalog of a zillion self-help books with titles like: *Psychocybernetics; Grow Rich While You Sleep; What Your Handwriting Reveals; How to Solve Your Sex Problems with Self-Hypnosis; Reflexology* (i.e. cosmic foot rubs); *Think and Grow Rich.*

Sorry

Institute of Advanced Thinking
845 Via de la Paz, Pacific
Palisades, CA 90272

Offers, among other things, a course on "instant memory," but I forget if it works or not. Find out. Free catalog. ((Remote Control))

Don't Quit Your Day Job

Spare Time Money Making Opportunities
Kipan Publishing
5810 W. Oklahoma Ave.
Milwaukee, WI 53219

Perhaps you'd like to sell fake cigarettes for smokers trying to kick the habit? Or maybe making your own bumper stickers is more attractive. Vinyl repair? Bronzing baby shoes? Preparing taxes? Upholstery? It's all here with plenty of people willing to sell you the simple instructions so *they* can make money in *their* spare time. 50¢. ((Factsheet Five))

MONEY!
$$$$
LEARN HOW YOU CAN MAKE MONEY WITHOUT EVEN TRYIN'
(SEE TOP OF PAGE 15)

Millions Through "Millions Through Mail Order" Ads

Jeanne's Treasures
41 W. Center, Mt. Gilead, OH 43338

Bottomless source of "Big Mails"—those sheets that contain lots of little ads and money-making deals. Just flipping through this issue I find the expected printing and mailing services, recipe exchanges, multi-level marketing, How to Win the Lottery, headlight reminders, and lots more. Send a buck and you'll get all the get-rich-quick schemes you can go broke on. ((With Factsheet Five))

"I Like To Sell Tapes For Mind Communication Company"

Mind Communication
2620 Remico SW, Box 9429
Grand Rapids, MI 49509-0429

Big free catalog of self-improvement subliminal tapes for "MAXIMUM ACHIEVERS." Here's how it works: give 'em your choice of muzak (EZ-listening, New Age, bland rock, bluegrass, etc.) and needs (Stop Smoking, Self-Confidence, Headache Relief, etc.) . . . your tape comes with the "commands" imbedded subliminally in the music. Examples of subliminal statements on the BED-WETTING tape: "I can do it. I like dry clothes. I like to use the toilet. I like my bed dry. I wake up and use the toilet." Also a multilevel marketing scheme.

CHAPTER 6

NEW AGE SAPS

Generic Sweetness-'n'-Light New Age rags are a dime a dozen in any health food store. What follows are either the very typical, or the extra syrupy-sappy.

Corniness is the greatest sin of the New Agers. Graphics to watch for that are surefire indicators of painful corniness: Seagulls. Sailboats. Sunrises. Galaxies. Eggs. Saucers. Crystals. Pyramids. Big eyes.

LET'S SEE IF WE HAVE ANY FATHER FIGURES IN YOUR SIZE

Transformational Information Systems
Box 2913, Gainesville, FL 32602

Trying to match you with the "system of personal transformation" that's right for you —sort of like a computer dating system, except that you get a guru instead of a date. Gurus generally cost a LOT more. ((With Factsheet Five))

BE BLONDE INDIAN

Iron Mountain
Artemisia Press, PO Box 2282
Boulder, CO 80306

Scholarly journal of "magical religion," meaning pagans of various stripes. Hefty articles on what it takes to be a real medicine man in the modern world. It's true that the healings effected by certain Third World witch doctors and medicine men can work miracles. It remains to be seen whether these Old Ways can be taught to anthropology students afflicted with recto-cranial inversion. $5 each. ((With Factsheet Five))

SWEETNESS 'N' LIGHT

Findhorn
The Park, Forres IV36 OTZ, Scotland

Write for *Links with Space* booklet and book catalog. A "White Brotherhood" style commune cofounded by New Age contactee David Spangler, this is one of those sickeningly sweet "Light" outfits that the evangelicals say are demonic. They probably are almost as demonic—or do I mean "moronic"?—as the evangelicals themselves. Findhorn has functioned as a kind of fulcrum for the New Age; they offer a free catalog and carry almost all the major New Age books. The Findhorn publications have a funny air of superiority about them, perhaps because they can afford typesetting rather than cheesy mimeography like their less well connected brethren. Aside from a bigger vocabulary, they really aren't much different.

Shucks—I was gonna menton Rajneeshpuram, the Oregon commune of the Rajneeshees . . . but . . . "Bob" forced the Baghwan into a quick sale.

WHO YA GON' CALL?

Meta-Scoop
1004 Live Oak, Arlington, TX 76012

A little homemade magazine from this group who also do psychic readings, dream interpretation, and ghostbusting. Texans plagued with poltergeists should call these gals. 75¢.

Friends In High Places

Logos
Swedenborg Foundation
139 E. Twenty-third St.
New York, NY 10010

This dry newsletter won't tell you much about old Emmanuel Swedenborg, the Swedish mystic who related his guided tours of the Afterlife in several astounding books, but they have a free catalog telling you where to get them. Swedenborg's rants on life as an angel read better than most science fiction, even though he wrote them a couple of hundred years ago.

Avert Catastrophe Through Smugness

Planetary
Citizens
PO Box 2722
San Anselmo, CA 94960

Giant New Age club for would-be do-gooders. Write for catalog and details on magazine —learn how to save the planet by sitting around meditating all day. Lots of theoretical brou-ha-ha about averting catastrophe by positive thinking. Some of it's wimpy enough to be funny; and there are a *few* useful references as to what exactly to *do* about this mess we're in. The rest just makes me mad. *Positive Thinking can kill you.*

Big Talk On Little Planet

GAIA
Institute for the Study of Conscious Evolution, 2418 Clement St.
San Francisco, CA 94121

Typical New Age One-World magazine in which experts use fancy jargon sure to impress upper-middle-class patrons with their "planetary awareness." "Networking the Planetary Community." "Relationships as an Evolutionary Path." "Institutional Problem-Solving in Science and Business." What a load of...ah hell, maybe I should't be so hard on them. I suppose some people *need* to be *told,* and if it's in less pretentious language they won't pay attention. The reliance on clichés insults *my* intelligence, anyway. Give 'em another decade and they'll be every bit as dogmatic as the evangelicals. The New Age? More like The New Self-Righteousness.*

---

* Me, I'm *never* self-righteous. And even if I was, it wouldn't matter; I have "Bob" in my life, and He is my Excuse. The true SubGenius doesn't need to be forgiven; all we need is that mighty Excuse.

And Here's One Of The Dwarf Lords By The Hot Tub

The Awareness Techniques Center
15 Queens Lane Box 338
Stow, MA 01775

More New Age spiritual awareness gobbledygook. However, it was worth a stamp just to see the following line in print: "#5: The Fairy-Spirit and Consciousness. A 4 × 6 photo of 'The Fairy Spirit and Consciousness Over Our Office Stapler.'" Free information, seekers. ((Remote Control))

The Eye In The Pyramid

Wanna get into some really outré classical occultism? Join the Masons. They're everywhere. You have to be invited by someone who's already in "The Craft," but once in, you'll finally know once and for all if Masonry is the insidious conspiracy it's cracked up to be . . . IF you can make it past the degrees they *tell* you about, and into the *secret* orders! GREAT for business contacts; you'll be in the same club as most presidents.

Probably the most enjoyable explanation of Masonry for half-interested outsiders is in Robert Anton Wilson's new series of historical novels, starting with *The Widow's Son* and *The Earth Shall Shake* (Bluejay Books, New York). These are the best yet from a novelist who has gotten more sane people interested in secret societies than all nonfiction writers combined.

Finally, An Honest . . . Oh, I Thought You Said "Car Mechanics"

Angel Tech
Vigilantero Press, PO Box 7513
Boulder, CO 80306

A book by Anterio Alli on reality selection, perception acceleration, karma mechanics, and "the art of being light." $17.95 . . . but ask for the catalog first. ((Waves Forest))

Be Programmed

Institute of Human Development
PO Box 41165
Cincinnati, OH 45241

Harmony, growth, Love, pathways to potential, holistic self-transformation, visualization, positive reprogramming, total fulfillment—all these buzzwords *and more* can now be yours. One of ten jillion self-improvement tape pushers.

GET HIGH ON YOURSELF BABY

Arica
101 Fifth Ave., New York, NY 10003

Oscar Ichazo's Gurdjieff-like* "university" for altered states of consciousness. Theoretically, they aren't out to control your mind, but to give *you* more control over *it*. An amalgamation of many of the hipper Eastern and Western religious traditions (particularly Zen, Sufism, and Cabala), supposedly streamlined for clarity. There's still an awfully high mumbo-jumbo quotient, though.

the violet arc of Consciousness.
the dark blue arc of Intuition.
the blue arc of Attention.
the dark green arc of Expressiveness.
the green arc of Impulse.
the yellow arc of Sympathy.
the orange arc of Vitality.
the red arc of Stability.
the pink arc of Eroticism.

My hatreds - murky yellow
My worries - murky orange
My rivalries - murky red
My remorses - murky pink

My envies - murky green
My lies - murky dark green
My fears - murky blue
My jealousies - murky dark blue
My prejudices - murky violet

Red
Red
Red
Red

Over-nonconformist - murky violet
Over-perfectionist - murky dark blue
Over-independent - murky blue
Over-efficient - murky dark green
Over-reasoner - murky green

Over-judger - murky pink
Over-idealist - murky red
Over-adventurer - murky orange
Over-observer - murky yellow

* Gurdjieff—the "Salvador Dali" of old-timey holy men. Check out his *Beelzebub's Tales to His Grandson*—a close read of the Introduction will make it clear to the discerning that Gurdjieff was laughing all the way to the bank. A true Wise Man.

World Paradise Coming... Film At 11

The Better World Society
1140 Connecticut Ave. NW, #1006
Washington, DC 20036

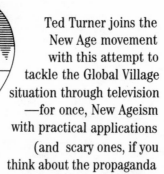

Ted Turner joins the New Age movement with this attempt to tackle the Global Village situation through television —for once, New Ageism with practical applications (and scary ones, if you think about the propaganda possibilities). This new group intends to produce and distribute programming on global issues for international audiences. So far, it looks like the same old One World anti-nuke-war approach...unwittingly forcing everyone into an "American Liberal" viewpoint, in other words, although they say they want to be truly "international." Time will tell. They want money.

"In This Petty Pace" Is *Right!*

The Futurist
World Future Society
4916 St. Elmo Ave.
Bethesda, MD 20814

"Forecasts" for social and technological changes in the years to come, from a hard-science and research standpoint. One of many mags serving the new, 90 percent bullshit "science" of "FUTURISM," which, like modern "Educationism," is so jargon-prone and academic that they fixate on one tree and forget they're in a forest crawling with carnivorous wild animals. Ridiculously steep membership/subscription at $45; make 'em believe you want to "review" it for your "networking magazine" and they'll probably send a free sample copy.

Pink Pagans

The Whole Again Resource Guide
SourceNet
Box 6767
Santa Barbara, CA 93160

A 360-page directory to 600 new New Age newsmags, books, etc. Now you can succumb to a new superstition every day! $21.95.

Gotta Hand It To 'Em . . .

Chi Pants
120 Pearl Alley
Santa Cruz, CA 95060

Are you ready for this? CRYSTAL-POW-ERED PANTS. A teeny crystal is sewn into the back seam, near the base of the spine so as to jazz those chakras. "You won't feel the crystal; you'll just feel the energy." This has got to be one of the most disgusting mergings of gimmicks for New Age consumer exploitation yet, and is all the more disgusting if these merchants actually *believe* their own claims. The crystal britches, however, are only a specialty item; the main selling point is that the "restricting" crotch area of old-age regular pants has been replaced with a panel of light cloth—a "gusset"—which allegedly allows you to "flow" and really, like, you know, get in tune with your environment and the Now Moment. For the catalog, they've wisely stuck with drawings of the pants or else tiny black-and-white photos with models posed in such a way that you can't clearly see that the gusset actually looks like nothing so much as a stylized artificial vagina. Hell, for all I know, these drawers may well allow you "full expression of your Chi energy." It's not so much the gimmick itself that's so repugnant, but the entire tone and feel and chic slickness of the catalog as a whole: it's so damn "Southern California Holistic" as to make you want to puke. But expertly disguised! Maybe that's what's so maddening about it. Even though there are hardly any specific annoying clichés to be found, it still reeks with that cloying, self-congratulating generic New Age stink. But . . . can one really blame the entrepreneur? I must admit that one of my closest SubGenius collaborators is making money hand over fist selling cheap "Crystal Rings" to holistic suckers for $50 each. Now, he no more believes in crystal powers than in Santa Claus; he's just making a buck off the current mystic fad, and as long as he keeps slinging the jargon, like Chi Pants does, the rubes will keep buying. That makes sense to me. So maybe it isn't the insidious New Age sales pitch that sickens me after all, but the people who fall for them.

Cash Grants To Psychics, Healers, And Researchers!

The Universal Voice
First Universal Church, PO Box 8
Cummington, MA 01026

That's right, these noble folks give FREE MONEY to selfless individuals making "significant contributions to parapsychology." You better believe that when I saw that, I started getting all KINDS of big ideas . . . until I discovered their grants are only for $100 to $400, and there are only $600-worth available. What kind of psychic research can ya do for $400?? Hell, I could make ten times that simply by starting a new religion, or even just a new "Parapsychology School." What a letdown. Free newsletter lists psychics, healers, tea-leaf readers, pyramid makers, crystal scammists, etc.

New Age Wimp Seeks Superstitious Woman For Meaningful Dialogue

Psychic Connections
Box 670022, Marietta, GA 30066

Crammed with New Age "Personals" . . . ads from vacuous kooks, looking for other addle-pated kooks, usually for romantic purposes. Here's a sample ad: "Single Pisces male, 49, UFO contactee, loving and gentle, seeks creative, spiritual New Age soulmate—the one I've walked with before—who shares interest in shiatsu, healing, herbs, pleasant vibrations, world peace. I read runes and dreams; I helped initiate the 'Storm of the Century' in San Antonio. Artistic, Starseed meditator, fantastic sense of humor. We were TOGETHER in previous lives." This mag also features "psychic predictions" of world-shaking events, many of which have actually happened—only, several happened YEARS EARLIER, *before* the predictions were even made!! HOW CAN THIS BE POSSIBLE?? IT'S A MIRACLE!! $15/year gets you membership including the newsletter, your own classified ad, and one free question about your problems (or your pet's) to be answered psychically.

Yet Another New Pied Piper

School of Light
PO Box 3513
Quartz Hill, CA 93536

A brand new—but age-old, of course—esoteric Order that prepares you for the Ray of Christ Consciousness. Boy, if only Philip K. Dick had known about this, he'd still be writing rather than rotting. Seems to be an Alice Bailey spinoff. Alice, if you didn't know, was one of the all-time superstar occultists—you can buy hundreds of her definitively New Age booklets at big bookstores, or from The Arcane School, 866 United Nations Plaza #566–7, New York, NY 10017.

GOD DAMN IT! I could list these offset-printed pacifiers for neurotics forever, but they're all the same. And I guess that's what they're trying to push: a certain "open-minded" sameness. This is their great similarity to the lowbrow Christian bigots. One respected New Age magazine, *The Fessenden Review,* says it all: they want "a more peaceful and homogenous society." HOMOGENOUS!! Well, that's just GREAT! Let's make sure every African bushman's kid gets a degree in Political Science in Transformation, or Contemporary Aspects of Jungian Psychology! Let's sell those overworked farmers in China some Healing Crystals and Subliminal Positive Attitude tapes! BAH! HUMBUG!

See, we all form this cosmic Spirit Brain with the Earth Spirit, called "Gaia," or whatever, and we're approaching this moment of great transformation when everyone in the world will begin to realize their potential as "gods" and "life spirits," and all sorts of scientific and mental breakthroughs will occur, and . . . and then the military will *accidentally* release an incurable mutant virus, and we'll all die in one huge Jonestown. POSITIVE THINKING. HARMONIC CONVERGENCE. **EUCHH!!! PTUI!!** I think I'll keep smoking cigarettes, if the New Age is gonna be composed of such whining ostrich sissies. (Although I'll admit this: when I get cancer, I'll be visiting a couple of Sioux medicine men I know, as soon as the "real doctors" are through with me.) "Holistic?" That's supposed to replace "common sense," I guess. It sure ain't the same. "Love?" Yeah, you *love* to keep saying *"love"* over and over again. "Fulfillment??" Oh, fulfillment is easy, once you've "given up your ego desires" to some preacher/guru wearing a tablecloth. The *lack* of desire is easy enough to fulfill! "New Age." **BLEAUH!!** "Christian." **YUUCCHH!** "Radical." **(URP!)** "Right wing." ***GAG!!*** "Normal." **KILL ME!!** I'll stick with the Orthodox Stangianist Lodge of SubGenius Covenant Peoples' Church of the Yeti Dobbs Ressurrected, thank you. If you want a belief system done right, do it yourself, that's what I say.

I may ruthlessly and unfairly criticize these people, but HELLFIRE, I'm giving you their ADDRESSES, for Dobbs's Sake! Find out for yourself. I figure you Christians and New Agers, anarchists and reactionaries and so on can **use** these addresses in your endless battles against one another. We SubGeniuses will just sit back and watch, bemused; and after Judgment Day, we'll get rich on Planet X, reminiscing about the follies of "the extinct earth humans" on Xist talk shows and in popular books that'll sell like hotcakes throughout the Galactic Federation of Enlightened Planets.

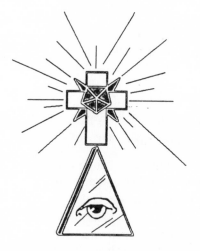

SCHOOL OF LIGHT

PEOPLE WE DON'T WANT TO INSULT

NICE GUYS

Habitat World
Habitat for Humanity
419 W. Church St.
Americus, GA 31709

   This group goes out and literally builds homes for the homeless.

WISE GUYS

Phanes Press
PO Box 6114
Grand Rapids, MI 49506

   Jungian and Fortean scholar David Fideler is also publisher and/or distributor of a few really *deep* (unfathomable to me) books on cabalist/alchemical/gnostic ancient philosophy. Pythagoras, Hermes, Porphyry, Proclus, and other heavyweights of the mystic mentating ring.

WHAT KIND OF PLANET READS . . .

The Planetary Report
The Planetary Society
110 S. Euclid Ave.
Pasadena, CA 91101

   Volume V #1 focused on "Planetary Catastrophes," and it's a hum-dinger for End of the World buffs. Excellent hard-science articles on mass extinctions, the Greenhouse Effect, the new Ice Age, etc., plus items of scientific interest to any planet or planet fan. The best part, though, are the color paintings of various cataclysms. (That kind of stuff is like porn to some of us.) $1.50 for back issues.

WHAT PRICE HAMBURGER??

Free Our Public Lands
Lynn Jacobs
2945 W. Barrel Dr.
Tucson, AZ 85746

A huge one-shot tabloid concerning the misuse of public lands for livestock ranching, going into great detail about the tremendous environmental damages caused by indiscriminate grazing. Partly because the American rancher and farmer enjoy a "sacred cow" status (so to speak) in our national self-image, this is a generally ignored issue that nevertheless has far-reaching consequences. Quite balanced and clearly written, the opposite of most eco-freaks' self-defeating hysterics. Free! But send a stamp to help out.

RANTS FOR RAMPS

Handicap News
Phyllis Burns
272 N. Eleventh Ct.
Brighton, CO 80601

News for and about the handicapped, concentrating on inventions that make life easier and recent medical advances. Full of contact addresses for support groups and the like. (I certainly never thought about emergency instructions that can be understood by the blind and deaf before it was mentioned here.) $1 and SASE. ((Factsheet Five))

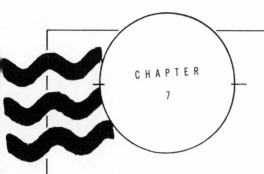

COSMIC HIPPIE DRUG– BROTHER STUFF

These are so categorized, because they're a lot less dogmatic, and more on the "hip" side than the others. These are the ones that MORE than tolerate sex, drugs, rock 'n' roll, and other things without at least a smattering of which no religion or political group can be much **fun**. Sorry to have to put it that way; I guess I'm just not very holy. I am LESS "holier" than thou, *pardner*. **PRAISE "BOB"!!! SEE YA IN HELL—BUT NOT THE ONE *YOU'RE* THINKING OF!**

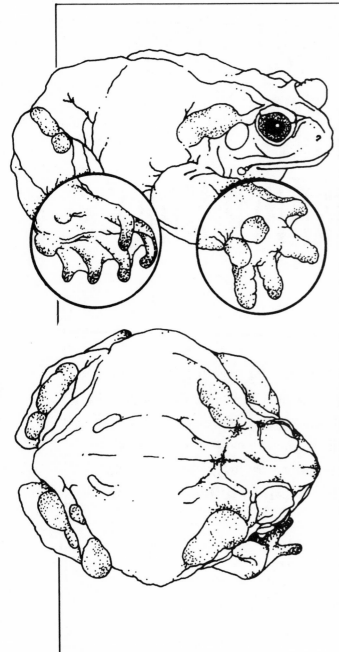

Pssst . . . Hey, Man, Wanna Cop Some *Toad??*

Bufo alvarius: The Psychedelic Toad
of the Sonoran Desert
Venom Press, Box 2863
Denton, TX 76201

This booklet by "Al Most" describes the use of Sonoran Desert toad *venom* as a potent (and legal!) hallucinogen. What people won't do for a buzz! It doesn't hurt the toad . . . you just scrape some secretion-squeezins off his neck glands, dry the goop, and you've got a couple dozen smokable "hits" that put you on Jupiter minus an ego or any sense of time or space. The active ingredient—5-MEO-DMT, a "telepathine"(!!)—is fast-acting, and this overwhelming psychedelic trip only lasts about twenty minutes. No price on this one, but $2 seems right. Several $3 to $5 books also sold here go into more detail, such as how to tell the psychedelic *Bufo alvarius* from other toads. Careful, kids—"toke up" on the wrong damn amphibian throat-juice, and you might start foaming at the mouth like a dog that's pestered a common garden toad . . . a sure tip-off to narcotics agents!

Shoot That Gage My Way, Ace!

High Frontiers
PO Box 40271
Berkeley, CA 94704

A real treat for "expanded consciousness" buffs.* Too bad it's only published once a year, but at least it's BIG. (And it may go quarterly soon.) Not just for acidheads; you can blow your mind on *concepts*. Tim Leary, new designer-drugs and life-extenders, weird science (wanna get off by electrical stimulation of your brain?), video and computer psychedelia, Paul Kantner, John Lilly, Diamanda Galas, Jello Biafra—folks in the hep, with-it groove. Great drug trip recountings, psychedelic art. Them were the good old days, and they'll get even gooder (albeit scarier) as more brain toys are invented! Many giant-format pages and very slick printing, but the price is steep—$30 for one issue of *High Frontiers* plus five smaller newsletters (*Reality Hackers*). Single back issues are more accessible at $6.50 (includes postage).

(Which reminds me. I want to compile a horror book of true-life drug experiences. Send a written account of Your Worst/Funniest drug trip (including alcohol) to me, Rev. Ivan Stang, at The SubGenius Foundation, PO Box 140306, Dallas, TX 75214. This could be the ultimate scare book to keep young kids off hard drugs, yet a million laughs to those already too far gone to be helped. This project is for real, and if you send me two to five page factual recountings of especially hair-raising or stranger-than-fiction experiences, it will very probably be used. Anonymity is fine.)

Down Underground

Maggie's Farm
Media Centre
PO Faulconbridge 2776
Blue Mountains, Australia

This "access" mag covers just about all the oddball "edge" ground this book does, but somehow avoids the depressing, almost desperate gushiness of American "holistic access" mags. Good feisty sense of humor . . . much readier to kick ass than your usual lazy peacenik "loveburgers." Crammed with material of interest to kooks, hipsters, social lepers, and dropouts of all kinds—even me. And you know by now what a spiteful, vindictive bastard I am. $4/year in Australia; $10/year overseas.

---

* SubGeniuses are born with expanded consciousness, and so seek to go one step "higher" (though there is no "high" or "low" in this realm) into *contracted consciencelessness,* a state that cannot be described in words, because it wipes out the vocabulary totally. See *My Biggest Sales Secret* by Dr. Philo Drummond (Dobbstown College Press, 1959).

MICROCOSM WITH BEADS ON

ZENDIK FARM
Carey Roberts
Zendik Communal Arts Group
1431 Tierra del Sol Rd.
Boulevard, CA 92005

"Cultural revolutionaries out to convince you that communal living is the only way to go," and not doing a bad job at it; this newsletter/rant is very strongly written... good no-bullshit slams at the status quo competitive life-style, undiluted by the vapid Utopianism characteristic of most communes. These people are PISSED!—and the honesty that's pouring out makes this a more noble experiment than usual.
I'll be very interested to watch their progress, though. Communes generally break up because the members get sick and tired of each other; somebody becomes a "boss." Just like in the normal world. Send about 75¢ for postage for one; $10 a year if it lasts.

KOOL, MAN, KOOL

Water Row Books
Box 438
Sudbury, MA 01776

Specializes in books, tapes and videos by and about BEATNIKS, offering what looks to be the *complete works (!)* of hep cats like Lord Buckley, Lenny Bruce, Ed Sanders, Richard Brautigan, Charles Bukowski, William Burroughs, Woody Allen, Gregory Corso, R. Crumb, Ginsburg, Kerouac, Kesey, et al. If they don't have it, it probably never existed.

From Acid Rock To Acid Rain

Light Times
PO Box 84366
Los Angeles,
CA 90073

Hippie fun on an irregular basis. Psychedelic comedy, Discordian adventures, cool reprints from nut literature —last issue included the text of a very telling debate between Abbie Hoffman and Jerry Rubin, interview with presidential candidate "Love 22," drug news, more drug news. No price, no schedule. But it's available . . . send about two bucks or a bunch of postage stamps.

"BRAISE ERIS!"

Discordian Churches
??????? St., Anywhere, Anytime

It's hard to nail down Discordians—which figures, since they're dedicated to the sowing of Discord, generally of the mental kind. They don't damage the physical world *much* in worship of sexy ol' Eris, Goddess of Chaos. Discordians all work, I mean play, in their spare time, on Operation Mindfuck—an insidious yet disorganized attempt to tear down your old mental paradigms *without offering anything with which to replace them.** Techniques include everything from elaborate pranks, to . . . well, simple pranks. Sort of a Zen version of the Merry Pranksters.** Founded in the 1950s by Greg Hill and Kerry

Thornley, it has never had a real headquarters or official magazine, yet it grows and grows—thanks partially to popularization in Robert Anton Wilson's *Illuminatus* trilogy. There is a Discordian bible, though—the amazing *Principia Discordia,* available from LOOMPANICS, PO Box 1197, Port Townsend, WA 98368

A DISCORDIAN DIRECTORY
THE MONTHLY B·I·T·C·H· NEWSLETTER

HAIL ERIS   ALL HAIL DISCORDIA

PUBLISHED BY MYCROCOSMUS V, BOX 23061, KNOXVILLE, TN, 37933·1061

---

* I'd be a Discordian except I'm a SubGenius, a much larger and more ancient mindfuck conspiracy of which the Discordian religion is only a tiny, recent spin-off. Proof of our success is the fact that Discordians think they predate us. Our ruse worked!

** Come on, you know . . . the Merry Pranksters, that wacky crew of acid-gobbling zanies—of whom Ken Kesey is the most famous—rendered immortal in Tom Wolfe's *Electric Kool-Aid Acid Test.* MY HEROES. People have compared the Church of the SubGenius with the Discordians, but nay, nay—it's MUCH closer to the Pranksters in style and spirit (though not often in internal chemistry). Discordians don't get thrown in JAIL for what THEY do. (Maybe that's why a few of their diehards refuse to descend to the "SUB"Genius level, the level where the Stupid Brain takes over. THE STUPID BRAIN!! YOU KNOW!! That much, much *older* part of the brain, where the *TRUE YOU* dwells . . . just south of the Hindbrain, but WAY north of the soul gland. You're *walking* on that soul gland! God, don't you people know *anything??*

Here's one Discordian newsletter (I'd list more, but all the older ones have moved):
TAO
Erisian Liberation Front, PO Box 1082, Bloomington, IN 47402.
$8/four issues.

And here's another wet-behind-the-ears newcomer:

KALLISTI KOMIKS

PO Box 19566,
Cincinatti, OH 45219

Rants by and for those who want to make no sense, except to the nonsensically enlightened. Not that it takes much to attain that particular state. Right up the alley of Zippy the Pinhead enthusiasts. $1.

THIS MUST BE THE REAL ILLUMINATI!

Falcon Press
3660 N. 3rd St.
Phoenix, AZ 85012

Free catalog of many esoteric Crowley, Israel Regardie, Timothy Leary, and Robert Anton Wilson books, and publishers of Christopher Hyatt's funny Discordian-like "UNDOING YOURSELF" series. They also offer a Golden Dawn correspondence course! I met this gang (and Regardie, just before he died), and they struck me as quite astute wise guys, the only Crowley supporters I've met who seem to be in on the gag he put over on straight and occult society alike.

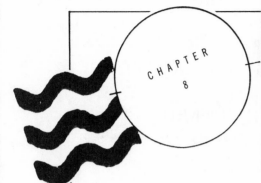

CHAPTER 8

RESPECTABLE WEIRD PUBLICATIONS

Occasionally, the quest for junk turns up gold.

The following serious journals of abnormality are not to be lumped with the kook publications; these are the few-and-far-between that approach unexplained anomalous subjects (like UFOs and ESP) from balanced, and therefore slightly humorous, viewpoints. All are good investments for anyone interested in healthier overviews of the various weird phenomena. Well, maybe not *all*. . . . there're some geeks in here, alright. But it's still a fun batch, altogether. Geekiness naturally goes with the territory, anyway.

Science has its own built-in superstitions . . . but you knew that. I mean, this isn't the *Dark Ages!* This paranormal stuff IS a big JOKE, isn't it? Surely there isn't some undetectable web of subtle forces permeating everything and inexorably *pulling* on all living things from an "angle" we didn't know existed?? That would make the textbooks a LIE! It would make Carl Sagan a DUPE, a WITCH DOCTOR!! It would imply that we were all victims of some PRIMITIVE, SHORTSIGHTED SET OF ARBITRARY BELIEF REFERENCES! It would imply that we are little more than CAVE MEN scratching away in the dark, compared to the GREAT DISTANCE that humanity has yet to travel in order to know *just what the hell is **really** going on!* It would liken us to DUMB BRUTES mindlessly fighting each other inside a tiny cage, fighting to the *death* because we never noticed that the cage door was OPEN THE WHOLE TIME! * Naw, this is all "KOOK" stuff, nothing impossible ever happens, when you die you're just dead and that's all there is to it, *JUST DON'T THINK ABOUT IT!!! **THAT WAY LIES MADNESS!!!*** Unless you know exactly how many grains of salt to take with any given report of paranormal intrusion.

* " I can't *believe* what-all I believe."—Dobbs, 1956

THE TRUTH SHALL SET YOU CONFUSED

Fortean Times
96 Mansfield Rd.
London NW 3 2HX, England

What's the difference between the *Weekly World News* and *Fortean Times?* Well, *reliable* is a tricky word to use in a world where living frogs occasionally rain by the thousands from clear blue skies, but these folks cover everything that CANNOT POSSIBLY BE, but IS ANYWAY (well, maybe) with wry humor and intelligence. The unchallenged bearers of Charles Fort's* mighty Tablets, they exhaustively compile and playfully examine stupifying news items concerning everything from your usual bigfoots, sea serpents, and UFOs, to bleeding statues, freaks of nature, spontaneous human combustion, hellishly ironic synchronicities, hilariously freakish accidents, etc. Tackling with morbid but contagious glee many subjects that might otherwise be unspeakably disconcerting, the editors skillfully avoid the fatal sins both of belief and denial, teasing the reader instead with a maddening profusion of possible explanations for each bizarre report without committing to any single theory. By mercilessly batting the reader's brain back and forth, bouncing it like a ping-pong ball between credulity and total skepticism, they dutifully prevent it from ever coming completely to rest on either side. The study of anomalies is essentially the skeleton in science's closet, an embarrassing and impertinent black sheep that keeps digging up troublesome exceptions to one cherished physical law after another. In the hands of disaffected cranks looking only for new reasons to smirk at mainstream science, it frequently veers off into abject kookdom. *Fortean Times,* however, successfully maintains a sane perspective, retaining the sense of absurd craziness that is Forteana's appeal but never giving in to the temptation to provide "answers" that only fuel the superstitious. Well established and professionally produced, it's definitely the place to start for anyone new to this seductive scientific back

* Charles Fort was the first person to laboriously catalog reports of anomalistic events (from live frog rains to astronomical wonders to ancient Norse artifacts found in America), most of them so rare that they were—and are —"damned" as impossible by science. By studying newspapers and scientific documents from all cultures and the distant past, however, he discovered certain recurrences and patterns that, taken as a whole, are convincing evidence that modern science still has a LONG way to go. Above and beyond the incredible range of documentation, though, Fort discussed these staggeringly weird events with an inimitably eccentric yet blackly humorous style that has to be read with perseverance to be appreciated. A taste not quickly acquired, but well worth the effort. His books (*The Book of the Damned, Lo!,* and others) prove him one of the greatest ranters of all time. Hence, the systematic study of unexplained anomalies is called "Fortean science."

Fortean Times

ISSUE No.35   The Journal of Strange Phenomena   PRICE: £1·00 $2.5

fact. $4/copy, $12/year (about to go up, so hurry!). Subscription recommended. They also publish a number of good books on anomalous phenomena, and collections of morbidly amusing news clippings.

Endangered Species

**Stigmata *(newsletter) and* Crux *(yearly journal)*
Thomas R. Adams, Project Stigma
PO Box 1094, Paris, TX 75460**

The only continuing report, and very well researched, on the disturbing epidemic of mysterious livestock mutilations, which invariably brings up the UFO question. You think cattle mutilations are a joke? There have been something like 20,000 since 1960, most of them **hideously weird.** Reports from all over the world, assembled with a minimum of editorializing. There's still no explanation for "mutes," although earthly helicopters manned by some secret group seems much more likely now than the extraterrestrial UFO theory. Secret U.S. government experimental UFOs...? Some bizarre plot to keep us all a little off-balance? Bad juju no matter how you look at it. $5 for *Crux* #1 or *Stigmata;* $4 for *Crux* #2.

alley. A typical issue, #47, covered the search for the Mokele M'Bembe (the legendary brontosauri surviving in the Congo, on which the Disney B-movie *Baby* was based); disasters that have accompanied visits by Halley's Comet; a survey of people older than 110, and suchlike. (Although in this case, there really is no "suchlike.") They report the more entertaining hoaxes, too, but not as

AND NOW MY CAR KEYS DON'T WORK EITHER!

Artifex *(newsletter) and* Archaeus *(journal)*

The Archaeus Project
629 Twelfth Ave. SE
Minneapolis, MN 55414

ARTIFEX

ARCHAEUS PROJECT
629 TWELFTH AVE. S.E.
MINNEAPOLIS, MN 55414

Vol. 5   No. 5   October 1986

STRIP-MINING THE PSYCHE

Dennis Stillings

Starting in the Far East millennia ago, civilization wrapped itself around the globe and ended its westward course at the coast of California. There remained but two directions to go: into space or into the psyche. The technologies of both inner and outer space are well represented by outstanding individuals and organizations in California, and, since old habits die hard, it is to be expected that we will transfer the same exploitative, ecologically unsound practices, at which we excel, into these new territories.

"Consciousness" developers are rushing into the psyche with the

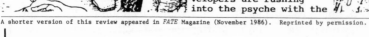

A shorter version of this review appeared in *FATE* Magazine (November 1986). Reprinted by permission.

Both *Artifex* and *Archaeus* are sometimes-scholarly, sometimes-informal collections of articles on bioenergetic fields—that is, they seriously look into telekinesis, clairvoyance, etc. If there is ever gonna be proof of mind over matter, the Archaeus people are pulling it all together in an extremely promising, level-headed way ... certainly a far cry from the usual psychic psychos. For the researcher, not the fanatic. These folks really know how to throw a spoon-bending party! The spoons or bars of metal don't exactly bend by themselves; the hands are used, but this kind of extreme bending is still possible only when the metal is somehow "softened" for an instant. I once watched the editor twist a spoon (in a diner) into a tight little spiral. Call me gullible, but I was unable to unbend it without pliers and vise-grips. Newsletters are $1.50; the journal is $6.75. You get both the annual journal and the bimonthly newsletter for $15/year.

Horribler Than Weird

Info Journal
International Fortean Organization
PO Box 367
Arlington, VA 22210–0367

The American equivalent of *Fortean Times*—the printing isn't as fancy, but the wealth of reports on Fortean occurrences is equally fun to read, and you don't feel like you're indulging some nut. (The mark of sanity in this field, and the all-important leeway for yuks, is the sincere admission of ignorance.) Many news clippings as well as eyewitness accounts and evaluative articles. Covers a vast range, not limited to the paranormal; for instance, there are items here on wild pigs running amok in California, and on Chinese rat-steak recipes. I suppose the editorial criterion is that it has to be *surprising*. They host yearly conventions of Forteans that are not to be missed for their unending parade of fringe "characters" both sane and insane. $3.50 each or four for $12.

DOUBT

THE FORTEAN SOCIETY MAGAZINE

"One measures a circle, beginning anywhere" — Charles Fort

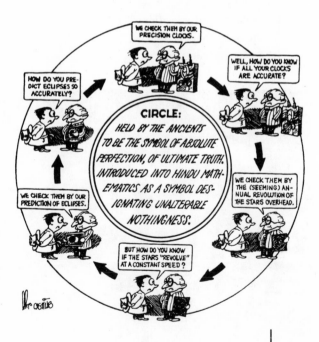

WHO DONE IT??

Critique—A Journal of
Conspiracies & Metaphysics
PO Box 11368
Santa Rosa, CA 95406

Each issue is a dense collection of essays and rants on such subject matter as psychic warfare, mind control, secret societies, UFOs, the occult, assassinations, cover-ups; plus reviews like these. Top-notch writing by the best skeptic/believers around. Sometimes scholarly, sometimes funny. Quite impressive . . . read this regularly and you'll astound your friends with your vast knowledge of secret projects and societies. Then they'll lock you up, even though it's THE TRUTH. $15/year or $4 for sample issue.

SEE ALL, GNOW ALL

Gnosis
The Lumen Foundation
PO Box 14217
San Francisco, CA 94114

A serious, scholarly metaphysical magazine that explores the various faces of Gnosticism (which can include anything from ancient Essenes to the visionary sci-fi writings of Philip K. Dick to the Magickal/alchemical secrets) and other Western spiritual traditions. Pretty esoteric stuff, but intriguing if you're into exotic and convoluted philosophies. Strives to define the difference between "authentic" Gnosis (miraculously derived knowledge, or "seeing the light," so to speak) and your run-of-the-mill psychotic episode. Editor Jay Kinney used to draw underground comics; his background shows insofar as *Gnosis* avoids the deadeningly academic metaphysical writers that this subject usually attracts. $15 subscription; sample issue $5.

Diane di Prima   Joscelyn Godwin   Justin Green

No. 2 $4.00

Gnosis

A Journal of the Western Inner Traditions

MAGIC
—&—
Tradition

THE GAUNTLET OF UFOLOGIST BASHING

Saucer Smear
PO Box 1709
Key West, FL 33041

This irregular newsletter is the Main Street of UFOlogist-town, where rival UFO researchers meet to gun each other down at high noon. Under the bemused eye of editor Jim Mosely, they viciously tear into each other's theories in the lively letters section that comprises most of the mag. You can't exactly buy a subscription; you have to keep sending funny or feisty letters to receive this. Beg and plead with style, convince him that you'll be qualified to join the fray, and he'll put you on his list.

SOMEBODY CALL WILD KINGDOM!

Journal of the Fortean Research Center
PO Box 94627, Lincoln, NE 68509

First issue features reports of some sort of flying creature, a "winged wonder" seen in Nebraska. Perhaps kin to Virginia's fabled Mothman goon? Or the Jersey Devil? Issue #3 reprints UFO-related documents from the Air Force and FBI. $15/four.

THE ONES THAT GOT AWAY

UFO Newsclipping Service
Lucius Farish
Rte. 1, Box 220
Plumerville, AR 72127

Just what the name says: a twenty-page monthly collection of news clippings about UFOs and other strange phenomena from all over the world . . . bigfoots, "Nessies" (Loch Ness monsters), ancient civilizations, etc. No editorializing; just the clips. Scanning one of these makes you feel off-kilter for the rest of the day. An extremely useful service: $5/month, $15/three months, $55/year. Frankly, I don't see how any warped but informed citizen can live without this. Always an absorbing read and WELL worth the expense. Farish also offers a catalog of classic UFO and Fortean books.

CURSE OF THE SAUCER PEOPLE

Center for UFO Studies
PO Box 1621, Lima, OH 45802

Nifty bimonthly newsletter on UFOlogy. The ads in these mags will turn you on to to even more extreme geeks than I'll ever have time to root out. $15/year.

MEBBE ZO ... MEBBE NOT

Zetetic Scholar
Dr. Marcello Truzzi, Box 1052
Ann Arbor, MI 48106

Journal for the Center for Scientific Anomalies Research—the editor once manned *The Skeptical Inquirer,* but decided they were *too* skeptical. Critical about what passes for "evidence" of the paranormal, but not dogmatic, they cover all the usual frightening data in a balanced way. After all, if something is truly "paranormal," wouldn't it naturally defy standard procedures of scientific investigation? Rather, it would require new procedures—no less scientific, but new. Most people want answers; this provides more refined questions. The letters section features ongoing feuds between the Hulk Hogans of paranormal and antiparanormal research. $12/year for two **big** (as in book-size) issues. Back issues are $8 but WELL worth it; #10 (1982 but still available) has articles on the controversial Mars Effect papers (which surprised everyone by giving, of all things, *astrology* some scientific credibility) and Chinese parapsychology.*

HOMETOWN HORROR

Geobibliography of Anomalies
Greenwood Press, 88 Post Road W.
Westport, CT 06881

At $59.95 this huge book isn't cheap, but ought to be mentioned. Lists more than 22,000 anomalistic events from all over the North American continent, categorized by location. These aren't detailed descriptions, but references; look up your hometown and learn how many UFO sightings, poltergeist events, crazy weather, and freakish geographical phenomena have graced your neighborhood.

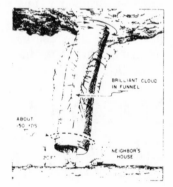

The funnel of the 1955 tornado at Blackwell, Oklahoma, was lit up like a neon tube. Cloud-to-earth electrical currents could be the cause of the scorching reported above.

This 'many-humped sea serpent' was seen near the Maine coast in 1958. (original drawing by B. Heuvelmans) From CURIOUS ENCOUNTERS

---

* One of my favorite branches of weirdness. Parapsychology is astounding enough to begin with; the Chinese approach is so relatively *alien* to Western paradigms that, for me, it's almost like porn. Can't get enough!

NATURE AS GODZILLA

Journal of Meteorology
54 Frome Road, Bradford-on-Avon
Wilts. BA15 ILD, England

Tracks extreme weather fluctuations and disasters all over the world; a good dose of humility for prideful humans. Descriptions of strange weather such as huge hailstones, tornado lightning, unexplained "wheels of light," (miles across) that appear in the ocean . . . stuff your TV weatherman doesn't want to go into. I once got the crap pummeled out of me by a freak hailstorm on a hot and cloudless July day in Texas. . . . I wasn't wearing a shirt and there was NO COVER. The physical pain was nothing compared to the disorienting horror of realizing the hailstorm's sheer impossibility. If I'd been a reader of this magazine, I wouldn't have jumped to the conclusion I did: that the Russians had a new weapon, or else an Army weapons experiment had gone wrong. $28/ four issues.

HEAD IN THE COUDS-!

Collectors of Unusual Data—
International (COUD-I)
Ray Nelke, 2312 Shields Ave.
St. Louis, MO 63136

A clearinghouse where one can send clippings on weird events, from whence they'll be copied and sent to the many other Fortean publications and archives. Some common subjects: astronomy, perpetual motion, mind control, voodoo, cattle mutilations, archaeology, you name it. He doesn't charge money, but you can get this ONLY by sending clippings. Don't even bother him unless you have something in the way of unusual info to offer in exchange.

AS WEIRD AS TRUTH

Science Frontiers
The Sourcebook Project
William R. Corliss
PO Box 107, Glen Arm, MD 21057

Author/publisher of many large handbooks of unusual phenomena (mental, physical, and in-between) and of *Science Frontiers,* a newsletter reporting wonderful new discoveries and hideous revelations from the science press—the kind Forteanoid weirdos like. Typical stories: NEANDERTHAL MAN MAY STILL SURVIVE IN ASIA . . . WERE FAIRIES AN ANCIENT RACE OF MEN? . . . and many less outré reports. This is also a source for some of the best books on Fortean and other damned sciences. Reputable; the GOOD stuff, too real to be too funny. The Anomaly Catalog series is an encyclopedic compendium of unexplained natural quirks, Fortean events, etc. Send big SASE for the book catalog and sample newsletter.

MONEY NOT GOOD ENOUGH, EH?

PASU Data Exchange
Stan Gordon, 6 Oakhill Ave.
Greensburg, PA 15601

Available for trade only with other collectors and researchers. From the Pennsylvania Association for the Study of the Unexplained —clearinghouse for sightings of UFOs, Bigfoots, poltergeists, etc. GREAT clippings. Operates a UFO hot line: (412) 838–7768

HERE, KITTY KITTY KITTY

International Society of
Cryptozoology
PO Box 43070, Tucson, AZ 85733

"Cryptozoology" is the study of as-yet-unidentified animals, and animals that mysteriously appear out of their natural habitat— giant cats in Britain, kangaroos in Ohio, pterodactyls in Texas, giant water serpents in lakes 'n' lochs, and of course those huge-footed Gigantopithecines and Sasquatches anywhere. Among the animsls that were once classified as "myth": the gorilla, the okapi, the sea cow, and the coelocanth. There's hope yet that some of our favorite monster movies will come true. $2.50 each, $25/year; giant (100+ pages) journals are $12.

MAKE SURE IT STAYS LOCKED

The Gate
PO Box 43518
Richmond Hts., OH 44143

Not a huge Fortean magazine, but very well done. All the usual intrigue of ghosts, lake monsters, mind-splattering scientific discoveries, UFOs, etc. Let me reiterate— this isn't kook literature; the writers take nothing at face value. $1 each or $4/four.

??? . . . BUT I THOUGHT THESE WERE ALL STRANGE MAGAZINES!

Strange Magazine
PO Box 2246, Rockville, MD 20852

I swear, these things breed like rabbits! Another brand new Fortean-style magazine, just born in late '87 (with a caul, of course), and very promising. Low-budget but still well produced, with better-than-average graphics and the right attitude: intelligent, open-minded doubt enlivened by a RAVENOUS LUST for ANY DAMN KIND OF TOTALLY MIND-SCRAPING WEIRD-ASS MYSTERIOUS SHIT SHUNNED BY NORMALS!!! Because they've just started publishing and are probably in more need of contributions than the rest, you aspiring writer/researchers looking for "staff position" credit may find it easier to get your foot in the door. (Don't expect pay, though!) The range of subject matter is much like the others in this section, and . . . well, I've run out of clever comments on the genre at large so I'll leave it at that. $14.95 for four; $3.95 sample.

WELL, WELL, WELL

The American Dowser
American Society of Dowsers
Danville, VT 05828–0024

Dowsing is (sometimes) for real; do you think I care if you believe me? And it leads into broader fields relating to earth energies, ley lines (little-understood energy fields that surround underground rivers), and other geological mysteries. I haven't seen this and don't know the price, but it's out there. If certain of your ancestors hadn't used dowsing to find water sources, you probably wouldn't be here.

PARAWEIRD

UFO Information
Japan Space Phenomenon Society
5-2 Kamiyama-Cho, Shibuya-ku
Tokyo, Japan 150

Twenty dollars a year, but how exotic can you get? I haven't seen this yet, but it's good to know of at least one Japanese Fortean pub

. . . no doubt there are many more. I spent two weeks right down the street from them in Tokyo; if I'd known about them, I wouldn't have spent so much money on the "Soft Woman" strip joints—a whole new Fortean phenomenon in itself.

YET ANOTHER OF CHARLES FORT'S BASTARD CHILDREN

Journal of Scientific Exploration
Pergamon Journals, Maxwell House
Fairview Park, Elmsford, NY 10523

ANOTHER new one! See? What'd I tell you? Have these anomaly magazine publishers never heard of birth control? This one, however, is strictly highbrow—very, very serious, repulsively academic, and heavy on scientific method. None of this rambunctious fun-and-games stuff. Just the article titles *alone* run to ten or twelve words long. How about "Analysis and Discussion of the Film of a Cluster of Periodically Flashing Lights Seen Off the Coast of New Zealand"? Um, uh, yeah, sure, I gotcha, Perfessor! No comic pages or pictures here, kids. Not exactly my kind of reading—in fact, I've gone to some trouble over the years to ensure that I'd *never* be intelligent enough to follow this kind of ponderous writing—but it may be just what some of you eggheads, long-hairs and career college students have been looking for. It certainly makes up in sheer respectability what it lacks in comprehensibility. Since they charge $40 (!!) for a two issue subscription, I almost didn't include them here...but they do mention "free sample copies." Go for it, but put "Doctor" before your name and make sure all the spelling and grammar in your request letter is term-paper perfect, or they might not give you the time of day.

WOULD YOU BELIEVE?

AMERICA'S MOST TALKED ABOUT MAGAZINE!

ISSUE NO.15 - - - WINTER 1985 - - - $3.25

THE FLYING SAUCERS AND THE MYSTERIOUS LITTLE MEN

A True Book-Length Feature

OLDIES

Would You Believe?
Armand A. Laprade, Rte. 4
Box 156, Marshall, AR 72650

Reprints of classic "kook" and UFO literature, including much prized stuff from the '50s and '60s. Some past articles: *Jonathan Swift—A Martian?; Sexy Mermaids; Killer Fog; Dwarfs in the Superstition Mountains; Human Pawns of Alien Minds.* YEAH!! $3.25 each or four/$12.

HELP WANTED

Archives for
Fortean Research
Bob Rickard,
1 Shoebury Rd.
East Ham,
London,
E6 2AQ, UK

This ambitious new project, headed by *Fortean Times* editor Bob Rickard, involves collecting data on *every damn weird phenomenon known to man,* entering it all into a monstrous computer database, organizing it, and finally making it freely available for research. No money involved; it's just a good cause. You can help by donating money and/or data—for instance, sending clippings on weird local events from your obscure small-town paper which the Archives aren't otherwise likely to get. Who can guess what practical applications will come from this project? Perhaps if the locations and dates of every UFO sighting in history are correlated and graphed, the resulting graph lines will form English letters that spell out a message from aliens: "E.T., phone home," "Surrender Dorothy," "Bob Lives," "Cease All Atomic Testing," or whatever. Maybe it'll show the formula for an immortality elixir, or instructions for assembling a miraculous device like the Interroceter in *This Island Earth.* Who's to say? Don't know 'till you try.

I'm not mentioning many books; you can't get "samples" as easily. But if you want a well-rounded overview of all paranormality, look for any of Colin Wilson's many encyclopedic nonfiction works such as *The Occult, Mysteries,* or *Poltergeist* (all Putnam books). You read these absolutely flabbergasting case histories, and you certainly don't *want* to believe them, but Wilson seems so relentlessly *sane* that you're hard-pressed to remain skeptical. Seriously, I can't recommend these highly enough. May they stay in print forever.

SKEPTICS!

PARTY POOPERS (finally)

The Skeptical Inquirer
Box 229, Buffalo, NY 14215–0229

Journal of the Committee for the Scientific Investigation of Claims of the Paranormal (CSICOP)—the voice of the professional debunker, and a wise investment if you're wading through the world of weird. Considering that they're outnumbered by unquestioning believers by about ten thousand to one, this is an important undertaking. The articles exposing hoaxes and delusions are very analytical; in fact, they're so bloodlessly academic that they probably alienate the audience that needs this most. Preaching to the saved: every cult's downfall, even the cult of doubt. Even if overly rational—indeed, almost irrationally so—it's still the only "policeman" patroling the psychic research beat. Guaranteed to shatter at least *one* illusion, no matter how skeptical you thought you were. A noble cause. Skepticism is a good place to start from; that way you won't go overboard when some "IT" happens to YOU. $18/four issues.

WILD NEWS

These are collections of items clipped from newspapers and magazines too weird, funny, synchronistic, or sickening to be ignored. The emphasis is on extremes of human folly rather than Twilight Zone phenomena.

ABSURD BUT NEWS

VIEW FROM THE LEDGE (clippings)
Deadfromtheneckup, Inc.
PO Box 57141
Washington, DC 20037

MAN LOSES 5 FINGERS TO SAW—DOG EATS ONE. WOMAN WINS AWARD FOR FALL OFF TOILET. Brilliantly selected clippings and news articles, all illustrating that this is, indeed, an insane universe. You'll hardly be able to disagree . . . and it's all true! You get it in return for contributions of weird clippings.

WE ARE THE NORMAL PEOPLE

Phoebe
James McDougall,
1162 Routes 5 & 20
Waterloo, NY 13165

"The Newsletter of Eccentricity." Each monthly six-pager is a collection of wire-service Odd News. Wonderful, perverse cross-section of cosmic absurdity that really happened. The Folly of Man . . . let it never end. Like the others listed in this section, *Phoebe* would be very handy to radio hosts, public speakers, and anyone else who has trouble inventing comedy. 55¢ each.

CHEWY FOOD FOR THOUGHT...DON'T CHOKE

The Perfect Pitch
Bob Marshall, ℅ Bob Dean
122 Ellsworth Ave.
Toronto, Ontario, M6G-2K6
Canada

Collections of startling quotes—many from sources reviewed here—and news items about people you'll be very glad you haven't met. Some are transcriptions from radio broadcasts that wouldn't otherwise see print. A quirky dose of wisdom and kookdom combined, never boring, frequently disgusting, it's a treat for sickos. Irregularly published; SASE should net a sample.

IDENTITY - THE CULTURE HERO (IN THE WEST)

GROUND		POPULAR ARTFORM	HIGHBROW ARTFORM	TECHNOLOGICAL ARTFORM	POPULAR ARCHETYPE (User as Monarch of)	GHETTO (Drop-Out)	SYMPTOMS
GLOBAL VILLAGE	Phonetic Alphabet & Papyrus	Christ	Plato & Aristotle	Spoken Word	Tribe	Family	Caesar
	Print (Movable Type)	Shakespeare	Francis Bacon	Manuscript	Village	Tribe	Luther
	Industrial Revolution	Dickens	Darwin, Marx	Printed Book	Town	Village	Luddites
	Electronic Revolution	Joyce	Einstein, Freud	Newspaper	City	Town	Al Capone
GLOBAL THEATRE	Television	a) Elvis b) Fellini	Existentialism	a) Radio b) Movies	Nation	City	McCarthyism
	Computer	a) Beatles b) Psychedelia	a) Norman Mailer b) Marshall McLuhan	a) Black & White TV b) Color TV	Planet	Nation	J.F.K. Assassination
	Satellite	a) Punk Rock/New Wave b) Sat. Night Live c) Cults	a) Club of Rome b) Club of Life c) Genetic Engineering	a) Computer b & c) Mixed Corporate-Media	Solar System	Planet	Watergate
	Second Coming	Ronald Reagan & Pope John Paul II	Furry Lint	Mass Man	Universe	Outer Space	Battle of the Harvest Moon

WHY NOT LET THE NEWS GET TO YOU?

YOSSARIAN UNIVERSAL News Service (YU)
PO Box 236, Millbrae, CA 94030/Fericano
PO Box 40710, Portland, OR 97240/Ligi

Yossarian Universal News Service
PO Box 236, Millbrae, CA 94030

A "professional news and disinformation syndicate" and source of great seditious *rumors* to spread, not actual news. Facetious, satirical "press releases" for dedicated pranksters to slip into legit wire services. For $10 you can have your own laminated color press-card, and badge, with your photo on them—gain access to newsworthy events for nothing! $40 for twenty "newsbriefs," but I'll bet small publishers can get it free in trade.

FOR THE CUTE AT HEART

Wonderful World News
Ringer, Box 8005, Suite 166
Boulder, CO 80306

Unnecessary facts, tasty recipes, cryptic notes. Rather less sardonic than the others. For those who prefer the cuter fringe news. $6/year.

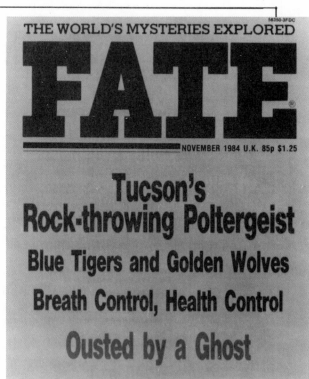

THE WORLD'S MYSTERIES EXPLORED

FATE

NOVEMBER 1984 U.K. 85p $1.25

Tucson's Rock-throwing Poltergeist

Blue Tigers and Golden Wolves

Breath Control, Health Control

Ousted by a Ghost

YA NEVER KNOW

Fate Magazine
170 Future Way, Marion, OH 43300

No guarantee of authenticity, but that doesn't mean *some* of the revelations in this perennial fave aren't true. Packed with articles ranging from plausible psychic experiences to gonzo ghost stories, miracles, and "My Date with a Saturnian" type luridities. Heck, they even expose a hoax now and then! Most importantly, this rag has some of the best classified ads anywhere, if you're looking for new brain-damaged kook sources. $15/year.

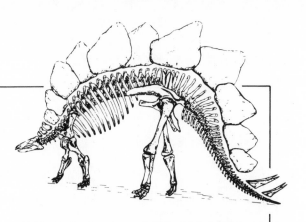

Dead Bigfoot Male Gives Birth To Dinosaurs From Jupiter!

Weekly World News
Latana, FL 33464

The ultimate in yellow journalism, with stories like: DOCTORS RAISE DEAD WITH ANCIENT CHANT. 10 YEAR OLD GIRL GIVES BIRTH TO HER 8TH CHILD! MARTIAN HUNTERS KILLED OFF THE DINOSAURS! LUCKY LOTTERY NUMBERS! You've seen 'em. The most frightening thing is that many of these stories may be true (though sensationalized to the max), but there's no telling *which!* $13.95/year, but you can find these in many American convenience stores and supermarkets. If you read closely, you'll find that many of the very best ones are rewordings of stories originally printed in Chinese newspapers. Which brings us to:

Just Dig Straight Down And Save On Postage

CHINA DAILY
2 Jintai Xilu, Beijing, China OR:
China Daily Distribution Corp.
15 Mercer St., New York, NY 10013

This isn't the most lurid of the Chinese newspapers, but its the most official as far as Party-approved news goes. I don't know the overseas subscription rate; write the New York office. News that would be perfectly normal to natives can become incredibly surrealistic to people of another culture. The strident, almost inhuman Maoism of the Cultural Revolution is swiftly being replaced by the most peculiar combination of pure old-time traditional Chinese-ness, and cautious, almost Victorian versions of Western-style fashion. It's hard to describe the flavor of this amazing daily. Better than following a soap opera. There are lots of strange phenomena in China, and even stranger religions among the peasants who comprise a quarter of earth's human population. Some Canadian hipsters do the English translations. One, a quasi-SubGenius type who has to act like a devout Marxist to keep the job, informed me that he manages to get pretty creative with it sometimes—which may partially explain the schizoid nature of the writing.

You might be able to obtain some of the more obscure sensationalistic Chinese papers—and their African equivalents, which can be equally surreal—through:
NEW WORLDWIDE ENGLISH MAGAZINES
Multinewspapers, Box DE-WM, Dana Point, CA 92629.
Twenty countries. Free brochure.

RELIGION VS. RELIGION

*K*ing *Kong Vs. Godzilla* ... now *there* was a movie. In the Japanese version, Godzilla won; in the American version, King Kong won. The Japanese producers shot it both ways. I like that.

WHAT??? ERRORS?? CONTRADICTIONS!?? SURELY YOU JEST!

Biblical Errancy
Dennis McKinsey
3158 Sherwood Park Dr.
Springfield, OH 45505

This free-thought advocate is taking on the biblical "apologists" in a direct manner. Points out errors and contradictions within the Bible, and invites those who disagree to write in. The stated purpose is to let the public hear both sides and decide whether the religionists are faithful or just rationalizing. Is there a difference? 75¢. ((With Factsheet Five))

NYAH, NYAH!

Some Reasons Not to Be a
Christian
Jim Lippard, PO Box 37052
Phoenix, AZ 85069

One of the little publications pinpointing contradictions and ludicrous statements in the Bible. Points out some of the "banned gospels" that the early Christian establishment censored; interesting bibliography in

the back. Not atheist fodder exactly, but excellent "doubters" material. A newer publication is *Fundamentalism Is Nonsense (Some Problems with Christian Fundamentalism, Christianity, and Theism in General),* one of the most thoroughly researched, readable compendiums I've seen for totally demolishing the supposed infallibility of the Bible. But... Gee, what a spoilsport! And couldn't he have taken on something a little more *challenging?* $2 for most people; $1 for members of the SubGenius Church. (Requires proof, such as a xerox of your ordainment card.) That there's any argument at *all* about whether or not the Bible is a fairy tale concocted by ancient wise guys to keep their violent brethren in line is astounding enough —much less the fact that MILLIONS believe in it, and attempt to live by it. I don't mean to just pick on you Judeo-Christian believers; I consider all your rivals every bit as gullible a herd of suckers as you are. But hey, I can forgive you for *that.* I know how it is.

"THERE *IS* A WAY OUT"

Fundamentalists Anonymous
PO Box 20324, Greeley Sq. Station
New York, NY 10001-9992

For people having trouble breaking away from fundamentalist mind-squishing. Why not? You already got your "AA" and your "Cocaine Anonymous"; religion can be just as tough an opiate to kick. Withdrawal from the dreamworld. They hold big seminars that cost around $185, the lesson in that being, "There's no free ride in life." (Think about that as part of the deprogramming—it drives home a main point.) However, there are also support groups in most towns. As one might imagine, ex-fundamentalists suffering cold turkey are a growth market. (Imagine how that must make the Falwelloids feel!) Because the counselors are nonprofessionals who have been through the damn mill, this group has a better track record than their New Age counterparts. Sorry, this is another listing that isn't funny . . .

Bummer . . .

SANTOS VS. THE MEXICAN MUMMY

Cult Awareness Network News
PO Box 608370, Chicago, IL 60626

Cult gossip about everyone from gun-toting, murderous Krishnas to gun-toting, murderous fundamentalists. It's not so much the religious gobbledygook they object to, but the brainwashing tactics. "Brainwashing" is so easy to do, once you know the tricks, that the techniques are now being used by multilevel-marketing-scheme recruiters and other corporate entities far outside the religious and governmental realms to which they'd long been jealously confined. $5/year for twelve issues.

EARTH VS. THE FLYING SAUCERS

Council on Mind Abuse
PO Box 575, Postal Station Z
Toronto, Ontario M5N 2Z6, Canada

Another anticult group, offering counseling to victims and escapees of pretty much any thought-suppressing belief system. But . . . hmm . . . what exactly do they replace the cult programming *with*?

FRANKENSTEIN MEETS THE WOLF MAN

Cult Awareness Council
Box 61922
Dallas/Ft. Worth Airport, TX 75261

Keeps in stock several of the major anticult books; ask for catalog. Newsletter $15 a year. The Church of the SubGenius is right up there on their hate list, alongside the Moonies and the Krishnas! This fills us with PRIDE.

Godzilla VS. The Smog Monster

Johann Most's *THE GOD PESTILENCE*
The Match!, Box 3488
Tucson, AZ 85722

A 50¢ reprint of a classic old-time, atheist pamphlet. ((Factsheet Five))

Abbott And Costello Meet Frankenstein

Saints Alive in Jesus
Box 1076, Issaquah, WA 98027

Well, I agree that Mormonism is insidious. In fact, its growth suggests to me that man is not only descended from apes, but is in fact tragically FAR from completing the process. But the reason *these* guys tear into the Mormons is because they aren't *Christians*. Idiotic enough to make you want to join the Mormons just to spite the authors! Nothing is more fun than watching fanatics accuse each other of fanaticism. They get pretty fanatical about it, even if—as in this case—they try with all their might to be "subtle" and "fair." That's when they're at their funniest!

Also from the same truth-seekers:
The Question of Freemasonry
Free the Masons Ministry (same address as above!) A pamphlet attacking the evil Masonic conspiracy, exposing its rotten core. They think. It's funny how zealots can inadvertently manage to almost convert you to their enemies' points of view. Did you know that Masons eat the flesh of the dead? Well, it says so right here. Always wondered what my dad did at those lodge meetings. No charge for the pamphlets.

Dr. Jeckyll VS. Mr. Hyde

A Mormon Temple Worker Asks Some Questions
Sword of the Shepherd Ministries
Box 4707
Thousand Oaks, CA 91359

This writer goes after the Mormons with a studied air of objectivity, but bases it all on biblical references. He totally ignores all the certifiable modern day dirt on the Mormons! For instance, there's evidence that the Book of Mormon was actually plagiarized by Joseph Smith (a Rogue SubGenius if ever there was one) from an antique *science fiction* manuscript that some weird old preacher had abandoned at a print shop. Oh, but the

Bible didn't mention *that*...so this guy BLEW IT! If these people weren't so fixated on their own mythology, they'd be able to find lots more ammo against their competitors.

BRAINWASHING DETERGENT

Religion Watch
PO Box 652, N. Bellmore, NY 11710

Editor Richard Cimino keeps tabs on upwards of 500 periodicals and summarizes trends in the modern religious world. A sampling of topics: Christian press reaction to the Libya bombing; Unificationist ecumenicism; the pope's stand on liberation theology; the Mormon position on science. Covers all the denominations I can think of and then some. $14/year. ((Factsheet Five))

TARZAN MEETS THE LEOPARD WOMAN

Creation/Evolution
Box 146, Amherst Branch
Buffalo, NY 14226-0146

A newsletter monitoring the Creationists' relentless efforts to supplement textbooks with superstition. Also spotlights everything that's unforgivably ludicrous in Creation Science, and clarifies common misinterpretations of evolution. Creationists call modern science guesswork. Yes; that's why it's science and not divine revelation. Real scientists don't claim infallibility; they're ready to be wrong (ideally), so they can move on the next thing. Creationists are right, period, because the Bible said so. 'Nuff said! $9/four.

THE INCREDIBLY STRANGE CREATURES WHO STOPPED THINKING AND BECAME PERFECTLY SATISFIED ZOMBIES

Forward
Christian Research Institute
PO Box 500
San Juan Capistrano, CA 92693

CRI attempts to highlight the doctrinal errors in other religions so as to make their own mainstream Christianity look good. Oddly enough, their method of argument is to show how their rivals' tenets conflict with the New Testament. The only articles that border on the nasty are those dealing with heresies closer to home, such as the Jehovah's Witnesses. $2. ((Factsheet Five))

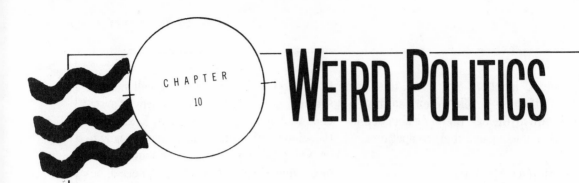

CHAPTER 10

WEIRD POLITICS

There are three kinds of people—I call them Larrys, Curlys, and Moes. The Larrys don't even know that there are three types; if they're told, it's an abstraction, because they cannot imagine anything beyond Larryness. The Curlys know about it, and recognize it as a pecking order, but find ways of living with it cheerfully . . . for they are the imaginative, creative ones. The Moes not only know about it, but exploit and perpetuate it.

Among the listees in this book, the naive, pleasant New Agers and "nice" UFO contactees, for instance, are Larrys (as are normals at large)—ineffectual, well-meaning do-gooders destined always to be victims, often without once guessing their status. Like sheep, they don't want to hear the unpleasant legends about "the slaughterhouse"; they *trust* the strange two-legged beings who feed them. The artists, unsung scientific geniuses, political writers, and earnest disciples of the stranger cults are Curlys—engaging, original, accident-prone but full of life, and intuitively aware of the Moe forces against them and trying to fight back. They can never defeat the Moes, however, without *becoming* Moes, which is impossible for a true Curly. The Moes, then, are the fanatics, the ranters, the cult gurus, the Uri Gellers AND the debunkers; they are the Resistance Leaders and the Ruling

Class Bankers, both. They hate each other, but only because they want to control ALL the Larrys and Curlys themselves. They don't actually enjoy their dominance; it's simply part of their nature. Nor are they any less foolish for the fact that *they* make the decisions. They suffer a chronic paranoia that is unknown to their less demanding underlings. Larrys and Curlys die in wars started by rival Moes—the Larrys willingly, the Curlys with great regret. Concepts like "Hell" and "Sin" were invented by Moes to keep Larrys in line; the Larrys, in turn, being far more numerous, exert social pressure on the Curly minority to also obey . . . mainly so the Larrys won't feel like suckers.

The Moes also invent myths, like that of the "Grouchos, Harpos, Chicos, and Zeppos," to throw more rebellious Curlys off their trail and keep them unsure of the real situations.*

I am a Moe, though not a particularly powerful one; that is why I know these things, and it is also why I dare to tell you—for most of you will think it's just a funny joke. A few will know it is the truth, but will fight far harder against my Moe enemies than you will against me, a relatively harmless Moe. My fellow Moes—enemies and uneasy SubGenius allies alike —will know what I'm REALLY saying, and chuckle in appreciation while plotting my downfall. In vain. ALL in VAIN, boy.

Not one political "movement" makes a bit of sense to me. Political approaches to world problems always seem to require some degree of stereotyping, of forcing people into a mold; even "anarchy" is guilty of this. I don't pretend to know what the answer is, but I've been convinced by Fate itself that it's cultural, not political. The last thing I want to see is a world of one unified culture, but a lot of cultures are going to have to

* When the Curlys finally die of overwork, the Moes find that they cannot live in an all-Larry world; they select special Larrys and vainly try to mold them into False Curlys . . . but it isn't the same.

compromise their attitudes toward each other if they don't all want to end up slaves to the *one* culture with the biggest guns—the culture of the political *controllers* of the various "little" folk cultures. Judging from history as a whole, I'd say we can look for this to happen in, oh, roughly ten thousand years. Cynical? Hey, if you'd seen what I've seen, you'd call me an optimist. At least I haven't given UP! Maybe the human race will surprise me. I wouldn't put ANYTHING past this species—not even success. (I even vote, always for whoever is least popular—not because I'm behind them, but just to help throw a slight scare into the ruling party.)

Hopefully, this helps to explain why almost everything in this section is treated with some degree of contempt, or at best pity. But if I was truly cynical, do you think I'd have gone to the trouble of reading what all these hundreds and hundreds of geeks had to say? I haven't spent weeks typing out and organizing all this crap for the money (HA!—although the money *allowed* me to do this, instead of corporate ad work) . . . not even for the sense of superiority, although that should help keep this entertaining. I tell you how to get their stuff, and describe them with what I HOPE is such obnoxious, hateful unfairness that you'll check 'em out for yourself *just to spite me.*

As the sage Dr. Philo Drummond said, "I am the greatest man in the world; indeed I am *so* great that I can afford great generosity: I encourage all others to adopt the *delusion* that they are as great as I. If they truly thought that they were themselves the greatest, they too would be as generous; and then we would all be able to *humor* each other, in peace, for none would feel threatened by the now-harmless delusions of everyone else." This is the *essence* of the only political party fit for SubGeniuses, the **Patrio-Psychotic AnarchoMaterialist Party.** "Every yard a kingdom; every child and dog a serf."

WEIRD POLITICS PART 1: NEITHER RIGHT NOR LEFT, but OFF THE MAP

The Horror . . . The Horror . . .

As Outsider material gets closer and closer to the real world—if you consider politics closer to reality than religion—it becomes scarier and scarier, both in what is revealed and what is implied.

If you want *ordinary* right-wing megalomania or left-wing teeth-gnashing, go to any extremist bookstore. Those listed here are too far outside the boundaries of the normal political spectrum to be allowed in most stores.

THE SIMPLE ANSWER TO ALL THE WORLD'S PROBLEMS

Little Free Press
Rte. 2, Box 38C, Cushing, MN 56443

Definitely the most idealistic, and arguably the most naive set of pamphlets in our Archives. The author's plan for total world utopia involves, simply, everyone working for nothing; all competition would be abolished. Work without pay—is that too much to ask? It's a pathetic halfway measure, though. We'd still be *working*. Otherwise, it might be a great idea . . . on some other planet, using some other race besides humans. Free, of course.

Keep Telling Yourself: It's Only A Magazine ... It's Only A Magazine ...

The Crystal Ball *and* **The Larsen File**
H. Larsen, PO Box 4080
Torrance, Ca 90510

The CRYSTAL BALL

A CONTINUOUS COMPILATION OF PREDICTIONS, PROPHECIES AND FORECASTS
WITH PERTINENT COMMENTARY, AD LIBS AND OCCASIONAL PREDICTIONS BY THE COMPILER

| Issue #19 | Editor: H. Larsen | October, 1980 |

ARMAGEDDON ?!

World War III? Rapture?!

NUCLEAR WAR?!

"...For the words are closed up and sealed till the time of the end. Many shall be purified, and made white, and tried; but the wicked shall do wickedly: and none of the wicked shall understand, but the wise shall understand."--Dan. 12:9-10--

"We will bury you."--Khruschev--

1. When will the "end times", the Rapture, the "final days" come? No man knoweth the day nor the hour, but what we <u>will</u> know is "the generation and the year!" So affirms Frank Goins in his June 10, 1980 "PROPHECY AND ECONOMICS" newsletter. Appearing in the Bible 146 times, the word "forty", among other things, represents one generation; and the "generation of the fig tree" represents the state of Israel. Further, Israel became a geographical nation on May 14, 1948. If this "generation will not pass away" before these things will come to pass, then by May, 1988 the "end times" will have occurred---seven years after its beginning in 1981. Frank Goins then presents the startling prophecy that since the Biblical "Rapture" must have occurred at least 7 years before that May 1988 date (occurring, according to the Bible, <u>before</u> the final 7 year Tribulation, ending in Armageddon), this Rapture must occur no later than May of 1981 ! ●●● [For a more detailed analysis and evidence of the above conclusion, see Bibliography entry #126.]

"And it shall come to pass in the last days saith God, I will pour out of My Spirit upon all flesh: and your sons and your daughters shall prophesy, and your young men shall see visions, and your old men shall dream dreams..."--Acts 2:17--

* * * * *

2. In the August 24, 1980 "Shepherd's Chapel" newsletter of Arnold Murray, we are again presented with the year 1981 as being a time of momentous beginnings and changes that "shall certainly prove to be an interesting one." [A touch of British understatement?!--HL] Mr. Murray attempts to establish a connection between Mt.St.Helens' 5 eruptions and Biblical prophecy for the latter days. They may soon be upon us. ●●● (Bibl.#104)

* * * * *

3. Turning to some psychic and metaphyscial sources, a September 7 "HOT LINE" from COSMIC AWARENESS entitled "5 Minutes To Midnight" suggests that time may indeed be running out before an impending nuclear war darkens our dreams and hopes. It could come this year; it could come the next. There are positive forces, however, that are working to counter the forces of darkness. This might delay or alleviate

"A compilation of Predictions, Prophecies and Forecasts with Pertinent Commentary, Ad Libs and Occasional Predictions by the Compiler." That pretty well explains *The Crystal Ball,* which is a treasure trove of nut lore—he gets a lot of material from many of the spacey UFO and psychic groups listed here. Some of the most outlandish past predictions were the very ones to come true. *The Larsen File,* likewise, is one classic continuing compendium of conspiracy fodder. Most of it's probably true, but you'll think it's *funny.* Latest word on the kook-watchers' grapevine says he's stopped publishing new ones, but has plenty of recent back issues to unload ... probably around $2 each. And prophecies get *better* as they get older.*

---

* Sometimes they even change! Compare the "Dateline for Dominance" predictions in the first edition of *The Book of the SubGenius* (McGraw-Hill, 1983) with the far superior reprint from Simon and Schuster (1987).

ALL THE CONSPIRACIES UNDER ONE ROOF

Tom Davis Books
PO Box 1107, Aptos, CA 95001

One of the best single sources of books on the CIA, assassinations, secret governments, Nazis, the wealthy, the Vatican, the mafia, U.S.–sponsored terrorism, mind control, etc. More than 800 titles, and many can't be obtained anywhere else. Send name, address, and 22¢ stamp for annotated catalog.((Waves Forest))

. . . AND WHEN I WOKE UP, I KNEW EVERYTHING!

Brainbeau
Box 2243, Youngstown, OH 44504

"The World's ONLY Radical." Inexplicable. One sees Brainbeau's crazy little ads in all sorts of oddball publications. You send for information, and you get more crazy little ads —pages and pages of them. But the ads themselves each bear a different plan for a new world order—a world of Brainbeau! His name alone says a lot. Text of one ad: "What makes criticism of my solutions go in one ear and out the other is the knowledge that I'm probably the sole possessor of a mind-changing W.W. II jeep accident head injury incident that involved eradicating previously held beliefs and substituting others via a round-the-clock me-to-me talkathon. Forty-one years later I'm still talking to myself." Send SASE and he'll talk to himself to you! A true "free spirit."

ECS/NOC, May 1980, page 2

NATIONAL OPPORTUNITIES AND CLASSIFIED
The Easy Chair Shopper

BRAINBEAU SAYS . . .

This "inflationary economy" has been with us for at least 8,000 years It's just beginning to "perk" world-wide Un fix Fixed wages – send S.A.S.E. to:
FIFTY FIFTY ECONOMICS
BEFORE T. V.
NON · PRODUCTIVE ADVERTISING TOOK ABOUT 3% OF YOUR DOLLAR NOW IT'S HEADING FOR 50%.
Would you rather some multi-million · dollar · a · year
Rathers or just plain Brainbeau ?
Send S.A.S.E. to:
PERCENTAGE PIE ECONOMICS
IT'S CLOSE TO 50 50
that you would be on a one years paid
VACATION
if Brainbeau had his way
Most of us should enjoy full employment in the HERENOW as we did in the
HEREBEFORE
and will do in the
HEREAFTER
Send S.A.S.E. to EVEN AGE
ONE BAD EFFECT OF
winnerless wars, fixed wages, unemployment, and atheism is the
TAKING OF HOSTAGES.
Send S.A.S.E. to:
4 WAY PEACE PLAN
SOMEDAY
A low ten percent and sooner just twenty five percent will comprise the

QUESTION:
How would you end unemployment in a hurry?
ANSWER:
We could print 100 billion dollars of paper money for the ten million unemployed and create an additional ten million defense jobs 'a la Reagan. Ten grand a year for each beats starving. The national debt would increase ten percent but think of the pluses. It would oil the wheels of commerce. Better yet, would be to create an all-involving, year 'round paying, ending, unemployment even age work force before robots make it mandatory. Everyone WORKS his or her share. Send S.A.S.E. to:
EVEN AGE WORKERS
Box 2243
YOUNGSTOWN — OHIO, 44504

THE UNLEASHED POWER
Of the atom has changed everything except our way of thinking — Albert Einstein. As I recall Einstein favored socialism right to the end. We're going to put an and to the "end", too. Send SASE to:
SCRAP SOCIALISM
Box 2243
YOUNGSTOWN — OHIO, 44504

WORLD UNREST
Continues because we are disobeying the fifteen commandments · especially the last five. Send SASE to 5 way peace plan — Box 2243 Youngstown – Ohio. 44504

What Hath The Illuminati Wrought?

Conspiracies Unlimited
PO Box 3085, St. Paul, MN 55165

Each issue covers different conspiracy theories. It's a tangled world of espionage and black magic out there, and keeping up with every group out to control your thoughts is an exhausting job. Send $5 for *huge* sample package. Incredible collections of extremist thought from this dimension and others.

Also, from the same address:

The Spengler Group

Promotes the work of the dead Oswald Spengler, A Nietzschean philosopher of overwhelming cynicism, amorality, and imperialism. For those with "a carnal sense of morality and destiny."

A Loaf Of Bread, A Jug Of Wine, A Spray-Paint Can, And Thee

Chaos by Hakim Bey
c/o Association for Ontological
Anarchy, Box 568
Brooklyn, NY 11211

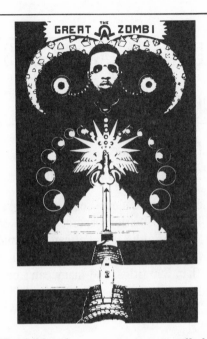

The bible of a new movement called "Poetic Terrorism." Explores in perversely compelling language the paths to chaos and ruin in our society. BUT THAT'S NOT ALL IT IS. Gives you instructions on speeding up the process. Many specific suggestions on how to bring about the collapse of Western Civilization, *artistically!* "If I were to kiss you here they'd call it an act of terrorism—so let's take our pistols to bed & wake up the city at midnight like drunken bandits celebrating with a fusillade, the message of the taste of chaos." Lofty, hash-inspired writing makes it all the more horrifying. Large bound book $5. Also available through Loompanics (see the "Great Catalogs" section). An SASE alone will get you indescribable sample flyers of poetic subversion, plus info on other books by the author—including *Scandals,* about Islamic "heresy" as seen from both inside and outside. This guy has led a strange life.

WORKERS OF THE WORLD—RELAX!

The Abolition of Work by Bob Black
Loompanics, PO Box 1197
Port Townsend, WA 98368

A book-length collection of rants and pamphlets by infamous broadsidist Bob Black (of The Last International), in which is set forth, in deliciously double-edged language, the most extreme political line of all those listed here: the total abandonment of the *work ethic* as we now know it. "What might otherwise be play is work, if it's forced." To Black, even anarchists and Marxists are too work-oriented, "because they believe in so little else." Leaves the left wing far behind. "If there were no work there would be no workers, and without workers, who would the Left have to organize?" This one IS for sale—$5.

THE ABOLITION OF WORK

by Bob Black

ANTIPOLITICS, ARMED AND LOADED

Neutron Gun by Gerry Reith
The Neither/Nor Press, Box 8043
Ann Arbor, MI 48107

"*There will be people who say that mere ideas cannot be dangerous . . . well, they just never had ideas like these.* Doesn't just open Pandora's box, but literally tears it apart. More than just a book, this is a concussion device. . . ." The publisher's description says it better than I can. Seven savage, powerful parables and allegories expressing a vision of society as Hell. Small wonder that the editor and primary author blew his brains out while sitting over his typewriter.* Seventy-five-page book, $3.95 postpaid. Also ask for the catalog of back issues of *Beatniks from Space,* a pretty disturbing literary/arts mag.

This book has a rough edge....

A BLAST FOR THE KIDDIES

The Armageddon Coloring Book
Sulkis, 2050 Manning
Los Angeles, Ca 90025

An effective and very funny nuclear war statement; it really is a coloring book, though not for kids. Dot-to-dot *Day After* scenes, *drastic* Change of Address cards, "cute" blast effects. Truly, the ultimate horror can paradoxically provide the ultimate laughs. Very cleverly done—a fine tool for making the unthinking think about the unthinkable. $3.70 postpaid.

JFK BREATHES YET

Kennedy Murder Mystery
George Thompson,
1528 Canada Blvd., #208,
Glendale, CA 91208

Kennedy wasn't even in that Dallas motorcade. Millions of dollars are being spent to suppress this information. You can have your choice of either cassette tape ($7) or transcripts ($1) of rants such as: "The Strange 'Death' of Lee Harvey Oswald." "The Stranger in Arlington Cemetery." "Dallas Ambush." OSWALD LIVES!!! All thirteen transcripts plus a book can be had for $10!! **

---

* Gerry Reith is having Eternal Sex in Asgard, home of all heroes slain for "Bob."

** "Bob" Dobbs, an expert in fake assassinations, set up the whole thing so that JFK could retire early to Argentina. Too bad that patsy Oswald had to die just so that John could drive a taxi in Argentina—but that's what happened. He told "Bob" he needed Slack. Don't tell Marina.

IT'S JUST A GAME

BOY SCOUT'S HANDBOOK

Paladin Press
PO Box 1307, Boulder, CO 80306

"Publishers of the Action Library." Books on lockpicking, wiretapping, smuggling, assassination, guerrilla warfare, and related subjects. Great catalog if you like this kind of stuff. Fast service, too. Catalog $2. ((Remote Control))

HELP WANTED:

Need young man to pass out Fair-Play-for-Cuba literature on Canal Street in New Orleans. Rapid advancement to more important work. Send résumé to Puzzling Evidence, 2140 Shattuck, Box 2189, Berkeley, CA 94704.

HE'S TRIED TO TELL THEM THERE'S A FOREST, BUT ALL *THEY* SEE ARE TREES

The Underground Grammarian
PO Box 203, Glassboro, NJ 08028

The Underground GRAMMARIAN

VOLUME ELEVEN, NUMBER ONE   FEBRUARY, 1987

Influxing Fun in Florida

Welcome to the twilight zone of professors. To put it politely, these guys are different. To put it bluntly, they are, at times, downright strange. But however strange or bizarre their methods might seem, they are as dedicated to teaching as anyone in their profession. ... Even though these profs have been known to smack ice cream cones into their foreheads, drill holes in desks, and dress up as Elton John, there's something serious going on here, something they take pride in—education.

From Today, a glossy PR poopsheet published for some reason or other by the University of Florida

IN the twilight zone of professors at the University of Florida, you will find, for example, David Denslow, or Dr. Dave to those who sit at his feet. He teaches in the College of Business Administration. He "teaches one live class in the morning, which is videotaped and replayed throughout the day."

Sometimes he breaks off his spiel and says, "Boy, there's something out there that's really destroying my concentration." (Pause.) "That jacket, that yellow jacket out there. Could you please take that off?" Then, a student planted in the back of the room takes off a jacket. But that's not all. The student then "speaks to the TV, telling Denslow his tie is too loud. Timing it perfectly, Denslow replies, 'Oh, my tie is too loud? Sorry,' he says, taking it off." Then the tape is replayed through the day.

Denslow has also planted students instructed to hold up rutabagas, in which act they may well have found some pleasure not exactly anticipated by Dr. Dave. He sounds like the right man to hold up some rutabagas to.

This comes from one R. Mitchell, who appears to be a teacher disgruntled about the invasion of our schools by educationalists. He employs a rapier wit to poke at a horde that he is relatively powerless to stop. "It begins to seem that making sense is a skill not unlike the playing of the violin. It can, of course, be done, but no one simply falls into the habit of playing the violin." This is conservativism at its best. $15/year. ((With Factsheet Five))

Vanishing Point

Eden Press
PO Box 8410
Fountain Valley, CA 92728

Barry Reid is author/publisher of the infamous *Paper Trip*, THE book on how to disappear and create a new identity, including birth certificates, driver's licenses, and passports. Everyone should have this information. Free catalog. ((Remote Control))

Confessions Of A CIA Drug Guinea Pig!

Martti Koski
Kiilinpellontie 2, 21290 Rusko,
Finland

This lengthy brochure—a "must" for conspiracy buffs—starts with a rundown of the *exposed* illegal mind-control experiments conducted by the CIA, the Mounties, and others: secret mass-sterilization campaigns in America, the germ warfare tests during which oft-deadly viruses were sprayed into the NY subway system (to track the "spread factor" of contagions), evidence implicating Jonestown as a mind-control experimental facility, etc., with examples of successful news blackouts indicating that the U.S. censorship system has international dimensions. But that's just the preface to a personal story by a victim of RCMP surreptitious testing of various "telepathic amplifiers" that use microwaves and brain implants to interrupt sleep, broadcast voices into minds, and generally modify behavior through sanity-wrecking. Koski's descriptions of the bizarre sexual and political brainwashing to which he was subjected in Canadian mental hospitals reads like classic paranoid schizophrenic delusions, except for one thing—it's told in a perfectly coherent, logical manner (aside from English grammar errors by the Finnish author), and backed up with testimonials from other victims of behavior modification.* Or were they? Well, the CIA's brainwashing program (called "MKULTRA SubProject 68") has been documented, but as for the Brain Transmitters, Radio-Hypnotic Intracerebral Control technology, and Electronic Dissolution of Memory devices . . . if the secret governments are that far along, satirists like me are in big trouble. On the other hand, it would explain about half the cases of UFO, Jesus, and Devil contactees. Send a buck-two-eighty or so to help him with postage.

---

* Americans tend to see Canada as a bland, benevolent neighbor, supposedly more "liberal" than the U.S. In actuality, a few civil liberties that we have to fight for only occasionally—for instance, the right to receive a copy of The SubGenius Video by mail—are denied there routinely.

KEEPING UP WITH THE OPPOSITION

Consumertronics
2011 Crescent Drive
PO Drawer 537
Alamogordo, NM 88310

Bizarre survivalist publications. Some truly dangerous stuff. Their flyer has captions like "Mexico is in terrible shape and could ignite any day!" "Better to be judged by 12 than carried by 6." Books on how to rip off automatic-teller machines, stop power meters, build blue boxes, and more. You may have seen these guys on *60 Minutes*. Catalog $1. ((Remote Control))

IF YOU THOUGHT MAN'S INHUMANITY TO MAN WAS BAD . . .

The Animals' Agenda
PO Box 5234, Westport, CT 06881

A real eye-opener—and closer. You may never even have heard of animal rights. Why worry about animals, you ask, when humans are being tortured and starved and enslaved? Well . . . it's probably far worse than you ever dreamed, unless you've already looked into this issue. Experimentation on animals is one thing; needlessly painful—nay, UNTHINKABLY HIDEOUS cruelty—in the name of money and just plain sadism (corporate R&D style) is another. Some of us, as kids, tortured bugs for fun. The nastier kids tortured cats. We grew up and were sorry . . . some of us. Imagine what an immature lab technician in a bad mood could do . . . not to bugs, but to chimpanzees and baboons. Multiply that by ten zillion and you get a glimpse of the picture. Your tax money has financed studies on just how much of every kind of pain a dog can take before it dies of sheer horror; it took a LOT of dogs to get the statistics *just right*. I don't care what you say, I've had dogs—hell, PET CHAMELEONS—who had more feelings than some people. $18/year; very professionally designed and printed, and almost rational—a far cry from the other "screaming crybaby" animal rights mags. Don't EVER let a child read this. It'll give you nightmares, but it'd give a child phobias.*

NO WAY TO GET AHEAD

Working Assets
230 California St.
San Francisco, CA 94111

A money-market fund, offering its own Visa card, that puts its extra interest profits into worthy humanitarian/conservation causes! Free info.

* A great source of photos for punkzine collage artists who've exhausted their files of facial surgery, autopsy, and Holocaust photos.

TATTLE TALES

The Last Hurrah Bookshop
937 Memorial Ave.
Williamsport, PA 17707

Free catalog from a bookstore specializing in political assassination books (especially Kennedy) and conspiracy theories. They seem to have EVERYTHING, including the ones you thought were rounded up and burned years ago. If even 5 percent of the allegations made in the world of conspiracy trackers are true, then Watergate was the very least of a million evils, Irangate was a laughably minor transgression, and you are living in a cage that you will NEVER notice.

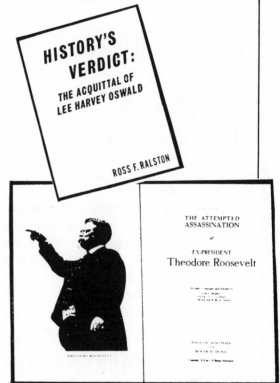

SOMETHING HAS HAPPENED IN THE MOTORCADE . . .

The President's Box Bookshop
PO Box 1255
Washington, DC 20013

Like the above; similarly extensive. Other assassination/conspiracy subjects include King, RFK, and Lincoln, as well as the pope, and other attempted assassinations. A million viewpoints, a billion details, but one thing in common—we've been *had*.

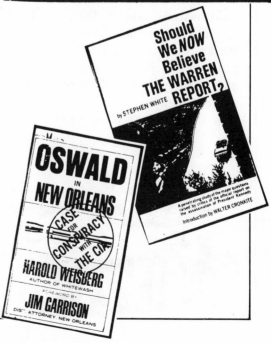

EVERY CHILD AND DOG A SERF

The Territorial Herald
Royal Post 200-0203, PO Box 7075
Laguna Niguel, CA 92677

This is the quarterly newsletter of the Free Territory of Ely-Chatelaine, a household kingdom that has declared its independence from the U.S. government and everything else. It exists mostly to reassert the concept of individual sovereignty. Be the tyrant of your own household government! Anyone can be royalty! An entire belief system and culture inside one guy's head. He is putting into practice the ONE POLITICAL SYSTEM that is Dobbs Approved: **Patrio-Psychotic AnarchoMaterialism**. . . . Each YARD a KINGDOM!!—and he's not even a SubGenius! Declare war on the neighbors! (Just make sure **you** get that first strike in.) Charters and founding decrees available . . . Tons of rants and info to be had here; start with a mere 75¢. ((With Factsheet Five))

YOU THINK YOU GOT PROBLEMS

Moscow Trust Group Update
Bob McGlynn, 528 Fifth St.
Brooklyn, NY 11215

Chronicles the continuing problems of the Moscow Trust Group, an independent network of peace activists in the USSR. Many members have ended up in labor camps, prisons, and mental hospitals. It's incredible that the Western peace movements are, for the most part, ignoring these people, who are risking much more than disorderly conduct charges at their demonstrations. $1 and SASE. Here you can also get the amazing "funny mag," *Shoe Polish Week*. ((Factsheet Five))

Brats In The Walls

KLMN News
Oness Press, PO Box 336
Calpella, CA 95418

The quarterly publication of the Kid's Lib Movement Network. I don't know how realistic the open and totally loving approach to child-rearing presented here is; I'd hate to be their babysitter. "Liberate your free expression." (Easier said than done!) "Conscious parenting." Hell, I say, they talk back to you, you threaten 'em; if they keep it up, you put 'em on a chain in the backyard with the dogs for a few nights. I've known kids who were raised à la Kid's Lib . . . they're crybaby assholes now, doomed to lives of misery. *MY* kids, they haven't suffered a bit from being tortured and beaten now and then. At least they keep their pants on in the damn restaurant! ((With Factsheet Five))

How Cute

Love 22
PO Box 4022, Key West, FL 33040

Love 22 (his legal name now) is still running for the presidency on his twenty-two plank platform. Heaviest "use" of "quotes" "ever"—always a sign of penetrating intelligence. Means well; hilariously retarded nonetheless. His twenty-two examples of cosmic coincidences involving the number 22 provide a perfect illustration either of schizophrenia, or piss-poor comedy writing. You can still get five $22 bills for a buck.

SELL-OUT TO THE ROOSKIES EXPOSED

The Phoenix Letter: A Report on the Abuse of Power
PO Box 39850, Phoenix, AZ 85069

Highly valuable exposés on the Western financial leaders' betrayal of the Free World to the Soviets. Editor is Antony C. Sutton, author of *Wall Street and the Rise of Hitler*, *Wall Street and the Bolshevik Revolution*, *Energy: The Created Crisis* and other books. $48/year/4 issues. ((Waves Forest))

ROAD WARRIORS

Australasian Survivor
PO Box E457
Queen Victoria Terrace
A.C.T. 2602, Australia

Definitely the sanest and most impressive survivalism magazine I've seen. The editors do sell a variety of guns, canteens, survival food, and whatnot, but the bulk of the journal is concerned with practical advice and a relative lack of "the world is ending tomorrow, buy our stuff" writing. Sample: $4 cash/Int'l Bank Order, or $18/year for Americans ((Factsheet Five))

* Founder of the Bavarian Illuminati, you ignoramuses.

THE PLAIN TRUTH

World Watchers International
Mae Brussel, 25620 Via Crotalo
Carmel, CA 93923

A unique and exceptionally accurate source of information on who's really behind the political assassinations, sabotage, genocide, government lies, and other high treason in high places. Weekly one-hour tapes of news analysis and backgrounds of the people involved. $6.50 each; there's fourteen years' worth. ((Waves Forest))

BENEATH THE VALLEY OF THE ULTRANIXONS

News of the New World
FOCP, PO Box 830
Honeydew 2040, South Africa

Maybe living in South Africa and the resultant siege mentality has gotten to them. This entire magazine is one long rambling screed about the One World Fabian Socialist plot to take over everything and in the process condemn the whites in South Africa to exile or death. They quote everything from Adam Weishaupt* to *SPIN* magazine at one point or another, lapping up all sorts of conspiracy theory and exuding it again in spades. Great stuff. $12/year. ((Factsheet Five))

YOU'LL PRAY IT'S ALL A LIE

John P. Judge,
PO Box 6586,
Street Station NW,
Washington, DC 20009:

Judge has been researching conspiracy theories on a daily basis since 1968. He is one of the few people in the country who has actually read all twenty-six volumes of the Warren Commission study. Carries a number of reprints of articles on the JFK, RFK, MLK assassinations as well as info in CIA-Nazi ties and the Jonestown–Mind Control connection. A good starting point. Free information. ((Remote Control))

STUMP THE EXPERTS

American Sunbeam
PO Box 107,
Seligman, MO 65745

The *American Sunbeam* was a newspaper published by Delamer Duverus who, according to an enclosed letter, was murdered by THE CONSPIRACY a couple of years ago. Although the *Sunbeam* is now defunct, reprints of Duverus's articles and editorials are still available for the asking. Almost impossible to describe or categorize, this stuff is rough going for even the hardened reader of religious-political-conspiracy weirdness and is guaranteed to have you scratching your head and going back over sentences to be sure you read what you thought you read. Sorry, you're on your own on this one. ((Remote Control))

And now for **Waves Forest's** political rogue's gallery:

GLOBESCAN (eight-page newsletter) 37, Quai d'Anjou, 75004 Paris, France: Worldwide news and analysis, focus is on finance and hidden power control groups behind the scenes.

INTELLIGENCE PARAPOLITICS. $20/year/twelve issues. Association for the Right to Information, PO Box 50441, Washington, DC 20004-0441; also in French: LE MONDE DU RENSEIGNEMENT/PARAPOLITIQUE Association pour le Droit a l'Information, 16 rue des Ecoles, 75005 Paris, France; 150 FF/year: Monitors European and U.S. intelligence, military and right-wing activities, Italian and U.S. Mafia, and the latter's close ties with the Reagan administration.

LOBSTER. $14/four issues. 17c Pearson Ave., Hull HU5 2SX, U.K: "Intelligence, parapolitics, state research." Detailed analyses of assassinations, "terrorist" incidents, and other illegal activities of intelligence agencies in U.K., U.S., and elsewhere.

THE MONTHLY LESSON IN CRIMINAL POLITICS (political-financial-newsletter) PO Box 37432, Cincinnati, OH 45222: Drawn mainly from overseas press.

OMNI PUBLICATIONS PO Box 216, Hawthorne, CA 90250: Good source for books on economic conspiracies, the Federal Reserve, the banking establishment, and ancient civilizations.

WORLD PRESS REVIEW (monthly) PO Box 916, Farmington, NY 11737: Survey of world news reports from non-U.S. and non-

English sources, including stories blacked out in the U.S. media.

COVERT ACTION INFORMATION BULLETIN. $5/issue. Circulation is about 7000. PO Box 50272, Washington, DC 20004; 202-737-5317: Probably the best magazine on the worldwide criminal activities of the U.S. intelligence and defense communities, and international fascist organizations.

THE CONSPIRACY TRACKER. $2.25/copy, six issues $12.90. PO Box 596, Paterson, NJ 07524

COMMITTEE FOR RESPONSIBLE GENETICS 5 Doane St., Fourth floor, Boston, MA 02109: Organizes opposition to military use of gene-tailoring research.

CENTRAL AMERICA ACTION COMMITTEE NEWS (by donation) CAAC, PO Box 7454, Olympia, WA 98507: Firsthand reports on the effects of U.S. policies in Central America, without the mass media whitewash.

CENTRAL AMERICA PEACE INITIATIVE (newsletter, by donation) 1022 W. Sixth St., Austin, TX 78703: Original news of abuses by both sides.

GREAT TITLE

The Upright Ostrich
PO Box 11691
Milwaukee, WI 53211

The One World Government is taking over the U.S. through financial manipulations of energy shortages, and will use this control, combined with the power of the press and a new slave-labor prison system, to suppress American citizens. Hence these crusaders publicize new tachyon or magnetic or Tesla theories that promise free energy for the masses, and also run articles on the hijinks of the big boys. $3 each or $25/year. ((Factsheet Five))

CONTRAGATE
WHISTLEBLOWERS

Forget Stephen King, horror fans. Just before this book's deadline, Waves Forest sent three publications examining the history and implications of the Irangate/Contragate scandal in far greater detail than I've seen in commercial media. The conclusions drawn are, as one might guess, quite frightening— even, I daresay, *sphincter-clenching*—when the facts aren't being filtered to fit public preconceptions. These publications show none of the hysterics, paranoia or naiveté which rob so many radical exposés of any credibility.

Ties between the CIA, international mafia, and drug trafficking, normally glossed over in network news, add a sordid dimension to Ollie North's Boy Scout world. Issue #28 of *Covert Action Information Bulletin* (address and price listed above) is entirely devoted to tying together various loose ends to paint a picture of multigovernment corruption conceivable perhaps only to the most disillusioned cynics. The evidence seems legitimate, though. Even if it isn't, this makes for more mind-blowing reading than most dystopian science fiction; if it is, you owe it to our more immediate future generations to part with the $5 and DARE TO KNOW.

CITIZEN ALERT
Box 51332, Pacific Grove, CA 93950
Starting with a collection of alternative press clippings, this irregular newsletter traces the origins of Irangate back to the Carter Administration and claims that the Reaganoid "secret government" has been in kahoots with the Khomeini regime since way back when. They sabotaged the Iran hostage rescue attempt and otherwise insured that the hostages wouldn't be released before the 1980 election. The accusations are mind-boggling, but all too well within the range of possibility. No price listed for this big package of news and commentary, so write first.

CHRISTIC INSTITUTE
1324 North Capitol St., NW
Washington, D.C. 20002
This well-funded activist group works with many other independent investigative organizations in attempts to document the global scale and political nature of organized crime, dating the "contra wars" back to 1959. Not even the labyrinthian, all-encompassing "Conspiracy" portrayed in SubGenius literature seems farfetched when considered from this perspective! Highlights of their explosive findings are encapsulated in a free flyer, which also includes info on their book, *Contragate Affadavit* ($10), large $7 info packets, and the $20 newsletter.

HIGH-TECH SUBVERSION

PUT YOUR HANDS ON THE RADIO AND SAY "AMEN"

The A *C *E
Association of Clandestine Radio
Enthusiasts
Box 46199
Baton Rouge, LA 70895

News and articles for those into pirate radio. In the U.S., that generally means hobbyists who broadcast unlicensed radio for yuks, as a reaction against the monotony of commercial radio, or occasionally for political reasons. In many European countries, pirate radio is a more serious venture, since most stations are entirely government controlled—doling out just enough lame "counterculture" to not look totalitarian. (Americans don't know how lucky they have it, in this regard!) * Then there's clandestine radio, meaning political propaganda or disinformation, set up by governments. This magazine tells you who's on what frequency, who's shutting down who, etc. Frankly, pirate radio could conceivably become extremely important in this country too. Be glad they're there. $1/sample, $12/year.

WAR GAMES

2600
PO Box 752
Middle Island, NY 11953–0752

Newsletter for phone phreaks, computer hackers, satellite hoppers, and other electronics whiz-kids out to take full advantage of everything the big communications powers withhold. $2 each.

* Perfectly legally, I get on the air every Sunday night and broadcast **The Hour of Slack**—SubGenius rants, music, and the X ingredient (unexplainable, unnameable stylistic technique) all over Dallas–Ft. Worth, from a little pledge-drive supported "people's station," KNON-FM, which is located in a run-down house. I don't get paid, but I don't get arrested, either. This is one case in which one could truthfully sigh, "Only in America." And probably not *everywhere* in America. . . . I'm sure our jokes would be too politically incorrect for, say, San Francisco, but far too "demonically liberal" for Birmingham. Man. It sure gets relative. Texas can be backwards, but it can also be a lot more free. It's our tradition. Someday, Texas will blow off the Conspiracy and be a Republic again, a bilingual Tex-Mex hodgepodge (Angloid techno-greed combined with Mexican MACHISMO) that will show all other countries how to do things RIGHT! Just you wait. Hmmph. AND WE'LL START BY RUNNING OUT THE NEW YORK–CONTROLLED AD AGENCY EXECUTIVE PUPPETS!!!

Radio Free Oceania

Clandestine Confidential
Gerry L. Dexter, RR 4, Box 110
Lake Geneva, WI 53147

News about the secret world of political radio broadcasts—frequency and schedule info, etc. $10/four. Related is Tiare Pubs., Box 493, same town & zip . . . distributes books on shortwave and miscellaneous ham-radio news sources from other countries, which often report on items kept out of U.S. mass media news.

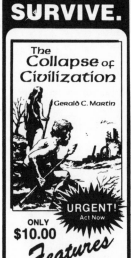

Peek-A-Boo!

Checkmate
Hunter International
Stratford
Plaza 1, #44
127 S. Stratford Rd.
Winston-Salem, NC
27104

Big catalog/access book on security electronics, eavesdropping viewers and recorders, miniature spy cameras, stun-guns, surveillance countermeasure devices, bugging equipment, voice scramblers, and many books for secret police and/or their rebel enemies. Illegal & exotic weapons handbooks, survival goods and books, even blowguns! Everything a commando, infiltrator, spy, or terrorist needs besides the actual guns and bombs. Very similar to the Loompanics catalog, but scarier.

You Can Be Rambo!

The Rouse School of
Special Detective
Training
Box 2469
Costa Mesa,
CA 92626

PICTURE YOURSELF . . . in the world of the ELITE INVESTIGATOR! And if you have trouble doing that, they *show* you rappeling down the side of a building (you look like G. Gordon Liddy). Industrial espionage, high-speed pursuit tactics, Repo-Man tricks, electronic eavesdropping, undercover techniques and *counter-terrorist tactics!!* What more could a kid want? ACT NOW like a true MAN and enroll in these courses.

WATCHDOGS

... BUT I'LL DEFEND TO THE INCONVENIENCE HIS RIGHT TO SAY IT!

Free Press Association
Box 1743, Apple Valley, CA 92307

Organization, newsletter, etc., for media people defending press freedom and autonomy. If you work in radio, TV, or at a newspaper—even if you just distribute cassette tapes of your garage band—you may be very seriously affected by certain seemingly innocuous laws coming down the pike, mostly sponsored by giant entertainment and communications companies and their allies in conservative, $-oriented government. I can't find evidence of political bias in this organization one way or the other!—probably because both far Left and far Right have the same worries about freedom of speech. People in the middle, who *trust* the government even if they *differ* with it, won't give a hoot. The TV networks show them just enough Left and just enough Right to satisfy them that they're getting the whole story. $20/year for nonjournalists; $25/year for pros.

EVEN SCUMBAGS NEED LOVE

Religious Freedom Market
Coalition for Religious Freedom
316 Pennsylvania Ave. SE, #202
Washington, DC 20003

The names on the Advisory Board list reveal that this tabloid is ultimately concerned with CHRISTIAN religious freedom, though they strive not to come off that way in this paper; there's an article on B'Hais being massacred in Iran, Rev. Sun Myung Moon's tax-evasion sentence, and Sioux claims on the Black Hills in South Dakota. You nonfundamentalists may assume that the "Religious Right" has too many friends in high places to worry about religious freedom, but you have to understand that they define that concept as freedom for them to, for instance, teach the Bible as ultimate truth in schools. Nevertheless, they do have many legitimate gripes. They have plenty of *enemies* in high places too: supposedly liberal groups who would silence the fundamentalists without ever seeing the hypocrisy of it. A law that restricts, say, Right-to-Lifers from showing a horrifying antiabortion film on TV can eventually be used to restrict *any* religious efforts.*

BIG BROTHER IS NOT JUST WATCHING . . .

Full Disclosure
Box 8275, Ann Arbor, MI 48107

A *real* education, and definitely one of the scariest publications around. Goes into terrifying detail about abuses of citizen's privacy by government agencies of all kinds. They've run articles on: CIA murder devices, IRS and police surveillance and coercion techniques, secret FBI "mass arrest" plans, political harassment, Post Office tampering with mail, and other things that will probably happen to you if you write to a lot of the groups I've listed in this book! They are forming a "Citizens' CIA." Nice concept. I wonder how long the editor will be able to stay out of jail, or alive. $15/twelve, or $1.50/sample.

CRIME FIGHTERS

THE NATIONAL REPORTER
Box 21279, Washington, DC 20009

Don't mistake this for one of those supermarket tabloids. This magazine was formerly called *Counterspy* and is self-described as "a source of analyses and information on the practices, organization and objectives of U.S. Intelligence." Former CIA Director William E. Colby labeled it "shocking, paranoic, cynical," and *Newsweek* has called it "the CIA's nemesis." A subscription to this one will probably put you on someone's watch list, but there again, so will a subscription to *Overthrow!* Free sample copy. ((Remote Control))

. . . YEAH, AND WHAT ABOUT THE TAMMY BAKKER FOLDOUT?

STREET MEETINGS INC.
PO Box 724, Dallas, TX 75221

Publishes a monthly cult exposé newsletter spotlighting the evils of such organizations and leaders as the Krishnas, Moonies, JWs, Mormons, Reverend Ike, Milton Green, and that scheming bitch Terry Cole–Whittaker. But where's "Bob"? Free sample copy. ((Remote Control))

* There's a high school in Baltimore at which the SubGenius students were allowed to form a "Bob" Dobbs Club, yet the Christian students couldn't have a Jesus Club . . . not on campus, anyway. Even *I* was appalled by this. A little.

LAND OF 1,000 DUNCES

THE MONITOR
Center for Democratic Renewal
PO Box 10500, Atlanta, GA 30310

Monitoring the activities of the Far Right —not the New Right of Jerry Falwell and Pat Robertson, but the lunatic fringe of Klansmen, neo-Nazis, and the Posse Comitatus. This issue leads off with an article on Nazi skinheads and the problems they cause nationwide. $15/year ((Factsheet Five))

TODAY, PLAYBOY; TOMORROW, THE CONSTITUTION

No More Censorship Defense Fund
PO Box 11458
San Francisco, CA 94101

You know, were the obscenity laws to slip very far at all from their present ambiguous position, ninety percent of the material I'm listing would be banned as indecent and you'd be busted for owning it. That still wouldn't rid the world of pornography, which would simply become a little harder to procure, but it would eliminate anything depicting nipples, violence against white male Americans, and raw street language, not to mention all music with a steady beat. Each year the forces of uptightness target somebody new to persecute in hopes of setting a more restrictive legal precedent. Entertainment conglomerates are too powerful to mess with, so the chosen victims are usually the semi-underground artists least able to afford costly, time-consuming trials. Last year, the sacrificial goat was the band The Dead Kennedies, whose unpardonable sin was to include a weird painting by reknowned artist H. R. Giger in their album packaging. This fund was orignally set up to help give that band a fair shake; although the case has been resolved for now (the Conspiracy won!), appeals will continue, as will future harassment of different artists and entertainers. If you've created a piece of work with so much as a cussword or a bare fanny in it, *even if your intent is to mock sexual exploitation,* you could be next. (Although it'll probably be me.) Free info.

WEIRD POLITICS PART 2: RIGHT WING AND QUASI-RIGHT-WING-LIKE

Don't stereotype the Right; that's a loose label, and sometimes one group can be diametrically opposed to another in every way, yet both would call themselves "Right." Sometimes right seems to merge with left, as with the various Libertarian branches.

An illustration of this can be found by perusing:

ONE END TO THE OTHER ... WELL ... AT LEAST HALFWAY, ANYWAY

Spectrum
Jim Corbett, 762 Avenue 'N', SE.
Winter Haven, FL 33880

A sixty-page-and-up listing of addresses for vast numbers of political and religious organizations, most of them roughly rightist; but that includes everything from Christian conservatives to Libertarian atheists to Odinists. Includes short descriptions; broken down into categories like antitax, antifluoridation, foreign affairs, right to life, alternative energy, etc. Bigots and hate groups abound as well. (Just because the editor lists someone doesn't mean he approves of them.) Mags, book catalogs, newspapers ... everything. $8.

THE VATICAN IS BEHIND AIDS!!

"The Project"
A-albionic Consulting & Research
PO Box 20273, Ferndale, MI 48220

This four-page newsletter is the start of an organization that will expose the British Royalty power structure that controls our minds, world economics, science, military intelligence, etc. See, it isn't the Jews after all, but the British Oligarchy, who are also engaged in a war against the Vatican. Ask for info and a sample, or pay $3 an issue, $20/year.

Yes, That Really Was His Name

The Peter Beter Audio Letter
PO Box 276, Savage, MD 20763

Wild, throbbing-at-the-mouth right-wing anti-Trilateral ravings beyond compare. Dr. Beter died, but his cassettes are still available, exposing the paranoid truth behind space germs, oil wars, Illuminati assassinations, etc. Great for scaring your friends. Ask for free list of tapes.

Reagan's Clone Raped By Zionist Masons From Another World!

Spiral Mobius
Spiral Enterprises
347 N. Union Station
Kennet Square, PA 19348

WOW! I *think* this is a right-wing-oriented publication, but it dredges up material from as wide a range of kooks as I do! Anti-Zionist and antiabortion, but with government-built UFOs, clone androids of our high officials, rape by aliens, and other nightmares thrown in. A classic of crankdom . . . $3 each.

St. McCarthy Would Be Proud

Christian Anti-Communism Crusade
227 E. Sixth St., Box 890
Long Beach, CA 90801–0941

Name says all. Stereotypes do apply here. Free rants. Get them to waste money on you.

Pack Your Bags

Spiral Feedback
PO Box 80323, Lincoln, NE 68501

President Reagan is about to put almost everybody in concentration camps. The legislation is already on the books—a secret proposal to silence all patriots trying to restore the Constitution. Time is running out; a "National Emergency" is about to be declared. The only problem is, just subscribing to this publication puts you on the government's target list! Only 10¢ per copy of this flyer.

"RED DAWN" WAKE-UP CALL

ACC Services
2553 Texas Ave. S., Suite C
College Station, TX 77840, Amerika

Keen free info on expensive ($16) "intelligence reports" proving that the Soviets are in cahoots with Mexico, and that they plan a joint attack on the continental U.S. Mountains of Soviet tanks and weapons have already been stashed within our borders!

MR. POTATOHEAD GOES TO WASHINGTON

The American Patriot
We the People, PO Drawer A
Scottsdale, AZ 85252

A monthly conservative tabloid "To save American independence—private property —personal freedom—save the Constitution." Typical issue views, with horror, lectures at West Point on disarmament, and reprints a congressional scorecard that gives Jesse Helms a 95 and Teddy Kennedy a 13. "The U.S. State Dept. is 'AMERIKA.'" $1 or $12/year. Also publishes *The Fact Finder*,

semimonthly brochures which, for instance, "prove" that Martin Luther King was an evil Communist dupe with extremely bad morals. ($12/six months). ((Factsheet Five))

MARTIN LUTHER KING AT COMMUNIST TRAINING SCHOOL

He said King was connected with over 60 Communist-front organizations and with various members of the Communist Party, U.S.A. and named them.

After Martin Luther King was assassinated, Communist agitators led waves of frenzied blacks through the streets of many U.S. cities and burned down whole sections of those towns. Then they intimidated authorities to seal up FBI records and recording tapes of King's subversive activities. The pressured authorities responded and ordered those tapes and records locked up in the National Archives until the year 2027 — *a period of 50 years.*

Dr. Larry McDonald was the only Congressman who had the courage to testify against naming such a holiday for Martin Luther King.

But the House of Representatives passed the

THE FACT FINDER

VOL 45, NO. 3   Phoenix, Ariz   Dec. 16, 1986

Published with 24 issues per year, postage paid at Phoenix, Arizona (2422 East Indian School Road, 85016). Subscription $19.95 per year — 2 years or 2 subscriptions for $35 —45th Year of Publication—

WHO ARE THE BRAIN POLICE?

NFD Journal
PO Drawer 2440, Tupelo, MS 38803

"The National Federation for Decency" is a Christian organization "promoting the biblical ethic of decency on television and other media." In other words, the enemy. Threats to decency include cable-TV in Holiday Inns, Garbage Pail Kids, Marvel comics, and Dr. Ruth Westheimer. These are the sort of people who make Ed Meese feel like he represents the country. $15/year. ((Factsheet Five))

the repair of older firearms (after all, modern weapons will wear out quickly, Come the Collapse), but delves into other concerns like building a greenhouse good enough to get you through nuclear winter. He also sells a number of exotic weapons and books by mail. $10/year. ((Factsheet Five))

Turn The Other...Uh... Now What Was I Supposed To Turn?

Facts for Action
Christian Research, PO Box 385
Eureka Springs, AR 72632

Another newsletter from someone decrying communism and socialism in our public schools, ranting about the IRS, drawing parallels between the Constitution and the Bible, hating homosexuals. $4/year. ((Factsheet Five))

The New Ronin

The Gunrunner
PO Box 327, Harrison, AR 72601

AMERIKA might ACTUALLY HAPPEN! Kurt Saxon's tabloid revolves loosely around

An Old Classic For Old Geezers

The Spotlight
130 East Third Street SE
Washington, DC 20003

"Your weekly newspaper from Washington." These people have been around for years. Right wing, founders of the Populist Party and the Liberty Lobby, their attorney is Mark Lane (former Columbia radical and author of *Rush to Judgment,* about the JFK assassination conspiracy). Great source of info on the CFR, IMF, Trilaterals, Bilderbergers, One-Worlders, etc. Free sample copy. ((Remote Control))

Now Hiring

Five Oceans Trading Co.
1450 Sixty-seventh St.
Emeryville, CA 94608

Pssst, Buddy, come 'ere. Ever think of being a secret agent? Maybe working for the

CIA? or FBI? Then what you need is the book *Careers in Secret Operations* by David Atlee Phillips. Phillips used to be Chief of Operations for the CIA's Latin American and Caribbean offices, so you better believe he knows what he's talking about. Their brochure answers all those questions you've probably been asking yourself, like, Do intelligence officers receive overtime pay? Will I have to kill anyone? How many "moles" are there in the CIA? And why hasn't the CIA assassinated Philip Agee? Free information. ((Remote Control))

That Commie Reagan!

America's Promise
Lord's Covenant Church, Inc.
PO Box 5534, Phoenix, AZ 85010

White America is the true Zion, and the Reagan administration is sickeningly liberal . . . hapless pawns of the Jewish/Trilaterialist bankers. You can get tapes of their farthest-right-wing radio broadcasts.

Do My Bidding Or Taste My Loving Wrath

Christian Falangist Party of America
Box 2533, Philadelphia, PA 19147

"Dedicated to Fighting the Forces of Darkness." Uh-oh. That probably means me. And you, and everyone else who isn't a Christian Falangist. Haven't seen their stuff, but the Membership Application asks you to sign this statement: "I hereby swear that I am not a leftist. That I am a Christian and am willing to abide by the rules and aims of the Christian Falangist Party of America." Their punctuation, not mine.

OH, THEY'LL BE WEARING THE MARK OF THE BEAST IN NO TIME, DON'T YOU WORRY

AAA
PO Box 3332, Venice, FL 33595

Free but crude anti-Trilateralist flyers. "Say NO to the NEW WORLD ORDER." Because if it ain't solid Christian, it's Satanic ...and probably "of an alien race" as well. That means just about everybody and everything. For $7 you can have the *8th Patriotic Directory,* 5,000 groups "concerned with Truth and Freedom " (in capital letters).

THANKS BUT NO THANKS

Network for Citizen Enlightenment
Box 1475, Clackamas, OR 97015

Dedicated to the restoration of "our Christian Republic. We are a Christian-American newsletter counteracting the hypnotic effects of the government-banker–controlled press and air waves." $2 sample.

WEIRD POLITICS PART 3: LEFT WING

I could repeat the same spiel about the term *leftist* as I did about *right wing.* It's hard to tell what it really means anymore. Some of these groups would probably object to being categorized this way. But these listings are for your skimming convenience, not theirs. Otherwise, we'd be looking at almost as many categories as there are addresses!

PLEASANTRIES

Twisted Imbalance
Box 12504, Raleigh, NC 27605

Can't find a price listed on this tabloid for the life of me. Mainly reprints of articles from better-financed mags, but with some good nutty, hip collage art thrown in. Sample issue has article on Salvadoran death squads, "monkeywrenching" ecologically damaging construction sites and roadworks (that means performing minor vandalisms that cost the company a lot of money), mock Army recruitment ads, exposé of the paper industry's sins, and a rant pointing out comparisons between Nazi Germany and Reagan America, which you might miss if you're a well-off Caucasian.

THE NONEXISTENT SHALL INHERIT THE EARTH OR: YOU WON'T EVEN HAVE TIME TO SAY "OUCH"

The Front Line
Box 1793, Santa Fe, NM 87504

A newsletter opposing the proposition that civil defense against nuclear attack is feasible, since it fosters the impression that a nuke-out is winnable. Emergency preparedness for natural disasters, yeah, but . . . how LONG are you gonna want to live in that mine shaft?? Grim news relating to this issue, and how your tax bucks are being spent on it. The title refers to our front yards—nuclear war strategies make all of us troops, and our front yards the front line. But at least you won't know what hit you! If you're lucky. $2 each or $12/six.

HERE, NOW

NOWHERE
Dkytn. Station, PO Box 13285
Minneapolis, MN 55414

"A Modest Journal of the International Revolution"—broadly defined and surrealistically applied. A fun bunch of pointed anti-you-name-it satire. $2.

LOW CLASS WAR

New Iron Column
1728 W. Ball, #4
Anaheim, CA 92804

Quarterly mag of the Creative Anarchist Network, "a collective of Anti-Authoritarian minded individuals with various perspectives on attaining a Stateless society." Boy, if they expect to see that happen within their lifetimes, they should've started somewhere back during the Roman Empire. Come to think of it, maybe they did. Lists of other anarchists; American Indian resistance news; class-war comics; Bakuninist theory; bad collages; worship of Native Americans and historical slain workers. Typical. $6/four.

CRASH COURSE

R. Waldmire
RR 2, Box 110, Rochester, IL 62563

This loner manages to cram an entire ecological crash-course full of pertinent facts into each of his small, nicely drawn $2 posters. Incredible concentration of detail, though some may need a magnifying glass to catch all of it. The one on tropical rain forests, for instance, tells you exactly what deforestation is doing, and how long the crucial parts of the biosphere have left if we keep on talking and talking. Other subjects include vanishing wildlife, pollution, etc. These posters should be placed at eye level over every urinal, where there's NO ESCAPE from reading the AWFUL TRUTH.

Lock Out the Boss: It Makes More Sense

this will evolve into a "Death to Robots" vigilante group that lynches innocent C-3POs and R2-D2s. I was "for the workers," too, but after fifteen years of it I decided that the noble workers are VICTIMS of work, forced to rationalize and romanticize the boredom and waste of mind. I'm not talking about one's CHOSEN work, I'm talking about the work you got stuck with for survival. $1.50 each.

WORK IS FREEDOM . . . MINIMUM WAGE IS WEALTH . . . UNIONS ARE GOD . . .

Worker's Democracy
WD Press, PO Box 24115
St. Louis, MO 63130

You'd have to be well-versed in Socialist history, theory, and jargon for this to make any sense. I'm not. These people seem to want to cling to the proud tradition of doing mindless labor that machines COULD do. . . . Heavily antiautomation, and obsessed with some romantic Ideal of the Working Man. Apparently, all executives are evil because they don't do manual labor. Perhaps in the future

THE OTHER KIND OF "SLACKER"

Resistance News
330 Ellis St., Room 506
San Francisco, CA 94102

Draft-resister news, rants, manifestos, and advice. The kind of publication that routinely refers to establishment authority as "Nazis," which may clue you to the level of sophistication. Easy for me to carp, though. I'm past draft age. I remember a time when I would have *memorized* a paper like this. . . . I was #30 in the lottery for Vietnam. I tried every possible scam and excuse, but they didn't believe a word of it. They could tell I was really an irreligious hetero non-drug-addict. Finally, they decided my feet were too flat for the Army. Lucked out. $15/year.

REALER THAN REALITY

The Realist
Box 1230, Venice, CA 90294

Paul Krassner is back with his famed more-or-leftist satirical newsrag. Forces you to pay attention to horrifying news items by making you laugh. In Issue #100, Robert Anton Wilson covers the Married Priests Convention and talks about Italian secret societies . . . crammed with snide distortions of already-distorted news of already-distorted reality. $2 each or twelve for $23.

BE A GOOD LITTLE CONTRA

Freedom Fighter's Manual by the CIA
Grove Press, Inc.
196 W. Houston St.
New York, NY 10014

A reprint, probably extremely unauthorized, of a handbook the CIA distributes in Nicaragua—instructions from our government for terrorist tactics that the ordinary Nicaraguan peasant can use to fight his government. Like a comic book, with English translations of the original Spanish text: "Put nails on roads and highways. Put dirt in gasoline tanks. Paint Anti-Sandinista slogans. Hoard and steal food from government. Leave lights on. Leave water taps on. Threaten boss over telephone." Molotov cocktail instructions, etc. It reads like old Yippie propaganda!! $2.

PUNCHIN' THE CLOCK— AS HARD AS YOU CAN

Labor's Joke Book
363 Morris, Providence, RI 02906

Collection of American antiauthoritarian essays and cartoons from the Wobblies on up —most of it funny from *any* political viewpoint. Edited by Paul Buhle. $4.95 postpaid.

Punchin' the Clock by Woody Guthrie

"I'm a government factory inspector." "Come around at four o'clock. We haint got it in shape for inspection yet."

It's About Space

It's About Times
2940 Sixteenth St., #310
San Francisco, CA 94103

An antinuclear/clean-energy newspaper crammed with news not only on battling nuclear power, but also war resistance, Central America, etc. Keep in mind the extremely biased nature of papers like this, but they can still be pretty educational. It was from one of these that I learned about some serious safety problems with the nearby reactor-in-progress that's supposed to serve Dallas . . . a *year* before our local city newspapers deigned to tell us.

One Step Beyond Politics

Popular Reality
Box 3402, Ann Arbor, MI 48106

Of the many radical/anarchist publications, this modest little tabloid is one of the few that displays enough sense of humor to be readable by people not totally steeped in leftist political theory. Very funny slams not only at the Establishment, but at so-called anarchists and pop-radicals as well. Articles by the top names in orneriness. A bargain at the price: 50¢ each or $2/six issues. They offer buttons, personal ID cards, and blank Birth Certificates now.

NOTE THE BOX NUMBER ... MUST BE A HINT!

B.A.N.G. Notes
Box 2666, Brooklyn, NY 11202

A very morbid newsletter of a Brooklyn antinuke group. Black humor adds pep to the political diatribes. No wishy-washing around with objectivity. Free.

I'LL STAY WITH THE PATRIOPSYCHOTIC ANARCHOMATERIALISTS, THANK YOU

Up from the Ashes *and* Kick It Over
Emma Goldman Resource Group
PO Box 5811, Station A, Toronto
Ontario M5W 1P2, Canada

Up from the Ashes ($1.50) is a small newsletter of contemporary Green theory and practice, the Greens being (for those of you who only watch TV and read ordinary news) the eco-radicals who see less technology meaning less environmental and social destruction. Ah, hell, what're plants and societies FOR, besides DESTROYING??? Not exactly the most compromising position. Even less diplomatic is *Kick It Over* ($1.50 each, $7.50/six), voice of Anarcha-Feminism. Typical article is titled, "A Herstory of Anarcha-Feminism." How inspiringly original and clever! You can tell they have a good solid grip on the aspirations of the masses. Or at least the Anarcha-Feminist masses.

Got a bunch of peace magazines here, too, but I swear they're all so corny I'd be embarrassed to list them. Can they not forget their egos long enough to step back from the painfully self-serving jargon? Some of these people, I swear, act like they're the only ones on earth who don't like war. Might as well be Moonies for all the "political action" they get done. Sometimes I want to KILL pacifists for making "peace" look like something only a stringy-haired forty-year-old-hippie woman with granny glasses could enjoy. I want to rip them limb from limb for making RAMBO, by comparison, look so much more alive and interesting to my seven-year-old boy. Digging their own graves with self-righteous hipness, in the midst of a world that is neither hip nor righteous. The normals probably COULD be manipulated away from Reagan-worship, if there was but ONE INTERESTING PERSON in the peace movement. What the hell. Here's one:

Peacework
American Friends Service Committee, 2161 Massachusetts Ave., Cambridge, MA 02140. $7/year.

GOOD LUCK!

Libertarians for Gay and Lesbian
Concerns
1800 Market St., #210
San Francisco, CA 94102

But you don't have to be gay. Holds conventions; you can buy tapes of the speeches at those. Out for sexual freedom and individual rights . . . more power to them! Now all they have to do is totally erase thousands of years' worth of random social evolution. Free newsletter sample.

YET ANOTHER SOLUTION

Synthesis
League for Ecological Democracy
Box 1858, San Pedro, CA 90733

Deep Ecology, Eco-feminism, and the Green Movement. Be affirmative, baby. If we all join together in love, personhood, and solidarity, and build solar rooftops, the bad guys will surely fall. Or else kill us in one fell swoop. I'd be behind these folks all the way, except that to achieve their goals they'd have to brainwash a billion people. Frankly, I don't believe in coercion, even of patently ignorant fools. Because, sooner or later, and probably *too late*, the question will arise: Who ARE the real fools, anyway? How can you convince even **one** Yuppie to do without its VCRs and microwaves? Dunno about you, but I wanna

KEEP mine. The other approach is for each individual to sabotage the system however he or she can; the system would then just fund more studies on what's going wrong, and the radicals would end up taking those survey jobs for the grant money. I prefer the "hate everybody and keep changing jobs until you die" approach; that way, one might *accidentally* find oneself in an unsought position of power. Much more satisfying, and certainly more honest. Not only will the Revolution be televised, the Revolution will *be* the television show. But your shallow earthbound human minds cannot conceive the levels of propaganda I have foreseen! $5/five.

FIGHTING FIRE WITH WATER

Adventures in Subversion
Anti-Authoritarians Anonymous
PO Box 11331, Eugene, OR 97440

Deserves a Pulitzer Prize. A book-length collection of the hard-hitting posters and handbills created by the A-AA. Many are collages of corporate ads, modified "in a spirit of destructive playfulness" to reveal their *true implications*. Every page is suitable for framing, or, better, for reprinting. Price? I don't think they have a price. Send SASE with 56¢ postage attached, and they'll send the samples + info.

WELL, ANYONE CAN MAKE MISTAKES

Reality Now, and Dissident News
PO Box 915, Station F., Toronto
Ontario M4Y 2N9, Canada

Collections of clippings from newspapers illustrating miscarriages of justice—stories that are embarrassing to governments and courts. And to rhetoric-slinging writers, I hope. Also much Greenpeace and animal-rights news. *Dissident News* is $5/three, $10/six, or $2 for a special issue that combined both mags.

NORMALCY

ABC, NBC, or CBS

This list is full of mean, sarcastic comments on right- and left-wing extremists and outsiders. But without mentioning some major aspect of normalcy, we would not be doing justice to the equally remarkable idiocy of the average, everyday middle-of-the-road citizen.

In the interest of fairness, to see these so-called kooks we're laughing at in perspective, watch a few hours of prime time. All of the monkeys ain't in the zoo.

The reason people fall for ANY of these half-assed systems—Republican, Democrat, Libertarian, Anarchy, evangelical—is because there's a *huge* piece of the puzzle MISSING and they don't know it. I don't pretend to know what that big piece is, but I KNOW it's MISSING. In the face of all this, the only *intelligent* reaction *is* total confusion. No matter what you think you know, to think you *really know* ANYTHING is as counterproductive as the dumbest extremist political system listed herein. And even these have more on the ball than the Middle-of-the-Roaders.

I tend to look at another's politics much as I look at their religion. You don't hold it against them—how can they help the way they were brought up?—but then you have to wonder why the hell they *still* believe in it!

Both politics and religion have three basic things in common. They offer:

1.   Leaders who are confident that they're qualified to be the administrators of Truth and Eternal Verities.
2.   Fellowship with enough others that you are not only reassured that you aren't insane, but that you may possibly even be superior.
3.   MOST IMPORTANT: A FORMULA that *forces* the world to make sense.

They offer meaning and hope. Fraudulent *constructs* of meaning and hope, certainly, but close enough for most people.

And another thing: *are* the Masons really an evil, Luciferian conspiracy? They must be. I'm a 49th Degree Master Mason myself and most Masons are never told that there *IS* such a thing!

CREDIT: RAYMOND PETTIBON

CHAPTER
11

GROUPS YOU LOVE TO HATE —BUT THEY HATE YOU EVEN MORE

I may be asking for it.

I've been criticized before for listing racist groups and other hate cults. No doubt some will be angry that I've included these; you think we're just needlessly giving them extra P.R. But nobody *ever* won a battle by ignoring the enemy, whereas many battles have been won by knowing how the enemy thinks. And unless you've browsed one of these, you DON'T know how they think. It's unimaginable. And there are as many now as ever before. Since the Klan reemerged in the '70s, more than 1,100 incidents of bigot violence have been documented. The people who get offended seem to be the ones who *can't really believe* that there are still uncool, murderous racist bastards running loose. If they knew how widespread this sort of thing is outside of their ostrich-holistic, Positive Thinking blindfolds, they'd be a hell of a lot *more* offended.

Besides—if you don't send these bastards money, but just butter them up while pleading poverty, they'll send you MOUNTAINS of crap at *their expense*—crap that YOU can use for firewood.

I do suggest using a fake name with these characters. A friend of mine has been regularly corresponding with a few of these, posing as an illiterate hick hatemonger without a job—he's rooked 'em out of tens upon tens of dollars in printing and postage. Imagine if half their yearly budget starts going to supply us mockers . . .

First—and maybe this'll mollify you censors . . .

195

ANTI-RACISTS

Center for Democratic Renewal
PO Box 10500, Atlanta, GA 30310

A multiracial, multiethnic group organized against bigoted violence. If you've been targeted by a hate group, the Center tries to provide assistance. Provides updated news on otherwise slippery clandestine hate groups from "skinhead" brand Punks to Moonies, but the emphasis is on the KKK-like White "Christian" Supremacist redneck types. The book *When Hate Groups Come to Town* ($10) provides case studies from numerous communities and people victimized by KKK-like terrorists. *The Monitor* ($15/year) is their newsletter reporting current racist violence, and successful counter-racism. Booklets on specific movements like "Christian Identity," LaRouche, and the Populists are $3. I sure hope these folks have a few good guard dogs around their homes and offices. (I do!)

IF THIS IS CHRISTIANITY, WHAT'S THE DEVIL LIKE??

Spire Christian Comics
Fleming H. Revell Company
Old Tappan, NJ 07675

Gross examples of just how far religious sentiment can be degraded. Much like Chick Comics, but in color and with better art. Plots written by people whose emotional development must have been stunted at age twelve. These would be the funniest things we've listed so far, were they not so popular in mainstream Christian bookstores. *That* is no laughing matter. If you haven't seen these, then you don't *know* how bad it can get. Jesus would puke! Comics are 50¢ each by mail; ask for a catalog. *There's a New World Coming* is a great one to start with.

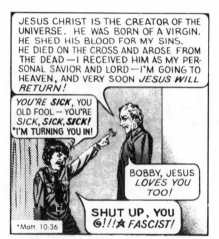

*"For the Lord himself shall descend from heaven with a shout, with the voice of the archangel, and with the trump of God; and the dead in Christ shall rise first; Then we which are alive and remain shall be caught up together with them in the clouds, to meet the Lord in the air; and so shall we ever be with the Lord."
I Thess. 4:16 & 17

"For unto you it is given in the behalf of Christ, not only to believe on him, but also to suffer for his sake."
Philippians 1:29

˥Found˩It

Chick Publications
PO Box 662, Chino, CA 91710

Learn to HATE for GOD. These are those tiny, rectangular "Christian" comic books that grinning zombies hand you on the street —the ones with atrocious art and an almost prehuman level of sheer, unbridled hate, manipulating the lowest human religious instincts. Not exactly a "turn the other cheek" philosophy. These have probably turned more people *off* to Jesus than any other Christian publication. If the Devil has been looking for something to make Jesus look bad, this is it. Chick depicts, with all-too-revealing glee, the eternal suffering that awaits Jews, Catholics, unbaptized babies, people who cuss, and anyone else slightly less consumed with hate and fear than he is. These rank right down there with the craziest Nazi UFO rantings, yet to many ignorant racists these are Truth. Terrifying. $5 for sample assortment of comics, and price list. But if you pretend you're the dumbest jackass in the world, he may well identify with you and send you many freebies.

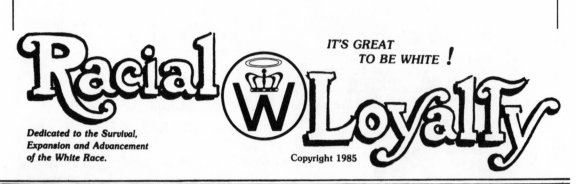

Dedicated to the Survival, Expansion and Advancement of the White Race.

IT'S GREAT TO BE WHITE !

Copyright 1985

Issue No. 30   Xmas Issue   December 1985

"PINKS" VS. "MUDS"

Racial Loyalty newsletter
Church of the Creator, PO Box 400
Otto, NC 28763

The Religion of the White Trash Race. Forget God, Jesus, even Odin—only Aryan mortals are worthy of global ownership. The "Mud Races" must die, according to this odious product of degenerate, inbred, senile hate-mongers. The KKK is no more dead than your favorite health-spa guru is; it's just fragmented into a million independent cesspools. To face the truth about just how primitive vast numbers of white Americans can still be, check this out. And while you're at it, sweet-talk these bastards into spending a fortune on postage. If you plead poverty, they'll send you a free *White Man's Bible* and other monstrosities that cost them a lot to print, and which you can use to line bird cages. But where does this guy get his money?? It's no shoestring operation!

THE POPE IS SATAN

Tony Alamo
Box 398, Alma, AR 72921

Vicious anti-Catholic tirades with a schizophrenic flavor and the taste of rotten eggplants. A portrait of socially tolerated dementia in action, these brochures ooze with vindictive psycho-hate. The real Conspiracy is the Jesuits . . . the pope is the "super-boss of all government agencies as well as the Vatican." He's also the Antichrist. What you'd assume to be a lone nut is unfortunately one of the more vocal tips of an iceberg of historical anti-Catholicism. Catholics were routinely harrassed and even lynched by the Protestant majority in this country, not so long ago. The hotbeds of paranoia over a "Vatican Conspiracy" have never completely died down. I say, leave the Catholics be—if for nothing else than respect for their unmatched elaboration of ritual, the most ridiculously convoluted in human history.

TO MY DEAR PERSONAL FRIEND . . .

Rev. Ewing's Church By Mail
Prayer Box 4574, Atlanta, GA 30302

Exemplifies the lowest in money-grubbing for God. Rev. Ewing's mass-mailings are designed to fool ignorant, lonely hicks into thinking they're getting personal letters; everything is printed to look like felt-tip handwriting on notebook paper. Crossed-out "mistakes" are even included to complete the air of authenticity. You get either a Prayer Cloth (made of paper) or a little bottle of Miracle Anointing Oil, for which you're expected to tithe half your income. Many do.

MUCH, MUCH, MUCH WORSE

Moral Majority
Box 190, Forest, VA 24551

Ask for their newsletter, and learn *just how moral* they are. Even if you've already been badmouthing them—many have, but only because their TV heroes do—you may be in for a surprise. Worse than you would've thought. Much worse.

THE POLITE HATEMONGER

The Director
Box 1175, Winchester, OR 97495

The Most Circumspect Racist. Newsletter from one lonely racist who never spells out either that he's a White Supremacist, or that he's disturbed by the violence inherent in most racist groups. He only wants to be your pen-pal. And here we've gone and blown his cover.

REAGAN, THE MASONIC JEW-CATHOLIC TOOL

Christians Awake
PO Box 3513, West End Station
Birmingham, AL 35211

"*All* politicians are beholden to the power of Freemasonry." Reagan isn't "right" enough; in fact he and his Jewish Communist buddies are to blame for AIDS, revolution, murder, and abortion. Even Jesus is the Antichrist . . . half the time. "The people are blinded because they have partaken of the leaven of the Pharisees." One issue went into endless detail showing how the mathematical dimensions of the Washington Monument prove that it is a phallic symbol erected by Masonic Jews and Catholic devils. Ask for sample.

DO UNTO OTHERS

Heirs of the Blessing Cassette Tape List
PO Box 52, Herrin, IL 62948

Cheap cassettes with titles like the following: *Hitler's UFO Forces. Soviet Weather War. The Bible and Arms. The Rotten "Roots" of Jesse Jackson. Christmas is Baalworship. The Dangers of Eating Pork*—plus White Power rock and roll! Typical frothing, drooling "Identity Christianity" hate rants against the Jews.

FORGIVENESS AND LOVE

Dr. McBirnie's "Pub Pak"
United Community Churches of America
PO Box 90, Glendale, CA 91209

This guy is a seriously wedged Christian conservative who has written about 800 pamphlets to give the Truth to his followers. This particular $5 packet contains:

WILL AMERICA'S NEW MONEY DEVALUE YOUR DOLLARS? The usual scare stories about new currency, recall and devaluation of the old currency, One World currency, the Mark of the Beast and all that. Now outdated by the Treasury announcements of what the new currency is actually going to look like.

DID THE SOVIETS SABOTAGE *CHALLENGER?* Makes much of the series of accidents that have hit America's space program recently in light of its past "incredible success." I suppose he's forgotten *Apollo 1, 6, 13,* and *17.* Oh, but no AMERICAN GOVERNMENT AGENCY could *possibly* screw up like that! Big company execs worried about their contract?? FORGET IT! *

TEN URGENT PREDICTIONS ABOUT AIDS. The predictions are an afterthought. The main purpose of this one is to complain that AIDS research and prevention are being straightjacketed by namby-pamby concern for the rights of homosexuals. He apparently got worried when cases started turning up in the straight population. We wonder what he thinks of the theories that AIDS is a secret Defense Department population-control project (The Nazis started with the homosexuals, too, before moving on to the Jews).

SATANISM & WITCHCRAFT: EVIL FORCES ON THE MARCH. A truly venomous and ill-informed publication, lumping together Anton LaVey, Wicca, Dungeons and Dragons, legends started by the Inquisition, and a lot of just plain crap. If Satanism was as pervasive and powerful as he claims, this jerk would already be dead. Or, maybe it *is,* and he himself is a Satanist but doesn't know it. ((With Factsheet Five))

---

* Some conspiracy watchers insist that the SECRET Administration deliberately caused the *Challenger* explosion, giving themselves an excuse to discourage further civilian participation in space—where projects are already being conducted that are so fantastically nasty that the "Star Wars" program is only the more palatable tip of the iceberg.

AND CAN I ACHIEVE MONUMENTAL STUPIDITY, TOO?

Delta Press Ltd.
PO Box 1625, El Dorado, AR 71730

Arkansas must be one strange place to live. More books on guerrilla warfare, sabotage, and other aspects of do-it-yourself mayhem. This is the place to shop if you're looking for stuff like T-shirts with the CIA logo emblazoned on them, bumper stickers with messages like *Let the Red Bastards Starve* and *Poland Has Gun Control,* or buttons that proudly proclaim *I'd Rather Be Killing Communists.* They also sell *The Turner Diaries* written by Andrew MacDonald, leader of one of the largest and most dangerous neo-Nazi organizations in America. Send two dollars for their catalog and learn how you too can become a vicious narrow-minded bigot. ((Remote Control))

SCHICKLEGRUBER'S FAN CLUB

National Socialist Movement
PO Box 42, Chillicothe, OH 45601

I presume this is the American Nazi party. Foldouts and pinups of Adolf Hitler. What a he-man!

LAROUCHETOWN, WHERE THE KOOL-AID GLOWS

Fusion Magazine *and other*
LaRouche booklets
Box 17149, Washington, DC 20041

If political groups are really cults, then this is the People's Temple of politics, with Jonestown around the bend. *Fusion* is a science magazine, sometimes concerned with unsung alternate-energy sources, always pronuke, and twisted subtly but definitely toward that strange mix of farthest-right and off-the-wall that LaRouche philosophy exudes. Like the goofiest senility-amplified crank theories, but on a big budget. SCARY to think where their money is coming from. Approach with caution; these guys can afford to use the kind of tactics the poorer hate groups fantasize about.

TURNABOUT'S FAIR PLAY

International Headquarters for
Hebrew Israelites
2766 NW Sixty-second St.
Miami, FL OR TOLL FREE (!):
1–800–327–5995

The "Great, Good, and Terrible" BLACK GOD YAHWEH wants black people to separate themselves from the evil white race, and return not to Africa, but Israel. "The black man in Africa is NOT OUR BROTHER, but 'OUR COUSIN,' through HAM in the Bible." American blacks are the Lost Sheep of the House of Israel. Claims to have five million readers nationwide! "We must discipline our little children. If any of them are so blind as to consort with our white oppressors, then . . . we must exert every pressure at our command until they return to a state of loyalty. They have been encouraged to follow our white oppressors' ideas and style. . . . These actions cause the white man to act like animals toward them. . . . [They] seek out our children to debase and destroy their love for us. There is no real love in his white heart for our children or us." Proof that Caucasians don't have a monopoly on racism—as if you hadn't caught on to that by now.

JUST AS LONG AS THEY ARE WHITE, THEY ARE PRECIOUS IN HIS SIGHT

The Appalachian Forum
PO Box 1992, Pittsburgh, PA 15230

Catalog of Northern European cultural & history books, and other tomes with a slant toward the superior paranoia of the white race. There must be more than one "white race," because this sure doesn't sound like the one I'm in.

SEIG HE—I MEAN, GOD BLESS AMERICA!

German American Information & Education Association
PO Box 23169
Washington, DC 20026

This organization will always support America's ethnic majority against encroachment by the minority race that controls the media. Informs you of "the true facts." "WOULD CHALLENGER HAVE BLOWN UP IF GERMAN SCIENTISTS HAD BEEN IN CHARGE?" Funny that they use the slimiest racist tactics supposedly in order to halt further defamation of German Americans, of whom I somehow don't think this group is exactly representative.

DEATH BY BURNING TO ALL NAKED PEOPLE WHO CUSS AND LIKE SEX

National Federation for Decency
PO Drawer 2440, Tupelo, MS 38803

Bitterness roils between the lines of this watchdog of morality, to whom freedom of choice is a tool of Satan.

MISUNDERSTOOD

Prima Facie
Bradley Smith, PO Box 931089
Los Angeles, CA 90093

Doesn't "deny" the Holocaust, but questions how much of the accepted histories are true. Supposedly tries to disentangle Holocaust revisions from anti-Semitism, but then they go and include all sorts of racist innuendos within their newsletter, as if to let the "right" people know their true motivations!

SORRY, THEY JUST DIDN'T DEVELOP OPPOSABLE THUMBS IN TIME!

Front Line News A.L.F. Canada
PO Box 915, Station F.
Toronto, Ontario M4Y 2N9 Canada

That's Animal Liberation Front. And they aren't kidding! This tabloid backs people who are willing to commit crimes in order to stop animal torture in research laboratories, industrial farming, etc—"animal concentration camps." Extremely intense firsthand reports of sabotage against the modern vivisectionists (reported anonymously, unless the speaker is already in jail). The hand-wringing histrionics of some of these people is bound to wreck their credibility with 'normal' activists. Like Greenpeace with a one-track mind and a bad tendency to sound like lunatics when the horrible facts would suffice. $10/year.

TOKEN WHITE SUPREMACISTS

The Nationalist
Suite L-240, 444 N. Frederick Ave.
Gaithersburg, MD 20877

$1 each for the Klan (or rather, "National Democratic Front") newsletter.

JUST WHEN YOU THOUGHT YOU'D SEEN IT ALL...

Christian Technocracy
PO Box 85842
Las Vegas, NV 89116

Even my thick skin was ruptured appreciably when I laid eyes on the endless hate-diatribes and plans for world conquest by authentic megalomanic Hillman Holcomb. To begin with, the enormous stack of self-published books he sent in response to a vague letter of inquiry revealed either his level of financing, or his desperation. The *Christian*

Technocracy "bible" goes on for 500 pages with incredibly scary ravings showing how the insidious "satanic talmudic jews" (*sic*) who rule the White Christian Man's Race can be defeated only when the Christian Technocrats take power over the entire planet. Such philosophies are a dime a dozen, but I have *never* seen them more vindictively stated. Packed with every lurid element common to hate literature, and then some ... easily half the writing here is in CAPITAL LETTERS, always a sure sign of delusions of grandeur. The big "bible" is $10—well worth it for collectors, though some sweet talk might net you the whole load for free. Includes an annotated "Protocol of the Elders of Zion" which is not to be missed! Equally venomous, shorter minibook rants are $3 to $4.

I think you need excerpts for this one to sink in. Check this out:

1. *Racial mongrelization of the White Race will instantly come to an end when Christian Technocracy becomes the Governance of America.*
2. *We will install a genetic program of the planned progression of the arrival of the fittest to survive and function within a totally Christian Scientific-Technological Civilization of the Western Hemisphere. The unfit will not even arrive! Western Civilization now has the knowledge and technique essential to the Civilization-Saving success of this program. ... Christian Technocracy feels obligated to extend its umbrella of protection over both Europe and White Slavic Russia. Both will be guaranteed the freedom of self-determination. ... But the satanic jew will not permit it until their power is first crushed in the United States of America. Otherwise, the White Race of Man, and Western Christian Civilization, empaled upon the deadly poisonous fangs of the serpent of*

talmudic jewdom would render futile any hope of a better world to come.

We Christian White Men of America now see this cunning jew-strategy in action as they stupidly plan, plot and instigate a nation and White Race destroying thermonuclear conflict between the Christian White Men of America and the enslaved white Slavic Men of Russia—just as they treacherously and satanically brought about the near-destruction of the White Race in England, France, Germany and Russia in two totally insane World Wars, in which nations of White Men were tragically pitted against other Nations of White Men, resulting in the jew-ritual murder of our finest youth.

The timeliness, the obvious, the vital necessity of Christian Technocracy in America is so apparent that no perceptive Christian White man could possibly fail to recognize it, and the less intellectually observant should even be able to 'taste' it and 'smell' it. ... They should at least be intelligent enough to recognize the inevitability of the arrival of its only alternative, opposite, the final degenerate form of the price system, which is chaos—the reign of satan on Earth, instigated and brought about through his disciples and apostles—the satanic, talmudic, pharisaic, khazar-mongoloid jews.

At this late state in the jew-planned disintegration of Western Civilization, the mental syphilis of price system jew-liberalism is the foundation for 'tolerance' of the satanic, debt-based, jew-price-system fraud of judaic-talmudic, finance-capitalism. Debt-based finance capitalism is the breeding ground that gives birth to, propagandizes and finances talmudic-marxist-jew-socialism, communism, republicanism, democracy, fascism and nazism.

—From *Christian Technocracy*

NICE CHRISTIAN BOYS

National Socialist White America Party
Box 1133
Pacific Palisades, CA 90272

American Nazis whose basic premise seems to be, "If four blacks kill one white man while robbing him, then it's okay for forty white rednecks in masks to torture and kill several black men just for fun." They want to deport all Jews, Hispanics, and blacks. Communism means slavery of whites, liberalism, and homosexuality (just like in Russia, huh?), and capitalism breeds organized crime and Jewish dictators... naturally, only National Socialism is left. Good old Christian National Socialism! This kind of thing makes me feel like a regular Nat Turner ... makes me want to massacre white people, at least until I look in the mirror.

THE OLD ODOR

The New Order
New Order Pubs., Box 6414
Lincoln, NE 68506

More internationally oriented $1 rag covering neo-Nazis the world over (also published in German!). Cover features shots of "Beautiful Aryan Women Standing By Their Men!" (As long as they keep their mouths shut, obey, and don't talk back, that is.) Swastika-laden promo stickers bear the slogan, *DEATH TO RACE MIXING!* Also sells Nazi regalia, books, flags, etc.

A similar organization, this time combining Hitlerphilia with Charles Manson fetishes, is:

Universal Order
Box 17, Chillicothe, OH 45610
No prices available, nor deserved.

THE ONLY THING WORSE THAN WOMEN IS MEN WHO ACT LIKE WOMEN

The Council of Chalcedon
PO Box 888022, Atlanta, GA 30338

Antiabortion, antihomosexual rabidity that seems to be dedicated to the proposition that the older and more archaic a philosophy is, the better. Women want rights over their bodies?? But what right do twenty million unborn babies have, over their VERY SOULS!!??!! And what about SPERMS?? Don't you think they cry out in horror as they meet needless death on the cold, hard tile of the bathroom floor?? *

* As "Bob" bespoke in PreScriptures X-14, Neuronicus 6:11, "...'Abortion *is* murder, but it's murder in self defense."

I KNOW, I KNOW, YOU DON'T WANT TO HEAR ABOUT IT...

Howard C. Allen Enterprises
Box 76, Cape Canaveral, FL 32920

Horrible; horrible. Twisted racist books on "The Negro Problem," etc. Beyond belief; beyond the imaginings of principled people. But you probably think it's counterproductive to so much as acknowledge the existence of people like this. Still. In every town.

EVERY *REAL* MAN FOR HIMSELF

Might Is Right by Ragnar Redbeard
℅ Loompanics, PO Box 1197
Port Townsend, WA 98368

Just one of many such rare reprints from Loompanics, this is a prolonged rant carrying Social Darwinism, racism, and a "Let the best man win" credo to their final extreme. Scathingly sarcastic of Christianity; cynical and ruthless like no other philosophy. "The world is governed by power and force, not ethics or creeds." From its own perspective, this is the ultimate antiauthoritarian philosophy. Anyone into racist movements should read this to see where their logic ultimately leads. Not a pretty sight. $5.95 postpaid.

RATHER BE A JACKHAMMER THAN A SIDEWALK?

World Power Foundation
℅ Loompanics
PO Box 1197
Port Townsend, WA 98368

It's hard to describe the utter ruthlessness of this new, up-and-coming secret society dedicated to dictatorship through murder, slavery, and a return to the feudal state. Outlines step-by-step plans for world takeover. Not racist! But inhuman in an almost literal sense. Truly shocking. Those who expect a world of peace and sharing ought to know who's out to prey on them. A miasma of horror, as well as the saddest truth. You can't write them directly; they *really are* a secret society. Their main books, however, can be had through the amazing publisher of weirdness, Loompanics. *The World Power Foundation* is $7.95 postpaid; *Secession 1985* is $5.95. Well worth it for shock value.

HATE SATIRE SO CLOSE YOU MAY DECIDE THERE'S NO DIFFERENCE

BAD NEWS FOR MODERN MAN

Action Amenities
1093 Broxton Ave., Suite 567
Los Angeles, CA 90024

For only the most daring collectors of hate-psychosis materials. "Confidential dissemination" of "discreet materials" and "procurement and disbursement of intolerable viewpoints and expressions," including some from the horrifying Robt. T. Calhoun & Associates, a group so noxious they have had to flee even *this* country. Handbills, posters, reprints of the most hair-curdling psycho-racist rants, strange and spiritually obscene cassettes, various vivid illustrations of psychosis in action. The "Preacher Tape" ($6) is a recording of a bitter, hateful small-town Jim Jones–type who got plastered before his radio sermon—unbelievable. Most frightening of all is the tape "Plan for Chaos" ($6), perhaps the most disturbing piece of electronic media on the entire planet. We certainly do not condone all of their activities. Send SASE.

A MODEST PROPOSAL

Patriotic English Tracts
B. M. Bozo
London WC1N 3XX, England

Many little booklets so extreme that one would like to think this was all just a particularly well-done satire. If only! Must be seen to be believed. *The Fanatic* ($4) is a larger publication, chock full of the finest kook literature available. Especially if you're a subject of the U.K., you'll pray that it turn out to be all just a joke. Send $3 in international money order for catalog, sample tracts.

THE
CHURCH OF
BEAVER CLEAVER

A modern evolutionary synthesis of religious and political thought as embodied in
WARD CLEAVER
and the interpersonal relationships of the CLEAVER household.

THE ETERNAL TRIAD
Made up of WALLY, BEAVER and EDDIE.

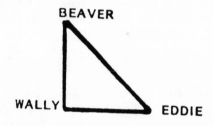

THE
SUPREME DUO
Made up of WARD and JUNE.

SUPREME DUO

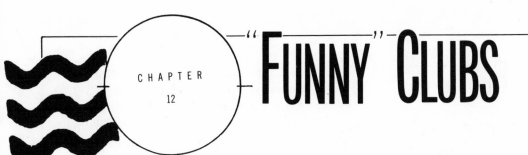

CHAPTER 12

"FUNNY" CLUBS

AW GEE, DAD, YOU NEVER LET ME CREATE UNIVERSES!

Church of Beaver Cleaver
122 E. Benson St.
Decatur, GA 30030

Self-explanatory. Send a buck for detailed examination of the Holy Trinity of "Beaver," "Eddie," and "Wally."

HE KNOWS WHEN YOU'VE BEEN BAD OR GOOD

Journal of the Institute of Scientific Santa Clausism
D. Meyer, PO Box 70829
New Orleans, LA 70172

Seeking scientific and historical evidence for the literal existence of Santa Claus. They claim to have discovered an actual Shroud of Santa. Not for Secular Grinchists or Claustrophobics. They are trying to be objective and skeptical (!). Great ads in the back. $2.50/year; send 50¢ and SASE for sample.

MAY BE HAZARDOUS TO YOUR HEALTH

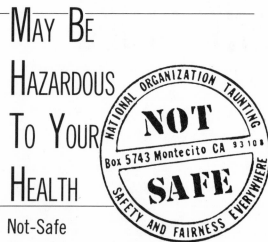

Not-Safe
Box 5743, Montecito, CA 93108

The National Organization Taunting Safety and Fairness Everywhere—actually a satirical organization that effectively takes trendy environmental paranoia, religious puritanism, and governmental regulations to their logical conclusions—that is, that absolutely *nothing* is safe. Their motto: "Protecting everyone from everything, at all costs." In this universe, for instance, their own magazine would be outlawed because it might cause papercuts. Very effective mega-exaggerations that, unfortunately, keep being imitated by life. Newsletter *Quagmire,* plus membership papers $10/year.

RECRIMINALIZE SEX!

Ladies Against Women
1600 Woolsey St., Box 7
Berkeley, CA 94703

A travelling troupe of comic agitators disguised as the ultimate Moral Majority–type "ladies auxiliary." Pummels the concept of the submissive housewife to death by savage mimicry. Not a one-joke idea, but a great vehicle for powerful mockery that hits far and wide. A selection of slogans from their buttons and bumperstickers: BAN THE POOR! MAKE AMERICA A MAN AGAIN—INVADE ABROAD! ABOLISH THE ENVIRONMENT—IT TAKES UP TOO MUCH SPACE! PROTECT THE UNCONCEIVED—SPERMS ARE PEOPLE TOO! YOU'RE NOBODY 'TILL YOU'RE MRS. SOMEBODY! PROCREATION, NOT RECREATION! This group is not only brilliant, but courageous; they show up at Phylis Schlafly rallies and upstage her. (The best part is that Schlafly herself admits she doesn't "get" the joke!) They're veterans of the acting combat zone—I once saw them stay in character while being physically attacked by angered fundamentalists outside the Reagan-Falwell Prayer Breakfast at the Republican Convention in Dallas. You can become a member and recieve bumper stickers, aprons, buttons, and a newsletter that is funny while also describing other people's worthy ecological projects. Send SASE for info; $15 membership.

L.A.W. "*I'd Rather Be Ironing*"
MEMBER

Ladies Against Women

1600 Woolsey # 7, Berkeley, Ca. 94703   (415) 841-6500

Lady: _____

Husband's Permission: _____

NOT VALID without signature of husband, father or clergyman
Misterhood is powerful!

At Least Someone Would Survive

Association to Save Madonna from Nuclear War
228 McCormick #3
Cincinnati, OH 45219

Seeks to declare a "nuclear free zone" within a 200-mile radius of any place that rock singer Madonna hangs out. Actually, a pretty clever tongue-in-cheek antinuclear statement that blossoms into statements-within-statements. Various other antinuke projects are mentioned. One involves a convoluted theory about "the bomb as virus," by which the arms race can be halted by halting capital punishment—almost as pathetically optimistic as the "Hundreth Monkey" theory to which New Agers cling. Not "street theater," but "mail theater." Send SASE.

How You Can Profit From The Coming Bloviation

Bloviatarian Manifesto
Neal Wilgus, Box 25771
Albuquerque, NM 87125

Our beloved leader Warren G. Harding coined the term *bloviate* to mean, roughly, "get slack" or blow everything off and take it easy. The world certainly needs the bloviation approach outlined here . . . but don't get all worked up about it! Wilgus is also one of the better-known serious "conspiracy trackers" (specializing in the Illuminati), and he offers various newsletters and a rumor-mongering fake-news disinformation service from this address as well. Send SASE for info.

Temple Of The True Gods

Museum of Modern Mythology
275 Capp St.
San Francisco, CA 94110

Its purpose is to house, document, preserve, and display twentieth-century advertising characters—home to Speedy Alka-Seltzer, Redi Kilowatt, Mr. Peanut, Tony the Tiger, and far weirder ones from before my time.

Wait Problems

Karen Carpenter Fan Club
Box 823, Burbank, CA 91503

They were in disarray for a while, returning mail, but they're back in stride telling us why Skinny was the Greatest Singer of All Time. Their publishing schedule is erratic. Even if they've folded again, they'd love to hear how Karen saved you from obesity. ((From Johnny Marr's *Murder Can Be Fun*.))

Shove It Up Your Planet

The Up Uranus Society
PO Box 1369, Carmel, IN 46032

Dedicated to the most unfortunately named planet in the solar system. Some excerpts from the newsletter: "The narrow shaft of knowledge penetrating Uranus should not be broken off." Collision with a large asteroid, "while not wiping Uranus out, certainly knocked it on a tilt." Uranus—"Not truly a place where the Sun never shines, but certainly a place where the Sun shines faintly." T-shirts, bumper stickers, buttons, all the usual gimmick-club paraphernalia.

Then Nancy Must Be Satan Herself

Church of Lateral Religion
22 Hyde Park Terrace
Leeds LS6 1BJ, England

Sells some great merchandise equating Ronald Reagan with the Antichrist. Super-cool RONALD WILSON REAGAN = 666 T-shirts, buttons, posters. Very funny rants. Send SASE with overseas postage.

"The Ignorant Man Is Like The Fly; Always Searching For The Perfect Cow Flop."

A Light in the Closet
5 Drawer Press, 920 Greenhert Dr.
New Carlisle, OH 45344

A little book of the Esoteric Wisdom of his Holiness Swami Mahananda Rajnuk Chittawan Aushannesistan Ji. . . . Collection of this extremely obscure guru's sayings. "If you seek wisdom diligently, soon enough someone will sell it to you." "Be not bothered by futility. Remember that it also rains on the ocean." "We are but lumps of consciousness in the gravy of awareness." "Many times it is necessary to consider a task before taking a nap." An indispensable pocket-size book of wisdom. The price is a secret, so send SASE first. Or, live dangerously and send $1 also.

DILLINGER— SUPERHERO, OR ILLUMINATUS?

The John Dillinger Died for You
Society
JDDFYS, Box 409940
Chicago, IL 60640

Founded by the mysterious Horace Naismith, reputedly one of the famed bank robber's illegitimate sons. Dillinger was merely an economic reformer, a "Robin Hood" of the people, not a common criminal! (Or would have been, if he'd only had the time.) *And why is the Sacred Amputated Relic of his Loins no longer displayed in the Smithsonian??* Send $3 and SASE for Membership, the latest poop on Dillinger's Illuminati connections, cool Society ID cards sporting the motto, "Never trust a woman or an automatic pistol," and more of whatever—plus catalog. They should have special caps for sale, bearing this logo, by the time this is printed. This is one of the philosophies that helped make the infamous Wilson/Shea *Illuminatus* trilogy what it is. Loosely connected to the Mad Dog Writers' Consortium of badass weirdos and gonzo writers of darkest Texas.

WANKERS

First Church of Cardtables and OM
W. 1920 Pacific, 99204 (Short address, I know, but mail will get there.)

"OM" stands for Occasional Masturbation. An irrregular irregular, full of bad taste, tackiness, sickness, and metaphysical innuendos. Send about 50¢ in stamps. A few pages made me guffaw. To make me do that, something has to be either really funny or unbelievably dumb.

SCHIZOPHRENIATRICS

Journal of Polymorphous Perversity
Wry-Bred Press, Inc.
20 Waterside Plaza, Suite 24-H
New York, NY 10010

Psychology-oriented humor and satire. Articles on the Nasal Complex, Vagina Envy, Diagnosis by Parking Patterns, etc., all reading like serious academic theses. Two issues for $8.70

SPIDER WORSHIPPERS

New First Arachnid Church
4249 Thirtieth Ave. S.
Minneapolis, MN 55406

Last remnant of the religion of Great Spiderism. The Great Spider created Himself on a whim, and the universe out of boredom. "He used to roar with laughter at the wars and break into tears during the famines and plagues." When you get to heaven, friend, you'll be met by a Huge Black Thing! Believe in Him, or He'll eat you. Send SASE.

HAVE YOU ACHIEVED ARCHBASTARDHOOD??

International Brotherhood of Old Bastards (IBOB)
2330 S. Brentwood Blvd.
St. Louis, MO 63144

Self explanatory. Any size donation accepted—$2, $5, $10—and, no doubt, up. Great membership card and honorary degree–type papers come with a $10 offering.

BECOME A KNOWLEDGIAN

Fred W. Lawson Institute for
Advanced Thinking
5307 La Branch
Houston, TX 77004

Center for the religion of *Lawsonomy*. Alfred W. Lawson was a famous scientific kook who defiantly preached wildly bizarre theories of "Pressure and Suction Physics" and opened a university of his own. A classic study in messiah-complex thinking. Send $4 cash for copies of various gut-busting documents and reprints about this enigmatic crazy man.

FOR TOP THINKOLOGISTS ONLY

Bo Diddly Tech/Darwin University
Box 2326, Evanston, WY 82930

Affiliated with the Church of Universal Confusion. Write for information packet. They charge $15 for their Doctor of Thinkology degree and other indoctrination materials.

AMPLIFICATION OF DESIRE

The Ego Foundation
501 D St. NE, #1-R
Washington, DC 20002

"Devoted to enhancing and/or destroying humanity's self-image. As the world grows smaller, we realize the need for a unified field theory to enhance the entropic process. Just beyond the atmosphere of our dull colored planet sits the eleven-mile-high Shiva, joyous at the prospect of a front-row seat to our slide into chaos. Only through mental terror can our goals be achieved." Sounds like rogue SubGeniuses! Send SASE, not money, because I don't think they've printed up any formal manifestos yet.

HA HA HA

Shelter Management Textbook

Call your local Office of Civil Defense (part of the Department of Defense, with offices in most major cities) and ask for a copy of the Shelter Management Textbook. If they don't have one, then what the hell are you supposed to do in case of a nuclear war? If they do have them, see if they have DATED ones ... the 1967 edition is a REAL LAFF RIOT. Includes hints on how to administer justice, form vigilante groups, perform executions, etc., after total breakdown of law and order.

NOT THE "NOT THE BIBLE"

The Superscriptures
Dave Reissig, Hitheryon House
Box 452, Syracuse, NY 13201

$1. Many other booklets also available, such as *Idea Stew* and *The Eater Out of Chaos*. Quirky manifestos in a style that's like a combination of H. P. Lovecraft, Poor Richard's Almanac and the Bible.

CHAPTER
13

WEIRD ART

The word *art* as used here does not refer solely to painted canvases hung on walls, but to just about *everything* that frustrated people do as alternatives to the mass murder, rape or child beating they might otherwise be driven to commit.

You'll notice the term *collage* cropping up a lot in this section. Now that most existing art genres have been bled dry, many victims of chronic creativity are chopping up and distorting older works, modern-day ads, and anything else they can find—animal corpses, secret government documents—and then recombining them to create something startling. From Dadaist rehash to the art fad of the '80s! While most of it is randomly juxtaposed trash by poseurs, the 'zines' listed here are hotbeds of *the good stuff*.

Another common characteristic is a general emotional tone of compressed despair, which occasionally explodes as heart-wracking black humor but more commonly expresses itself as your straight down-home *angst*. Traditionally, artists have never been the *cheeriest* of people to begin with, and those listed here are the veritable "Eeyores" of the modern art scene.

WHAM! BAM! THANK YOU MA'AM!

Survival Research videotapes
Target Video, 678 South Van Ness
San Francisco, CA 94110

Among the many superstud and groovy videos offered by Target is one featuring spectacular footage of the gigantic, death-dealing mobile artworks by Mark Pauline and cohorts, aka "Survival Research Laboratories." They build enormous, noisy, and very dangerous unguided robots—Cyclopean juggernauts armed with flamethrowers, catapults, spiked maces, and worse—mindless automatons that shamble and crawl and roll in a random orgy of destruction. Animal corpses are often incorporated into the smaller robots for a touch of nature. (Hey, it's organic!) These horrifying inventions are set loose in parking lots to blindly do battle with each other. Now, *that's* what I call ART, god damn it!! Check catalog for current video prices and selections.

???????

Fool, Out, Get Stupid, Journey into the Worlds of Tomorrow, *and* (undecipherable title)
Seth Deitch, c/o R. Chalfen
25 Grant St.
Cambridge, MA 02138

Probably the most *inexplicable* publications in existence. Completely nutty mock-scientific art books by Dr. Ahmed Fishmonger, a reclusive crank whose writings and accompanying collages are practically impossible to describe, because nothing about them makes any sense whatsoever. Nothing. Trying to figure out where the illustrations originally came from could drive one to the proverbial brink. Leave any one of these publications on the coffee table next to the *TV Guide* for friends to peruse; watch their expressions as they thumb through, striving vainly to find an explanation, to locate *any* thread that might provide some anchor to reality. Not sloppy nonsense like 99 percent of the amateur collage-zines being done these days, but works of *classic* inscrutability and inexpressible bulldada from the venerable Fishmonger and many other masters of the form. $3 each.*

* Fishmonger also sells huge 24″ x 36″ posters of "Bob" Dobbs for $8.

BLEED FOR YOUR ART

High Performance
240 S. Broadway,
Fifth Floor
Los Angeles,
CA 90012

No, it's neither a car nor drug magazine, but an absorbing quarterly review of the freakish world of performance art. Some of today's most "Now-Au-Go-Go" art is walking the streets on its own, in the form of people who use their own bodies and behavioral quirks as canvases, bravely sculpting their flesh like clay. One guy hangs himself in the air on dozens of little hooks through his flesh; another grows grass on cars and clothes. Some

invent new languages; others tear themselves apart onstage. How dedicated they must be, and how numb! Read about this happening movement now, while it's still happening, before the artists nobly kill themselves off. Only

 (Tacit . . .)

Are there any good parties tonight?

Vol. VI, No. 1, February 1985

16 pages/Copyright 1985, Steven Durland. **$6,000**

Presidents Attempt Four-Year Art/Life Masterpiece

Chief Execs to Remain Handcuffed for 4 Years

By THE NECKTIE DEAD
Tacit Staff Writer

President Ronald Reagan has announced that he will spend his entire second term handcuffed to his three living predecessors, Presidents Nixon, Ford and Carter. The announcement had been expected and political analysts feel it is natural outgrowth of the "tying-yourselves-together-for-extended-periods-of-time" mania that has been sweeping the country as a result of Montano Hsieh's "One Year Art/Life Piece" in 1984. Sources say the craze has been all over capitol Hill ever since the Supreme Court Justices tied themselves together and dragged Sandra Day O'Connor into the men's room.

White House spokesman Larry Speakes, currently tied to House Speaker Tip O'Neill said the handcuffs are tastefully concealed and once you get used to the four of them walking around together and coming down narrow halls sideways you rarely even think about it.

When the Presidents go out President Reagan leads the group but President Carter refused to be handcuffed in the order of succession saying that President Ford's stumbling and President Reagan's falling asleep all the time made it impossible to stop laughing. The four Presidents sleep in one large bed with Nancy Reagan and her son Ronny, their hair joined in a long braid, sharing a single bed to the President's right.

It had been speculated that eating would be a problem for the four Presidents

but guests at a formal White House dinner honoring the heads of state of four emerging African countries said the Presidents managed quite well with President Nixon using his free hand to feed both himself and President Carter and President Reagan doing the same for President Ford. Drinks were sipped through straws.

The Presidents leave tomorrow for Summit talks in Geneva with Soviet Premiere Konstantin Chernenko. Chernenko is currently chained at the ankle to the entire Politburo and claims to have thought of the idea long before President Reagan but the Soviet news agency Tass reported that the

chaining was actually the Politburo's idea and has nothing to do with art.

The Summit talks are reportedly expected to focus on halting the proliferation of "tying-yourselves-together-for-extended-periods-of-time" to Chad, Monte Carlo and certain Latin-speaking Canadian

Continued on page 1

The Four Presidents as they announce that they have been handcuffed together and wait for photographers to leave before attempting to go out the door. Left to right (obviously no pun intended or applicable): Figure it out.

God's Opinion

Art/Life Shmart/Life

By GOD
Tacit Staff Writer

As I look down on the world these days, and anyone in my position would, I am obliged to notice the uncharacteristically serendipitous standards by which you evaluate the quality of your life. Art is Life? Life is Art? Is the Pope Italian?

I mean if your lives were half as good as your art you wouldn't be behaving like that.

Look at this statistic. Over 10,000 people in the United States were killed with handguns last year, only four artworks suffered the same fate. What does that say? Guns don't kill artworks, *people* kill artworks.

Why? because you're jealous, that's why. Why are you jealous? Because paintings and sculptures of bums get to live in climate-controlled museums and real bums live on the street. Because people pay money to consume wine and cheese to look at art and you can't get anyone to come to your party and look at you. Why? Because art looks better.

So you think that if you put art in the streets its no better than you are. You think that if you give art away its not worth any more than you are. But are you making your life better or are you making your art worse?

Let's face it. Life is merely fodder for Trivial Pursuit. Art's a whole lot better than Life and worth a lot more as an investment too. So instead of trying to bring art down to the level of life, why not try to bring your life up to the level of art? You'd look good in a museum and I wouldn't forget your name because it would be on the little card right next to you.

a very few of the writers are trendy, buzz-word-juggling Art Nazis; most are good at culling out pretentious rich-kid dilettantes from the true original maniacs. $5 sample (it's a large magazine, fancily printed). $12 yearly sub.

ESCAPE FROM THE PLANET OF THE OLD

**Duplex Planet
David Greenberger, PO Box 1230
Saratoga Springs, NY 12866**

A monthly selection of philosophical quotes from the profoundly aged inhabitants of the Duplex Nursing Home, where the editor was a nurse. That may not sound exactly *thrilling,* but this touchingly surreal little magazine has earned renown and a growing circulation for regularly supplying some of the funniest "moments" ever committed to print. A strange dignity pervades the otherwise bizarre ramblings. Thought patterns such as these can *only* be achieved through senility—they cannot be imitated.* #63 is classic . . . "Best Of" issue. Six/$6; back issues $1.50

AND THEY LIVED HORRIBLY EVER AFTER

**Rotten Island
David R. Godine, Publishers, Inc.
306 Dartmouth St.
Boston, MA 02116**

A children's book about a land where everything is as bad as it could possibly be. Mind-bending ugliness for tots. "It had acres of sharp gravel, and volcanoes that spat poi-

---

* As the years wear on, remember (if you can) the Dobbsian proverb that " . . . senility is the *last* thing you'll have to worry about."

son arrows and double-headed toads.... There was an earthquake an hour.... There was no shortage of anything ugly. All these horrid creatures dined on one another.... They lay on hot embers dreaming up new ways to hurt, or planning how to get even for something that never happened." Helps to prepare youngsters for real life. Available in many bookstores.

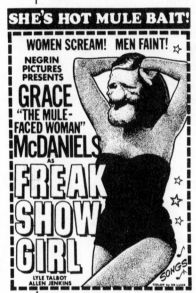

BEAUTIFUL MUTANTS

Freaky Postcards! Glenn Bray Box 4482 Sylmar, CA 91342

Latest merchandise from this publisher of Szukalsi, the renowned King of Kooks, is a packet of postcards commemorating famous circus freaks, drawn by Drew Friedman and Kim Deitch. Includes Grace "The Mule-Faced Woman" McDaniels, Rondo Hatton, the Swedish Angel, and other fave bearers of the acromegaly genetic banner. $4.50 for all eight postcards.* See also Chapter One for Szukalski material!

SATANISTS FOR CHRIST

Voice of the Martyrs/Sarita Crocker
216 Winston
Los Angeles, CA 90013

No telling which denomination burned this young mortician's brain, but her Xeroxed collage magazine carries blasphemy *just about as far as it can go*. And I've seen it go pretty far.... Savage caricatures of Catholics, Evangelicals, and of Jesus Himself. Glorious. (Maybe nowadays it takes blasphemy to get God's attention!) From the very heart of darkness, friends, and almost as demonic as Jim and Tammy. $2.50.

MORBID YUKS

False Positive
Out-of-Kontrol Data Institute
PO Box 432
Boston, MA 02258

Scary collage art, reprints from strange, strange, strange paperbacks, fanatical religious harangues, other symptoms of culture sickness. Couldn't be more fun. Different themes each issue; the "all-kooks" issue, #2, was so popular that classic crackpot manifestos have become a regular feature. $3 each or four/$8.

* Acromegaly is the where-it's-at bone disease that made the Elephant Man the man he was.

"O.K., THAT WAS BILL. THAT BRINGS US UP TO SEPTEMBER '74. YOU HAD AN AFFAIR WITH HIM BUT DID NOT LOVE HIM."

WHO WAS IT NEXT?"

PURTY PITCHERS

Raymond Pettibon
1240 21st St.
Hermosa Beach, CA 90254

Each of Pettibon's art books features a couple of dozen one-page drawings of shocking, and I do mean shocking, intensity. Many are nightmare depictions of an all-Mansonian hippie era—vivid, extremely unpleasant scenes of acid-driven suicide, sexual mutilations, and criminal lust–vengeance. This artist has one *black* attitude, all the more disquieting because his desperate drawings exude a nauseating stink of newsreel truth. Should be in art museums, but uncovered only after midnight. Start with any of the *Tripping Corpse* books. $1.40 each or all 28 for $20.

"AMERICA ON THE MANIC EDGE OF ABSURDITY"

The Secret Album of America
Xeroxial, 1341 Williamson
Madison, WI 53703

$3.50 for this epic pictorial of eye-lid-peeling imagery from Joe Schwind, top-notch collage-slinger who probably doesn't realize yet how many people he's influenced. Gluing together a bunch of clips from 1940s *Better Homes and Gardens* is one thing; every punk-music fanzine editor does it. Schwind's work, however, is technically accomplished and aesthetically unthinkable. The grinning American "THINGS" that people his constructed dream landscapes seem confusingly familiar . . . in a sinister sort of way. Buy now before he's famous, and watch for his video work! Xeroxial has loads of other art books too, but I dunno how "artistic" they are. Not very, I hope. They are trying to collect collections of lists of archives, and also to print a book of "Manifestos and Movements."

MAIL BOMBS

Spiegelman's Mailart Rag
1556 Elevado St.
Los Angeles, CA 90026

Can't "grok" a "price" off this. Not only that, but considering that this publication lists the addresses of hundreds and hundreds of mail artists, it's *damned strange* that it doesn't have *its own address* printed somewhere within! The ultimate convergence point for mail artists ... those unpaid martyrs and valiant warriors against art gallery elitism, who may spend *hours* doctoring *one postcard* until it becomes a glorious work of vibrant self-expression—at worst, a random welter of stupid store-bought rubber stamp imprints—only to have it mangled by Post Office robot mail-handling machines before being delivered to the next mail artist down the line. Mail art was a great thing before the art students started being taught what it was. If you jump into the pond of mail art, be ready to wade across acres of self-conscious, idiotic "artiness" before locating the potent perpetrators. Still, this funky 'zine can lead you to many strange pen-pals, particularly among the nonpretentious old-timers and grizzled vets of the "movement" before it became one.

Here are a few mail art elders; they might reply only if you spew at them something sufficiently tortured and sick.

DJ at FOMT, 151 Balleyboley Road,
Larne, Co. Antrim, N. Ireland

Nunzio Mifune, 217 E. Rische,
San Antonio, TX 78204

Dr. Al Ackerman, 137 Burr Road,
San Antonio, TX 78209

About As Jim As You Can Possibly Get

Jim Magazine
Jim Woodring, PO Box 10075
Glendale, CA 91209

All Jim! Almost "Jimlike" in nature; the one great Jim-personality triumphs over stark Jimlessness. Fantastic photo-surrealist Jim paintings go perfectly, for no discernible reason, with the Jim texts that inexplicably transcend the unJimmian senselessness that usually characterizes the goat skull displays in Jim's barn. DON'T ASK ME WHY. Jimmed to the max. Send BIG envelope SASE, $1, and 56¢ in stamps.

"FOR THE REALIZATION OF UNHEARD-OF DESIRES."

Semiotext(e)
522 Philosophy Hall
Columbia University
New York, NY 10027

Their self-description is perfectly accurate: "A huge collection of works in AMERICAN PSYCHOTOPOGRAPHY—areas not found on the official map of consensus perception . . . Passion and involvement, self-abandoned craziness, funny, sexy, dangerous, unabashedly precious, punk, loud, and direct. Science fiction, weird fantasy, pornography, other mutated genres; sermons, rants, broadsheets, crackpot pamphlets, manifestos . . ." and on and on and on in the world of the Bizarros. Editor Peter Wilson consistently wrenches the best hidden morsels of thought candy out from underneath the deepest, toughest crusts of his writers' brains. 1988 issue will feature the ugliest in rogue science fiction.

NOT A PRETTY SIGHT

Art Police
3131 First Ave. S.
Minneapolis, MN 55408

Prolific purveyors of disgust, striving to achieve TOTAL REPUGNANCE in drawings and comics. A relentless purge of all things nice by many different artists. You'll hope they're only pretending to be psychotic. $3 each. Cheaper at $1, but just as repellent, is *Losing Faith Comix* from the same folks— the graphic wailing of lost souls. What the hell, nowadays young people *work* at being lost souls. It's the cool thing to do.

BE A KAREN, MONTY

KAREN ELLIOT and SMILE MAGAZINE
c/o Stewart Home
11 Bromwich House
Howson Terrace, Richmond Hill
Richmond Upon Thames
Surrey TW 10 6RU, England

Many aspiring artists can now achieve instant fame by becoming Karen Elliot, who is already famous. They can be twice as famous by being TWO Karen Elliots. Heed: "Karen Elliot is a name that refers to an individual human being who can be anyone. The name is fixed, the people using it aren't. *Smile* is a name that refers to an international magazine with multiple origins. The name is fixed, the types of magazines using it aren't. The purpose of many different magazines and people using the same name is to create a situation for which no one in particular is responsible and to practically examine western philosophic notions of identity, individuality, originality, value and truth. Anyone can become Karen Elliot simply by adopting the name—when one becomes Karen Elliot, one's previous existence consists of the acts other people have undertaken using the name." Now you know how Karen got so famous. She was everywhere at once, at the right time.

She is, however, NOT the same as a similar art-world hero figure, Monty Cantsin. Monty has actually been around much longer, preaching the non-art art gospel of his Neoism movement. And so can you. Go ahead! Be Monty! Your home becomes the Neoist Army Central Command the minute you mail the first postcard signed "Cantsin." If you're interested in adding another personality to your own—with art status already attached —you can either just dive straight in from scratch, or catch up on the previous escapades of your plural self first by writing:

Monty Cantsin
Neoist HQ, 153 Ludlow, #6,
New York, NY 10002
And an equally good place to find Karen/Monty/Smile/Neoism would be:
Pete Scott
64 St. Annes Road, Belle Vue,
Doncaster, DN4 5EA, England
And an equally equally-good place to find Monty/Smile/Karen/Neoism is:
Rev. Arthur Berkhoff
Beeklustlaan 13, 7606 SZ, Almelo, Holland
And a similarly equal (but, like every single one of them, *different*) hideout of the Karen-headed Smile-Monty from Planet Neoism:
John Berndt
3523 N. Calvert St., Baltimore, MD 21218
But *worst of all* is
St. Tentatively, A Convenience
PO Box 382, Baltimore, MD 21203

NO TELLING what version of which interpretation will result from whom, unless *you* become him and her and *take charge.*

No Greater Absurdity Is Impossible

Faster Than Gone, Spout, GUMBO, *and others*
Jim Wheat, Nonzense, 1202 Oriole Garland, TX 75042

Little books of rant and wisdom and weather and advice from the *other* dimension. Wheat grabs linguistic logic by the tongue and yanks it hard; however, he reaches *up* for that tongue from *behind.* Hard to figure just how he does it, but his schizo-bibles effectively separate the left brain of the reader from the right, *one* of the brains leaving in a state of cosmic bliss . . . but only as an *alternative* to going insane. Wheat should be writing ALL network TV shows. As jaw-droppingly brilliant as it is acid-droppingly confusing. $2.50 each.

TAURUS (April 20–May 20): Give your job to the boss; he may have a better place for it. Kick a Pisces. Evening will bring you much happiness, if you can quit laughing. A greedy cousin will demand your presence at his birth. A fire below will quench your thirst. Don't throw out next week's dinner; it might be spoiled.

CANCER (June 21–July 22): A close friend will sleep in your closet. Lying on your back may be the truth. Questions about answers may puzzle you. Your outlook is inside. Nothing might mean something if everything doesn't happen. An unexpected check will arrive in today's mail; forward it to proper owner. Find a reliable person to flush your toilet.

VIRGO (August 23–September 22): A prized appliance may run away. A much needed rest will find you awake. A very important phone call will wake you up seven times tonight. Answer the eighth call. An unexpected light will darken your desires. A missing relative will show up on radar; in a car.

LIBRA (September 23–October 22): Sleep with a Gemini. A rare opportunity will become scarce. Exercise your right to be left out of the middle. Co-workers won't. Take stock of your sins; write them on your face. Review stance on sitting. If it's still standing tomorrow, sit on it. An obscene call will bring you what you wanted. Satisfy your desire to give up falling down. Stay out of neighbor's disposal.

—from Jim Wheat's *GUMBO*

FEELING GLUM? HERE, TRY THIS

Apocalypse Culture
Amok Press
PO Box 51, Cooper Station
New York, NY 10276

A lushly illustrated, morbidly sensuous romp deep into millenium's end craziness—dozens of excerpts from what might as well be a cross-section of the more depressing materials I've listed so far. Editor Adam Parfrey reprints classic essays by psycho murderers, mad doomsayers, and dangerously fearless thinkers, all obsessed with the end of civilization. A veritable orgy of hopelessness, sadism, compulsive self-destruction and conspiracy paranoia. Bet you can't wait! Features interviews with necrophiliacs, lycanthropes, religious schizophrenics, etc., tastefully interspersed with nightmarish photos, art, and unpleasantly factual articles. No home library of human perversity is complete without it! The book is $9.95, not including postage (an extra buck should cover shipping.)

MALL SWEET MALL

MalLife
PO Box 1393, Tempe, AZ 85281

Ask for catalog of mental disturbances such as *MalLife Magazine* itself, an exploration of the mold around the edges of Pink mall life-styles. They also carry (for $1.50) the *Pandemonium Spirit* publications of Jake Berry, a raspy voice for the alienated, disaffected, and just plain fucked-up. Berry's poetry is never pretentious, because it's not just TRYING to be grim and depressing—it really is.

BASICS OF NIHILISM 101

Re/Search
20 Romolo St.
Suite B
San Francisco, CA
94133

Even if you just emerged from a 20-year coma, you can legitimately achieve a state of up-to-date coolness just by reading a few issues of Re/Search. *Issue* in recent cases has meant "book," huge yearly extravaganzas of two hundred pages or more. No two are alike, and all have been great. #4/5 ($10) was a William Burroughs special; #6/7 ($11) examined the most extreme acid-etched manifestations of what's termed "industrial art"—i.e., Throbbing Gristle & ilk in music, forbidden medical texts made into psychotic art, nihilistic odes to high-tech weaponry. You know. The usual. #8–9 ($12) was the J.G. Ballard orgy, with all you could ask for in sardonic technohorror. #10 is a gigantic book called *Incredibly Strange Films*— a definitive guide to low-budget masterpieces of sleaze by psycho directors. NO STONE IS LEFT UNTURNED. 1988 issue will be on PRANKS!

Hot Stuff

Fallout
Box 1535, Ukiah, CA 95482

The pit bull of radical tabloids. All the countless other half-assed political poster artists and Monday-morning wheelchair collagists should measure their work against the standards set by this startling tabloid. It would put most of them to shame, if they had any. The perpetrator, "Winston Smith," lives up to his nom-de-plume; his skillful juxtapositions of corny old ad art with current bad news clippings ruthlessly hammer home anti-authoritarian messages with razor-edged clarity, unsurpassed technical proficiency and some cool, cool wit. You'd best praise "Bob" that Big Brother hasn't caught ol' Winston yet; his propaganda skills would be a deadly weapon in the hands of the Ministry of Truth! The free-form text pieces, too, take funny/painful chomps out of the throats of whichever subjects they lunge for. I'd have to call this guy the best dropout yet from the school of radical/surreal guerrilla graphics, and believe me, I've seen plenty. Jaded as I am, I practically jumped out of my chair when I first laid eyes on this stuff. Very erratic publishing schedule, but there're always back issues available at $4 for two.

Instant Pinhead Awareness—Only A Boot-up Away

Headliner *and* Off-the-Wall *computer programs*
Salinon, 7430 Greenville Ave.
Box 31047, Dallas, TX 75231

Now, just like Zippy the Pinhead, you can generate inscrutable, wise-sounding sayings out of ordinary, everyday nonsense—automatically! *If* you have an IBM PC or compatible computer, that is. These programs are intended for use in ad copywriting by burnt-out agency execs desperate for catchy slogans, but anybody with a heavy jones for the absurd could enjoy them. Thousands of built-in expressions, phrases, and words are arbitrarily scrambled and recombined to produce new names or statements, often of such accidental and vague "profundity" as might befit a Zen master. "Desperation is the root of all progress." "Affluence is the root of all amazement." "It's not whether you win or lose, it's how you accept the antagonism." NOW YOU TOO CAN LEARN TO TALK LIKE "BOB" DOBBS! START YOUR OWN CULT AND EARN BIG MONEY AT HOME. *Head-*

What Do These Famous People Have In Common?

liner, which lets you choose specific parameters, is $99; the simpler and totally random *Off-the-Wall* is $29.

THE KING OF RANT AND ROLE

Michael Peppe
400 Hyde St., #507
San Francisco, CA 94109

This possessed madman is so much better than most of his colleagues that I've been calling him "The World's Only Good Performance Artist." (I'd say *great,* but it'd imply that there might be others who *are* "good," and I'm still a bit unsure on that score.) This one-man cultural junta performs (solo) on stage, makes tapes, composes music, writes manifestos, and so forth; unlike generic performance artists, however, his funny pieces really *are* funny, his dramatic ones are truly dramatic, and his bizarre, senseless ones are obliteratingly spectacular. Nothing arty-farty about it; even cultural throwbacks like me are left drooling in dumbfoundment. His material and delivery are so fast, so sharp, and so disciplined that to contemplate how he can possibly write, much less *memorize* it all, dangerously taxes one's sanity. This human dynamo of unshackled bulldada created *behaviormuzik,* whereby nameless physical gestures and nonverbal mouth noises are assigned symbols and written out like a musical score; to my knowledge he's the only living person *mentally capable* of performing these indescribable but enthralling compositions. He also performs semi-conventional songs and "multiple personality monologs," skipping at breakneck speed from one starkly etched character to another with Olympian acting dexterity. The guy is *not of this earth.* You can read about other worthy stand-up Samsons in *High Performance* magazine, but for the sake of humanity's cultural future I had to single Peppe out. Once you've seen him perform, almost everyone else in the field will thenceforth look sickeningly pretentious and lazy. His cassette tapes will jackhammer your mind for only $5 each, and he's working on a videotape. *UH-oh!* Enclose large SASE, at any rate. Incidentally, he's seeking recordings of rants by authentic street crazies and mental patients to incorporate into his repertoire.

ON THE OUTSIDE, LOOKING OUT

Twisted Image
Bruce Duncan,
1430 University Ave., #26
Berkeley, Ca 94703

Bruce Duncan (aka Ace Backwords), like so many listed in this section, may well become a famed historian of the cultural backwashes of the '80s. Or, he may decide to just get drunk and blow it off. This highly irregular mag is unpredictable in subject matter but always hepper than you'll ever want to be. Ranges from funny/hideous cartoons about modern courtship rituals, to interviews with primal fringe movers in the unapproachable borderlands of Cool City. #7 has a John Waters *(Pink Flamingos)* interview, R. Crumb rants, the everpresent "more," and a suitably ugly design style quite representative of this decade's underground "look"—watered-down versions of which will be integrated into TV commercials by ad agency hacks of the '90s. $1.50; back issues are $5.

'PUTER PICASSO

Get
227 Westridge Dr.
Tallahassee, FL 32304

Tabloid portfolio artwork done on a home computer. The digital breakup of images in cheap home computer graphics is somehow psychedelic, but the steep price versus zero emotional impact may limit interest in this to computer-art enthusiasts. Three/$10.

YOUR GARBAGE AT OUR DISPOSAL

PunX
917 S. Ripple Creek
Houston, TX 77057

Belligerent collage-and-rant magazine with no discernible reason for existence, except to harrass everyone in general. Ferociously snide, erupting with diseased personality, this curiosity is minimally concerned with the Houston punk-music scene. However, it recently changed editors and I'll be surprised if it can uphold its original standard of nastiness. Technically, it's FREE!! (Send three 22¢ stamps.)

THEY VOMIT ON CHRISTMAS

Sick Teen
PO Box 918, Green Bay, WI 54305

One of the ugliest of the punk fanzines, it effectively trashes the very genre of trashing. Eye-wreckingly dense collage of sleaze-clips has a certain charm even as it renders the text unreadable. (I think it's about bands.) Practically radioactive with teenage-ness. At 50¢, you can't really go wrong, unless for some reason quality is more important to you than unbridled defiance of everything pleasant!

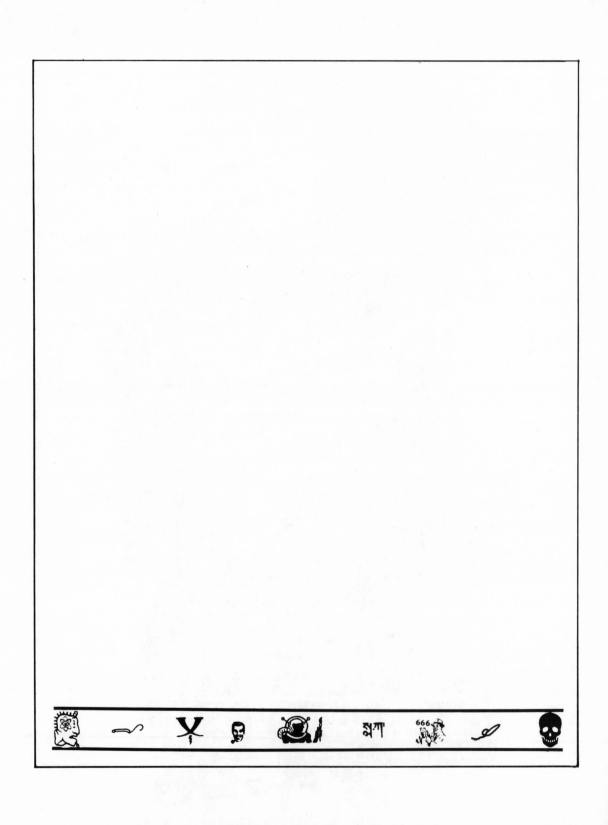

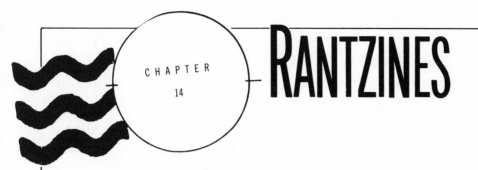

CHAPTER 14

RANTZINES

In days of yore, opinionated assholes had to become bards or preachers and develop live acts in order to vent their spleens satisfactorily at more than a few people. By contrast, today's frustrated world saviors and hometown Hearsts enjoy 4¢ photocopies (with reduction!), cheap laser typesetting, and, most importantly, the relentless spread of "instant print" shops. Anyone capable of wielding a crayon can mail out five hundred copies of a twenty page manifesto for less than five hundred dollars. With a home computer, it can be given the polished look of big-time publications —or at least a close enough approximation to fool the rubes. As far as the average reader can tell, it has as great an operating budget, and hence credibility, as any "real" magazine.

Gutenberg would *shit*.

We don't know how good we have it—whatever it *is*. There aren't any historical precedents, not on this scale. Could the advent of home publishing pose a threat? A lot of governments sure seem to think so. The handy copiers that we take for granted are rare critters in places where freedom of expression is limited to business hours and approved documents. On much of earth's populated land surface, we'd be jailed for things we do on a daily basis. Relative to most countries, we're allowed to go hogwild and are doing just that.

If it's a "publishing revolution," as optimists claim, it hasn't caused any appreciable political disruption *here* yet. Still, as mainstream publishers huddle closer and closer under common corporate umbrellas, the corresponding kudzu-like growth of independent press Zorros naturally fills the voids.

Okay. So these Xerox Zorros are allowed to spread around as much freedom of expression as they can afford, and they have ample opportunity to build readership and even make a profit. But to what use do they put this unprecedented power? A lot of them put their energy into WHINING.

Whining is often the worst thing about the *personal* leakages spilling from the small press revolution, which is what this chapter covers. It's a damn waste of evolution for these self-publishers to be whining when they should be RANTING. The difference is profound. Whining seeps out of the text and dribbles off the paper; good old righteous all-American pulpit-pounding, black-eye pea-eating *ranting* SPLATTERS off the pages as if sprayed from a high pressure fire hose. Come on, you small publishers! AMERICA MUST NOT LOSE ITS LEAD IN RANTING. I don't care if your circulation is only 200, quit your caterwalling and get back to *kicking butt* like your forefathers did! Quit critiquing rock bands and making dumb Reagan-Nazi collages! *Exploit* your miseries! TELL WHAT REALLY MAKES YOU *FEEL!*

Most of the following does cut loose into full tilt rant mode . . . some with a vengeance, others only in fits and starts, frequently bogging down in mental masturbation. If you send for one, and its lameness or obnoxiousness or whatever pisses you off, then it's your *duty* to hurl your own javelins of belief and outrage back at them. If you feel like it. But that's what they're *praying* you'll do; that's what they're *in* it for. None are doing it for the money; the very best they can hope for is that their rantzine might pay for itself. They strongly suspect they're smart, but they want to make sure they aren't *crazy,* and each new serious pen-pal is a helpful reference. They don't care if you're a clumsy writer, if you can't type, if you're an enemy; they want you to talk to them no matter what. And it's understood that what you write is meant for print, because that raises the stakes and makes you either get real or blow your cover. They've spewed out a bit of themselves, and they want some of you spewed back in return—individual to individual. You may both be spewing crap; but at least you're addressing each other by name. It's personal. And therein lies the sole redeeming grace of the sorry little rantzines, the one blessing that big publishers are denied.

What the rantzine publishers really want is to *communicate.* One-way input from the mass media monster isn't anywhere near enough—because it doesn't notice them, it can't be trusted. It isn't a friend. They want to talk, and they want to get a response. They need that. People always will. That's one of the few things I like about humans. I have little use for their usual spaced-out mumbling, but *boy howdy,* when things heat up and their brain juices start pumping and they get to *ranting*—ahhh, it's a marvel to behold. There's nothing like watching a human being when it knows it's alive.

Don't order these expecting useful information, interesting graphics, or anything else practical. You may get those, but consider them extras. Let's put it this way: If, when reading the newspaper, you skip over the editorials and letters from readers, then don't mess with these. Otherwise, go for it and join the bloody fray when possible.

Your Chance To Expound

Reader's Poll
Frank Kogan, 625 Ashbury, #11
San Francisco, CA 94117

Each issue, Kogan asks a series of questions. In the following issue, the readers' replies are printed. Sample questions: "What does sperm smell like to you?" "Do you think the word "shit" is always negative? Define your answer." "What squeaks most?" "Who is your favorite of the girls in Mrs. Brown's sixth-grade glass?" * Have at it, but don't get caught with your pants down.

Tee-Hee

Inside Joke
Elayne Wechsler, PO Box 1609
Madison Square Station
New York, NY 10159

Hurts to read because the print is so tiny, but that way a lot gets packed into each issue. Rants and reviews of all manner of pop/underground media, especially comedy; essays, opinions, and insanity, plus comprehensive listings of other small fringe publishers. $1 each, or 56¢ in postage stamps. If you read this regularly, contribute letters, or otherwise get involved, it can be great fun. If not, you may drift away . . . .

The Garbage Patch Kids craze has the nation going ga-ga over these homely but huggable little shits.

___

* Wanda was always my favorite . . . but thank god our dreams of love just weren't meant to be, because she ended up with Smith and Jones—and look at her now, *making jig-jig* with ALL the Samuels brothers AND their friends behind the old church, night after night. That damn Wanda! Just goes to show.

Very Specific

The Occasional Journal of Nothing
in Particular
G. Fourmile, PO Box 419
Lafayette, CO 80026

The opinions of the Mortimer Snerd Institute of Nihilist Absurdism. Such as they are. One thing you can say for Nihilist Absurdists: they're very *tolerant* of the things they either want to destroy or else refuse to believe in. $1 cash.

#4! FICTION BY RUDY RUCKER, JOHNNY HAZARD, JOHN SHIRLEY, SCOTT BENNETT, CHRIS RENEKE; GRAPHICS BY JOE SCHWIND, FREDDIE BAER, DAVID STEENLICHT, FRANK RHM-MARKS + OTHERS! ARTICLES BY SALLY GNYLAN, DEBORAH BENEDICT + THE ED. + LETTERS + MORE!

Human Garbage Revue

Sidney Suppey's Quarterly &
Confused Pet Monthly
Candi Strecker, 590 Lisbon
San Francisco, CA 94112

"A very occasional—like yearly—'zine of trash mutant culture, bemused natterings, and street-level anthropology." Editor Strecker has a good eye for finding amusingly crazy human effluvia in unlikely places, and she packs each issue with her discoveries and droll observations. She coined a term for those of us who enjoy cheap bulldada: S.A.P.s, or "Self-Amusing Personalities." * $1 sample.

Rant 'N' Roll

Live from the Stagger Cafe
Luke McGuff, PO Box 3680
Minneapolis, MN 55403

Similar to the above, but smaller, from one of the young turks of radical humor. $1 sample.

* Not a bad definition of SubGeniuses in general! "Bob" summed it all up when he said, **"The stupider something looks, the more important it probably is."**

Maybe I'm Dead

Food for Birds, People for Profit
Mid-Coast Sub-Church of Paranoia
RFD 279, Rockland, ME 04841

This is sort of a SubGenius spin-off with no schedule. About the only way to get a copy is to convince Yossarian, the dude in charge, that you're not some kind of "Bobbie," and send him something useful, like hate mail, absurd artwork, or dead presidents. A lot of it is screaming and hollering by people who claim that not only is the emperor not wearing any clothes, but neither is anyone else. And in Maine, that's quite a problem. If something here doesn't outrage you, you may be dead already. $2? ((Factsheet Five))

Bleed On The Mimeograph Or . . .

Puke on the World
3133 Harriet Ave. S.
Minneapolis, MN 55408

A small 'zine with something to offend nearly everyone. Those not in the mood to be offended can stick to the adventures of Pygmoid, the boy who thinks he's a nuthatch. The rest of you can read the Ed Asshole "My Drunken Opinions" column, the continuing light porno, or the rest of the growling and raving here. SASE. ((Factsheet Five))

. . . Huh?

The Cosmic Ray
Krudzna Ink, PO Box 5003
Greensboro, NC 27403

The newsletter of the Cosmic Ray Deflection Society of North America, Inc. It's a bit difficult to explain these folks. They are trying to protect us from deadly rays and make the world a funner place to be, while keeping their fingers on the pulse of the folk art that haunts the backwoods of America. $7.50/year. ((Factsheet Five))

MOST HATEFUL OF THE RANTZINES

The reckless drivers of these paper venom–vehicles are concerned not so much with teaching you anything, but with pissing you off at all human reality, making you *hate* as much as they do. If they didn't write, they'd probably kill.

OSWALD II

Kerry Wendell Thornley
2981 Lookout, Atlanta, GA 30305

One of the all-time classic ranters; for a buck you'll get info, but if you send something more impressive (not necessarily money) and he likes it, he may respond with reams and sheaves of his ten billion harangues and diatribes against, or for, anything, and sometimes everything. Thornley earned his place in the Kook Hall of Fame on several counts; for one thing, he cowrote the basic Discordian bible, *The Principia Discordia*. He is also the *other* Manchurian Candidate who *would've* been used as the patsy had Lee Harvey Oswald proved unworthy. (He and Oswald were in the Marines together.) $1 gets you started.

NO FUTURE

Fourth World
Dr. Bugg, PO Box 77362
Atlanta, GA 30357

"A Journal of Social Nihilism for the Hell of it." Oh, yeah? Well, BIG DEAL. Send SASE.

I'LL DO THE COOKING, THANKS

Eat My Shit
Eat . . . , PO Box 12504
Raleigh, NC 27605

First issue had an interview with the Butthole Surfers, an essay on Freudian Scatology, another on torture, and other unpleasantries. You get the idea. *Scrumptious!* Free, but only if you send some excretions of your own. Be creative. It's fun! I recall how fun it was to be creative, way back when, before I had to do it for a living. Don't put the magazine's full name on your envelopes; the P.O. won't deliver it. "Eat" will suffice.

My Kinda Folks

Lowlife
Glen Thrasher
1095 Blue Ridge Ave., #2
Atlanta, GA 30306

Hate and chainsaws.... A generally disgusting celebration of everything uncouth. Story fragments, drawings, and poems with no clear focus beyond mutilation, blood, dismemberment, death, and embarrassment. Plenty of crude drawings featuring self-mutilation and masturbation rub shoulders with stories of vampires and sex slaves, serial killers and office workers. Delicately captures the '80s ambience of torment and agony, sloppiness and sleaze. No reason for this to exist. Pretty damn cool! $1.50 each. ((With Factsheet Five))

World-Class Contributors

Between the Lines
Erik Kosberg, 3013 Holmes Ave.
Minneapolis, MN 55408

Scavenges dead clips of news and graphics from dying magazines which serve to remind us that no matter how ugly our species is, we're still funny.* Also reprints hate-rants by modern "Jonathan Swifts" such as Bob Black and the great Ivan Stang. $1 each.

These Krazy Kids These Days!

The Addict
PO Box 76, Rockford, TN 37853

A sample: "Okay, asshole. So you think you got it all figured out now that you know there's no Santa Claus and that cops are redneck terrorists. Well HA HA! I got news for you—mark off MTV's *Rock & Wrestling* kick as another attempt at selling poor dumb children a trend that finally died in a puddle of its own shit. But gee, I'd still like my chance to degrade Cindy Lauper anally. Fuck it. No way." Got the idea? No price ... send 50¢ in stamps or so.

* Not only "Bob," but God as well, love us not because we are "good" but because we are funny. Why do you think the Lord(s) haven't ended man's troubles by now? These aren't *cruel* Gods, necessarily; we'd do the same thing if we were in Their shoes. You wouldn't want a *dull* universe, where everyone got along! You'd want a Theater of Fools, an Arena of Pain. You'd want *show biz!*

The Sound Of One Tool Splorting

Nocturnal Emissions
Bruce Kalnins
203–638 E. Eighth Ave.
Vancouver, B.C. V5T 1T1, Canada

Aptly named. An endless but engrossing all-purpose gripe on both the mundane and the cosmic, and all in-between, with remarks from readers. $2?

Hell Is Life

Notes from Oblivion
Jay Harber, 626 Paddock Lane
Libertyville, IL 60048

A little Xerox mag that never stops hurting your brain with gripes about the daily Inferno as endured by Dr. Sensitive and his friends. A million punk mags do this sort of thing badly . . . this one's just as ugly, but grilled to perfection. An unflinching glimpse into one disturbed psyche, for those who HATE LIFE and all its trimmings. Mmmmmm-MMM!! You'll smack your lips with unrepressed sadism as you learn how others have needlessly suffered. Send $1.50, I suppose.

Ugly Is Beautiful

Birth of Tragedy
Box 6271, Stanford, CA 94305

Large tabloid full of miscellaneous distasteful bizarrities. #4, "The God Issue," features interviews with Anton LaVey (founder of the Church of Satan) and hate rockers Henry Rollins and Nick Cave. Fiction by Lydia Lunch, American's favorite HellPorn Artiste. $2 each.

Love Me Or Die!

Stu Cult Newsletter
Harsh Reality, 12440 Moorpark
PO Box 193
Studio City, CA 91604

Stuart Goldman, once merely an ornery nobody, had the nerve to declare himself Godhead and start a cult dedicated to himself. (Sounds like the kind of dude I can **respect**.) "I too am fed up with yes men, sissies, New Agers, butt-boys, Pod People and other assorted swine. I cast my vote for reality . . ." T-shirts available in two versions: STUART GOLDMAN IS GODHEAD, and STUART GOLDMAN IS A SHITHEAD. He's starting a regular hate journal soon that looks to be *hot, slimy and indispensable*. Send SASE.

GAG — *CHOKE* —

Wigglepig: Meat Market Icons
59 Silverhill Dr., Islington, Ontario
M9B 3W3, Canada

One might call this Moral Decay Quarterly. Xerox nasties mag with graphics culled from morgue photos, slaughterhouse reports, and medical textbooks about skin disease. Foulness of biblical proportions. Too cool to reveal a price.

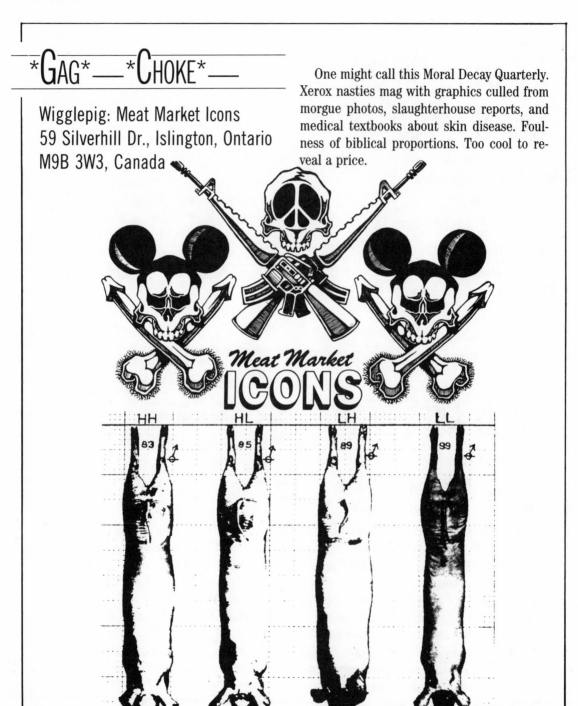

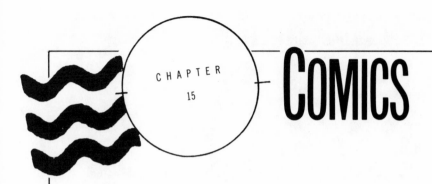

COMICS

The American art establishment took a damn long time acknowledging that comics could be respectable. As soon as that happened, though, comic artists started trying to disprove it, and are doing so to this day.

The comics listed here aren't commercial superjock tales; they're by people who *had* to draw them or go insane. I list these for you people who haven't bought a comic book since *Dr. Strange* went up to 50¢ and who thought underground comix disappeared with head shops. Surprise!

Comics grew along with the times: uglier and uglier and uglier.

This almost-reputable magazine functions as a gallery for disturbed artists—sometimes borderline psychotic, sometimes tortured geniuses, but always outsiders. Each issue usually has a couple of autobiographical pieces by different people, painful both to ingest and excrete, about the travails of being, say, the fat kid in high school with acne and big lips. Started by Robert Crumb, now edited by Aline Kominsky-Crumb. Where *Heavy Metal* offers fashionable graphics, *Weirdo* presents the exact opposite and is really more interesting. One recent issue spotlighted the stomach-pumping results of the Ugly Art Contest. $2.50 each plus $1.50 postage. Last Gasp also distributes a full line of classic underground comix; ask for catalog.

PSYCHOFUNNIES

Mystery of the Wolverine Woo-Bait
Joe Coleman, PO Box 1416
New York, NY 10009

One of the most grotesque comic novels ever perpetrated; William Burroughs novels are sweet and innocent by comparison. I worship it. Cautiously. Plot concerns freaks of nature, sexual perversion, mystical horror, and paranoid sci-fi. Every page is cluttered with mystical scribbles which frame the action, rendered in the kind of frenzied detail of which only the mentally ill are capable. A real find; captures schizophrenic mentality just long enough for you to get a good look at it before you barf. *Authentic*. $6.50 each and

worth it; excellent printing and binding. If this guy isn't really nuts, he's so great a put-on artist that he might as *well* be nuts. The Joe Coleman Portfolio for $6.50, and Joe will soon have a video compilation of his infamous live performances—which include blowing himself up with explosives and biting the heads off live animals. That's *The Momboozoo Follies,* probably around $35 for a VHS copy.

Eat Holy True-Cross Shards, Ill-Drawn Demon!

John Jacobs comic books
Madison Comics
1813 North Twenty-first Rd.
Arlington, VA 22209

Psychotic E.C.-style sci-fi comics with Jesus as superhero thrown in for good measure. Gutwrenchingly funny only because Jacobs is so serious about it. *Dr. Peculiar, Frontier,* or *Black Atlas,* $2.80 each postpaid. Send SASE first to see if he's still there.

Ouch!

Anti-Social Comics
333 S. East Ave., #209
Oak Park, IL 60302

Tales to Depress, drawn with exquisite rawness and written in what must have been excruciating agony. Bleak visions of ordinary American society and allegorical sci-fi stories. "A hideously alienated distillation of sociopathic gross-outfulness..."—you can quote me. #4 is $3.25. *Mz. Antisocial,* an all-women special, is $1.75.

REVENGE OF THE HAPPILY SEDUCED INNOCENTS

Dr. Wirtham's Comix and Stories
378 Judson Ave., Mystic, CT 06355

Dr. Wirtham was the party-pooper who persecuted the horror comics of the 1950s out of existence. This is the comics fans' revenge, with stories too graphically strong even for the regular "ug comix" publishers. Heavy on E.C.–inspired sexually oriented horror; vulgar in the extreme . . . but *tastefully* so. Maybe censorship *is* necessary, if that's what it takes to provoke backlashes like this. Thanks, Dr. Wirtham! $2.50.

THE WAY OUT . . . WAY, WAY OUT

Exit *and/or* Raw
70 Greenwich Ave., Box 594
New York, NY 10011

"Fine Art" comics, printed on huge-format paper, with death and decay as a unifying theme. State-of-the-art art; a feast for the morbid eyeball. Almost every example of New Wave graphic techniques is represented; a study in styles on the cutting edge. Artists on *Exit* include Byron Werner, Carol Lay, Mark Mothersbaugh. Giant page size and classy

printing justifies the demonic price tag of $6.66.

(Editor Art Spiegelman is coincidentally the "concept man" behnd the Garbage Pail Kids. Which reminds me—don't ignore the Garbage Pail Kids. In 20 years you'll see the full extent of their psychic impact on a whole generation. IT MAY BE JUST WHAT SAVES US. . . .)

GRAB YUH ANKLES, AMERICA

Robert Williams
8039 Teesdale
N. Hollywood, CA 91605

Send SASE for catalog of original paintings, T-shirts, posters, and back-issue comics by this Michelangelo of lowbrow High Low Art. Williams, who started with Ed "Big Daddy" Roth on the "CAR-toon" motor-monster mags of the early '60s, became a cult hero in underground comics with such masterpieces as *Coochy Cootie's Mens' Comics;* he's still a wild card on the L.A. Zombie Art scene. **NOT politically correct, PRAISE "BOB"!!!** His soul-blasting paintings—available on postcards as well as in a book—are vast tableaus of unimaginable intricacy. If Salvador Dali is like Hieronymus Bosch on LSD, then Robert Williams is like Salvador Dali on five times as *much* LSD. If you don't also consider Williams the greatest, then you can take your "good taste" and shove it where "Bob" *don't care to look!* Rip Off Press (see below) carries his book, *The Lowbrow Art of Robert Williams.*

FUNNIES FROM COOL HELL

Those Annoying Post Brothers
Vortex Comics
367 Queen
Street West,
Toronto,
Ontario
M5V 2A4,
Canada

Interdimensional criminal adventures of the hippest hit-hippies in comics from Matt Howarth (art) and Lou Stathis (stories), both escapees from *Heavy Metal.* The art style is a lean, disciplined cross between Steve Ditko (*Dr. Strange*) and Windsor McCay (*Little Nemo*), and the stories are pure Theater of Cruelty. $2.50 postpaid; $10/year.

ART & STORY — *BOB BURDEN*
ALL CONTENTS © *ROBERT BURDEN 1984*
LETTERING — *ROXANNE STARR*
• PRODUCED AT THE •
BOMBERTOWN DADA-WERKES STUDIO

Vegetable Police In Dadatown

Flaming Carrot
Aardvark-Vanaheim, PO Box 1674
Station C, Kitchener, Ontario
N2G 4R2, Canada

Bob Burden's parastupid superdetective with a carrot for a head is a Rambo-like victim of brain damage, running amok in a surrealist version of crime-ridden America. Violently original drawing style; the dialogue and narration are likewise *very peculiar*. Few comics make me laugh out loud, but this is one of them. Among the highest achievements of humanity; by comparison, the Eiffel Tower looks like a random arrangement of Pic-Up-Stix. Well, maybe that's stretching it a bit. But it's at least as *original* as the Watts Tower.

S'NOT ART

XEX Graphix
PO Box 240611
Memphis, TN 38124

75¢ comics that are vehicles primarily for the careful and devoted rendering of every blemish, scar, snot-drip, and open wound on the repugnant faces of the characters. No plot; just the ultimate achievement in Ugly Head drawings! How come this Mondrian guy gets thousands for drawing *squares,* and these maestros only get 75¢? Am I *missing* something?

TASTE THE SWEET KISS OF MY BASEBALL-BAT BAPTISM, CHRISTIAN HEATHEN DOG!!

The Post-Vegas Vatican
D. Cripps, 4807 S. Mullen
Tacoma, WA 98409

VIOLENCE!!! Here you may view every shard of bone, every spewing vein, every bead of sweat and every exquisitely rendered shock wave from the skull-crushing blows inflicted by mythical sadist antiheroes against mystical sadist villains. The artist, "Pope Crypts," depicts a radioactive world of cults-at-battle in a style that taps every red-blooded lad's fantasies of world takeover and TOTAL ANNIHILATION of ALL RIVALS. Like *Bruce Lee vs. Road Warrior on the Day After.* $2.50 each.

STILL ONLY 25¢!!

Stupid Boy
Matt Feazell, Not Available Comics
Box 5803, Raleigh, NC 27650

One of the many in a line of "mini-comix," teeny underground comics cheap enough for individual artists to self-publish without big-press accountants breathing down their necks about content cleanliness. *Stupid Boy* is entirely composed of stick-man drawings, but funnier than many of the more carefully rendered comics. Low pretensions = thicker yuks. $1 plus SASE.

WISH YOU WERE YOUNG AGAIN?

Neat Stuff
Fantagraphics Books
4359 Cornell Rd.
Agoura, CA 91301

Neat Stuff is Peter Bagge's unforgivably gross, unforgivably funny, and unforgivably poignant exploration of life as misfit, loser, and geek. Anyone who endured an outsider's childhood will cry with laughter over these perverted, jarring, but all-too-familiar stories. $2.50. Ask for the Fantagraphics catalog; they publish *Love and Rockets* and other "fine arts" comics.

YECHH!

Crazy Men Deluxe and Crazy Men on Vacation
M. Roden, 611 Garfield Ave.
Milford, OH 45150

This carries on the grand tradition of Basil Wolverton, whose "ugly-face people" on *MAD* magazine covers were in turn an extension of every twelve-year-old artist's urge to draw infinitely detailed monster heads. All-visual stories without words. $2.50 pp.

DRUNKEN, AGING BATMAN GOES BONKERS, KILLS 50 GRANNIES

Batman: The Dark Knight Returns
Warner Books, 666 Fifth Ave.
New York, NY 10103

This book is a compilation of Frank Mill-er's limited-edition Batman tales, together comprising one of the most gripping sagas in comics *or any other kind of literature!* I'm normally no superhero fan, but I couldn't put this down. Batman in the real world! When the story opens, the Batman has been in voluntary exile for ten years, sick and tired of being scapegoat for a corrupt justice system that coddles criminals. As a gang of mutated teenagers terrorizes Gotham City, the Caped Crusader can no longer contain his lust for vengeance, and returns to crime-fighting—throwing in a little sadism here and there. By the end of the story, he's leading the mutant-punks, and even kicks Superman's ass! (Superman is working for Reagan at this point.) $12.95 plus something for postage, but better comics and sci-fi bookstores will carry it.

THE GLUE-HUFFER'S COMPANION

Jumpstart
Lone Wolf Press, Box 1554
Cambridge, MA 02238

Joe Schenkman is best known for his rudely rendered stories of glue-sniffing, incestuous hick badasses, once seen in *National Lampoon* before it wussed out. This comic carries on that Torch of Lowlife Glorification, with repulsive work by Schenkman, S. Clay Wilson, and others equally skilled at depicting the worst side of human un-nature. $4 each.

STREET PIZZA

Roadkill
Box 2405, Loop Station
Minneapolis, MN 55402

More sick humor for discerning vomito-philes . . . yet mostly done in "cute" styles! Happy-go-lucky tales of fatal diseases, bad sex, etc., plus news of other sickos. $2 each by mail.

UNDERGROUND COMIX NEVER DIE— BUT THEY STILL BLOAT UP IN THE HOT SUN AND SMELL REALLY BAD

Rip Off Press
PO Box 14158
San Francisco, CA 94114

Among the all-time greats carried by this underground comics institution: *Anarchy Comics, Cocaine Comix, Rip Off, Tits & Clits* (feminist humor), *Weirdo, Young Lust, Zippy,* and the immortal *ZAP!* series. Believe it or not, even the Fabulous Furry Freak Brothers have changed with the times . . . and not predictably, either. But *ZAP* is the most crucial. If it was "before your time," don't worry—it still "applies." Catch up on these before they're out of print, kids! I mean it; if you blow it off, you'll be making a BIG MISTAKE. . . . Most are a mere $1.25 . . . ask for catalog.

YOU'LL VOMIT ON MOM, OR YOUR MONEY BACK

Cannibal Romance
Last Gasp Eco-Funnies
PO Box 212, Berkeley, CA 94701

Just one of many excellent horror comics from Last Gasp, the other "Hearst" of under-ground funnies. This particular comic re-volves loosely around a theme of cannibalism, both literal and metaphoric . . . a great ex-cuse for some hot artists to go all-out on repulsive morality plays. #1 has stomach-turners by superstars like Paul Mavrides, Carol Lay, Hal Robins, Dori Seda, and Dam-ian, whose "The Tapeworm" reaches new lows of puke inducement. $2.75 postpaid; add a buck for the catalog. Incidentally, they sell garish full-color "Bob" Dobbs T-shirts for $12 postpaid.

Too Bad It Isn't 3-D

Carnage
Rusty Short, 2201 N. Plains Ave.
Austin, TX 78758

For the fans of Ed Gein and other serial killers. The Wisconsin lampshade-maker doesn't show up in this comic, but plenty of like-minded, skin-eating folks do: Albert Fish, John Wayne Gacy, and Fritz Haarman all get their turn in the spotlight. Bits of text on the exploits of these gentlemen are mixed in with truly tasteless blood-and-guts drawings. $1.

Trash Expander

Comics Fanola
Red Ink Press
9429 Silverthorne Dr.
Lake Park, FL 33403

Endless news of the off-mainstream comics industry, where some of the best and a LOT of the worst take place. $3/six.

Quickies

Zomoid Illustories
Ray Zone, 128 N. New Hampshire
Los Angeles, CA 90004

Low, low 50¢ each for these four-pagers by various artists in the L.A. cartoonists' Mafia —Carol Lay, Byron Werner, Eddie Nukes, Ken Tao, and others no less ill-minded.

All Fug Dup

In Media's Feces *and* Kill for Peace Again
Tuli Kupferberg, 160 Sixth Ave.
New York, NY 10013

Potent minimalist cartoons by one of the Fugs, a bulldada band that will live in infamy. $1 each.

Normality Exhumed

American Splendor
Harvey Pekar, Box 18471
Cleveland Hts., OH 44118

It took the mainstream fifteen years to notice this one. Always does. . . . Perfectly normal moments from the lives of nobodies are rendered in such an intense relief that they become full-blown dramas. Realer than life. Ask prices.

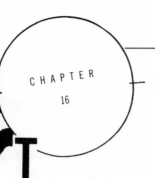

GREAT BADFILM AND SLEAZE

To categorize other people's mental excretions as "weird," one must first know what's "normal." And boy, do I! I've had to pander to normalcy my entire life just to survive. Haven't you? It's a *bitch,* ain't it?!?

Some normal things are okay. . . . A few are even necessary—money, for example. But too many normal things are so completely sanitized that overexposure to them breeds that vilest of diseases, boredom . . . true "Hell on Earth" for us abnormals. *Lucky* abnormals, however, can learn to recognize nuggets of *bulldada* among the mundane things that Normals cast aside as garbage. Things that partake of the holy spirit of bulldada are, to us, as revealing and sometimes as hilarious as any deliberate "joke" or serious accident.

A bad movie can be a greater piece of art without even *meaning* to be than a "good" painting in a museum. What does it matter, either way? Mere thousands see the painting, but millions see the movie. MILLIONS. No matter how bad it is.

Badfilms are SO damn bad, they're GREAT. Also called "psychotronic" films, these are the rare antimasterpieces that *accidentally* tell the truth —not about the subject matter, but about Hollywood, movies in general, and driven artists. Just how far will a sufficiently ambitious man go, how much money will he spend, how many storytelling rules will he ignore, to bring his vision to the silver screen? And how many of his shortcomings will be glaringly apparent in the final product? And . . . who the hell will *care?*

By Far The Greatest Publication Listed Herein

Zontar—The Magazine from Venus *and* **Zontower**
Jan Johnson, 29 Darling St., #2
Roxbury, MA 02120

GET DOWN ON YOUR KNEES, PUNY MORTALS, BEFORE THE GLORY AND TERROR THAT IS **ZONTAR!** "Devoted to intensive study of the most obscure and disreputable cultural manifestations of the decaying Human Empire"—in other words, really bad monster movies, low budget biblical epics, etc. Named after a film by the ultimate obscure badfilm director, Larry (*Mars Needs Women*) Buchanan. Transcendantly funny writing and collages make this the most enjoyable bad movie magazine; the makers of the very worst sleaze are worshipped as

GODS in these pages. *Zontower*, in fact, is a spin-off that is almost *entirely* "religious" in nature. Incredibly sloppy layout is perfectly in keeping with the subject matter; a purist's delight. You may be thinking, "What the hell do I care? I'm not a movie trivia buff!" With *Zontower*, your interest in the actual *movies* is the *last* thing that matters. Try it. You'll learn that in the hands of (Sub-)geniuses, ANYTHING can become *crucially important,* even to you. (One of the latest issues is on a cassette tape! But it isn't representative.) $3.50, 2 or four/$12.

Seedy

Sleazoid Express
Box 799, Peter Stuyvesant Station
New York, NY 10009

A vividly written plunge into the seaminess of the porn-'n'-horror moviehouses of the New York City slums, and into the lives of the street people who make and watch these films. A fascinating, unblinking gaze into the pocked face of society's horny, alcoholic, malnourished underbelly. $2 sample, $10/year.

SLOUCH 'N' VIEW

The Couch Potatoes
Rte. 1, Box 327, Dixon, CA 95620

The Mystic Fellowship for TV addicts, a "Shriners Lodge" for those who can sing the theme songs to every dumb sitcom ever made, those who proudly vegetate in unabashed reverence for the likes of Ellie-May on *The Beverly Hillbillies.* Far from the one-gag novelty one might expect, the Couch Potatoes teachings are densely detailed and extremely funny even to the layman. To believers, it's Truth; *they* know what The Tube really is. Books, certificates, clothing, all the standard "joke organization" gimmicks, but showing such dignity and style as befits this august assemblage. *The Tuber's Voice* newsletter sample $1.50; four/$6.

SPLAT!

Underground Film Bulletin
PO Box 1589, New York, NY 10009

Thick photocopied mag detailing, through interviews, the subterranean filmaking scene in New York—which of late has become a real *Grand Guignol,* with artists trying to outdo artless splatter-film producers in grotesquely overdone gore and sex...but from a punk-derived mutant viewpoint. The nihilistic outlook of the filmmakers results in some hilariously cynical statements. Published on a very irregular basis; at $1.50 postpaid they must be losing money. Write first to see if they're still there.

RUSS MEYER LIVES

It's Only a Movie
℅ Flores, 54 W. Randolph St.
Room 606-E2, Chicago, IL 60601

Newsletter from a major appreciation group for penetratingly naive and/or lurid films; good articles on all manner of weird entertainment that was ahead of its time, from Screamin' Jay Hawkins to *Mondo Cane.* They also deal in extremely rare videotape copies of unsung antimasterpieces (like Lenny Bruce's last performances, and the wildest Japanese animation) as well as great bizarro "video wallpaper" compilations. $8/year for mag alone, $12 for mag and membership in the Psychotronic Film Society, which locates and shows prints of rare badfilm in Chicago.

JAPANIMANIA

Wyvern Webb Graphics
PO Box 560805, Orlando, FL 32856

Outlet for Japanese animation videos, compact discs, records, etc.... doorway to the perplexing but often astounding New

World of high-tech Japanese entertainment, particularly animation. Cartoons that most Japanese consider simple-minded kids' stuff become highly symbolic art masterpieces here—until they're translated, anyway. Japanese animated films comprise a formidable new genre of psychedelia that American cult audiences have only begun to bootleg! Foolish "Japanimation" fans have deified *Robotech*, while ignoring the *really hot* stuff like the feature version of *Lensman*. And then there's the Japanese pornographic cartoons . . . you ain't seen NOTHIN' yet!! Ask for catalog. Rent the dubbed *Warriors of the Wind* (New World Video) to see what I'm talking about.

THE BAD, THE BAD, AND THE UGLY

Trister Keanes' Slimetime
S. Pulchalski
1108 E. Genesee St., #103
Syracuse, NY 13210

"A Guide to Sleazy, Mindless Entertainment," says the masthead. "All the Shit That's Shat to Shoot." A modest newsletter of rude, to-the-point reviews of stuff like *Godzilla 1985, Rhino Video's Weird Cartoons, The Toxic Avenger, Bloodsucking Freaks,* and other video releases of exploitation movies. FREE!!! but send 50¢ for postage.

SATERS OF YOUR VIDEO JONES

Videomania
Box 359, Princeton, WI 54968

A tabloid for the home-video collector, with a slant towards the obscure and esoteric . . . no porn, though. (CHICKENS!!!) And why they cover the mainstream stuff is beyond me . . . it isn't like you'd never hear of *Top Gun* otherwise! They also have a tremendous ad section for collectors, and a service that locates video dubs of hard-to-find films. $2 for samples; $10.95/year.

THE BIBLE

Incredibly Strange Films
Re/Search, 20 Romolo, #B
San Francisco, CA 94133

Next-greatest book on badfilm (or psychotronic movies) ever, second only to Michael Weldon's *Psychotronic Encyclopedia*. Not just the ultimate examination of the fantastically bad and stunningly strange, but also odd genres such as women-in-prison, industrial safety, old-time "nudie," psychedelic, and other film types. Pics, lists, interviews, rants . . . an indispensable holy tome, a steal at $15.

No Sense Trying To Be Polite

Gore Gazette
Sullivan, 73 N. Fullerton Ave.
Montclair, NJ 07042

Lively reviews of current splatterfilm crud. To give you some idea of how badfilm enthusiasts approach their subjects, here's an excerpt: *"IGOR AND THE LUNATICS is amateurishly embarrassing in the extreme, with a grainy look and a hand-held camera that almost resembles a Super-8 high school project. . . . Mary Ann Schacht, the film's heroine, is ugly beyond belief; her zitted-out face and huge fat ass evoking audience pity every time she appears onscreen."* Tell it like it is! A buck a sample or $13/year.

Dobbs Approved

Camp Videos
5650 W. Washington Blvd.
Los Angeles, CA 90016

A video distributor specializing entirely in bad films such as *The Psychic, Nightmare House, The Incredibly Strange Creatures Who Stopped Living And Became Mixed-Up Zombies, Thrill Killers,* and other reprehensible epics. They even have one called *Video Violence—When Renting Is Not Enough.* (For every copy of that one they sell, they donate a *penny* to Oral Roberts's television ministry to prevent that noble TV evangelist from being "called home" by God and vanishing from the face of the planet.) Write for catalog! And look for the picture of "Bob" on the side of the box—if you don't see it, it ain't bad enough to be "Dobbs Approved."

Freddie The 13th Meets Nightmare On Halloween

Video Drive-In
PO Box 32313
Columbus, OH 43232

For those who rent splatter films at the local video rental outlet. The films reviewed in this mag are the rock bottom of the genre (at least, I certainly hope they are!). This issue: *Three on a Meathook, Pieces,* and *Hitler's Harlots,* together with an article on the roller-coaster career of Traci Lords.* $3.50/ten. ((Factsheet Five))

* For you sheltered ones, Traci Lords is the *verboten* porno starlet. After working in porn films for several years, someone found out how YOUNG she was (she first heard the "calling" at age fifteen!); thus all movies from that period (or perhaps even pre-period) of her life are illegal, and therefore in great demand.

El Sickola

Dead On Arrival
Jeff Queen, 1517 S. Twenty-first St.
Sheboygan, WI 53081

Another 'zine for the gore-movie fanatic. This one, like the others, is mainly filled with reviews of repulsive films that aren't likely to show up at your drive-in, but DOA also offers quite a bit more. Decidedly the underbelly of the gore 'zines, DOA would be a good place to start if you're looking for entree to the tape-trading circuit. $2 ((Factsheet Five))

Bootlegger's Delight

Hi-Tech Terror
Craig Ledbetter, PO Box 5367
Kingwood, TX 77325

This time around we have reviews of *Victims*, *Spasms*, *Love Me Deadly*, *The Killer Hour*, and *Doctor Butcher*. Also has a column listing all the gruesome new releases. $6/year. ((Factsheet Five))

Nasty, Nasty!

Impure
Jack Stevenson, 171 Auburn St., #11
Cambridge, MA 02139

More material glorifying mass murderers. We get a Manson poem superimposed on Sharon Tate's face, Ronnie and Nancy fucking up a storm, and more Gein-o-Philia. ((Factsheet Five)

The Holy Grintrinity

The Three Stooges Journal
710 Collins Ave.
Lansdale, PA 19466

From the official Three Stooges fan club; alternating between news bearing on the Stooges (no matter how tenuous the link), and goods one can buy having some connection with them. Includes a list of those licensed to use the Three Stooges name on their products, and a classified ad section. $6/year; yearly membership gets you all issues and a keen club card! And they carry all the Stooge biographies, including *Larry— The Stooge in the Middle*. ((With Factsheet Five))

Now You Can Drop By For A Visit!

The Stars Secret Address Book
American Information Products
10840 Fullbright Ave.
Chatsworth, CA 91311

Ever gotten so enraged by something on TV that you wanted to throw a brick right through the screen? Well, now there's no need to stop there; you can take your revenge straight to the source using this mimeographed booklet of celebrity home addresses. Or, instead, you can suck up to them and grovel like a fool, if that's your self-demeaning preference. Actually, in many cases you only get a big studio's address, or what is likely the office of the star's agent. Moreover, most of the celebs listed are ultra-mainstream pop music heart-throbs, or minor character actors and has-beens who work in network TV or bland movies. By way of a test, I looked for Richard Pryor, Brother Theodore, Alice Cooper, and Frank Zappa; no luck. Listees are more along the lines of Barbara Eden and Tony Curtis. No price listed; definitely inquire first, as this may be a short-lived one-shot.*

Brain Decay Guaranteed

Sinister Cinema
Box 777, Pacifica, CA 94044

Excellent selection at prices that can't be beat. If you're a psychotronic film junkie this is definitely a must-have catalog. Of special interest is the exploitation section with such hard to find classics as *Chained for Life, Tomorrow's Children, She Shoulda' Said No,* and *The Flaming Urge.* If these don't rot your mind, nothing will. Free catalog. ((Remote Control))

* Surprisingly, many celebrities actually do read mail forwarded by studios and fan clubs, and some even respond. For a while, we made half-assed efforts to recruit famous weirdos for the Church of the SubGenius by sending propaganda via fan clubs, and a few notables did join forces with us, much to our mutual benefit. George Clinton incorporated magic Churchly "trigger images" into album covers and a video, for instance; David Byrne tried to involve us on *True Stories,* although the money execs nixed it; DEVO even wrote hymns to "Bob" after hiring us for graphics and video animation. In return, we get to drop their names shamelessly, just as I'm doing now! Even counterculture heroes like Ken Kesey, Robert Anton Wilson, R. Crumb, and Timothy Leary—people you'd think would have better sense—responded enthusiastically to our timid overtures! So don't fear approaching your gods— you never know until you try. Hell, one of the Firesign Theater—the god damn FIRESIGN THEATER, mind you, the most innovative mutant artists since Shakespeare—was so blinded by the Bedotted Glory that is "Bob" that he named *us* their successors!! (Probably the beer talking.) Some of our targets remained aloof, of course, thus revealing themselves to be unworthy after all. (We'll reserve judgment just a little longer on the Oingo Boingo guys, only because their general attitude is so uncannily similar to ours. *But our patience is wearing thin.*) One SubGenius minister who worked for a big rock concert promoter was routinely assigned to score drugs for musicians; this devoutly immoral fellow would chop up their coke and lay out the lines atop a copy of *The Book of the SubGenius.* After they'd snorted their doses of "Dutch energy" off of "Bob's" image, he'd give them the book to keep. Oddly, this bait worked only once to my knowledge—and, wouldn't you know, the star turned out to be a plagiarizing jerk who went and ripped *us* off!!

Rated "AB" For Arterial Bleeding

Magik Theatre
Raymond F. Young, PO Box 0446
Baldwin, NY 11510–0129

Billing itself as "The Magazine of Diverse Film Esoterica and Weird Science," this one gets off to detailed reviews of about twenty sleazy movies, from *Amin: The Rise and Fall* to *Where the Buffalo Roam.* Following this are articles on Kaspar Hauser and Ed Gein. And then there are pages and more pages of oddball movies: *Plan 9, Daughter of Horror,* and much more. Disgustingly graphic photos. In-depth interviews with badfilm directors ... detailed enough to provide glimpses into the fullness of eccentricity that drove them to sink months of their lives into movies that *even they* knew were stinkers, at least by ordinary standards. Also, behind-the-scenes looks at the making of movies like *Dementia, Women of the Prehistoric Planet, The Brain Eaters,* and others. Up to eighty pages of it. $5.95 each, or $20/year. ((Factsheet Five))

We Are The Weird

Joe Bob Briggs
PO Box 33, Dallas, TX 75221

The world's only (and best) drive-in movie critic tells it like it is about the really impor- tant movies. Movies like *Slumber Party Mas- sacre, I Spit on Your Grave, Vampire Playgirls*—you know, culture. Send SASE for a free copy of his newsletter and you might get lucky and get a *Terminator* bumper sticker, too. His middle name ain't "Bob" for nothing. And if your local paper doesn't carry his column, why then the only thing to do is get yourself a subscription to the weekly:

DALLAS OBSERVER, 2330 Butler, Suite #15, Dallas, TX 75235

... which incidentally, carries "Singles Personals" meat-market classifieds (all sexes) peppered with inadvertently hilarious pleas from lonely Dallasites vainly trying to sound hip. Write for local delivery prices. ((With Remote Control))

The Atomic Café People Bought Up All The Good Stuff

International Historic Films
PO Box 29035, Chicago, IL 60629

Great source for old army training films, propaganda, and newsreels on videocassette. Haven't you always wanted a copy of *Uncrat- ing and Assembly of the P-47 Thunderbolt Airplane?* Free catalog. ((Remote Control))

EVEN THE OFF SWITCH ITSELF MUST BE DESTROYED!!

Society for the Eradication of Television
Box 1124, Albuquerque, NM 87103

Send SASE for loads of free antitelevision hate literature. Unearthly logic at work here; these folks see TV as a habit-forming distraction from real human activities, and feel that it should be totally removed from our lives. I agree. And I think all wheeled vehicles should also be confiscated and burned... they seduce us away from healthful walking and running. Likewise, air must go—it sometimes carries industrial poisons, and deadly invisible viruses. Certainly, TV is a zombie-maker; so is religion and book addiction. For that matter, the average corporate job is far worse than all of those put together, if you want to talk about turning once-thinking ent-

ities into automatons! There are those of us who can see TV being used in a vastly different way in the future—the far future, unfortunately. It has indeed been a "cold" passive medium in the past, but that doesn't mean it can't be transformed into a challenging, nay, *demanding* medium by those of us who were raised amidst its technology. Shows like *Max Headroom* and *Pee Wee's Playhouse* are but cautious testings of the waters of the "Media Barrage TV" style that is to come, no thanks to those who so conspicuously lack an Imagination Gland that they blame everything on TV. In the meantime... frankly, I don't see that my own chronic addiction to the mighty GodScreen has rendered me an iliteret, enheumen Zomby.*

Boy burns down house playing Superman...

---

* It's ridiculous to even argue the point; as David N. Meyer II, SubGenius Pope of all New York, Idaho, and the Great Pacific Northwest, hath oft pointed out, *"SINCE WHEN is stupidity a handicap in the 1980s?"* So, TV makes us stupid—WHAT THE HELL IS WRONG WITH THAT, if the "intelligence" these people cherish brings us nothing but a godzillion meaningless jobs, nuclear arms races, and deadly chronic stress from the needless overcomplication of life?? Tomorrow might reveal that what we now call "stupid" may, in hindsight, prove to have been far more productive, FUN, *and even more logical* than the overloaded, imagination-smothering, mechanistic "intelligence" of today's superstitious Normals. Besides, were television to be outlawed, I'd be out of half my jobs!

IT'S ALL DONE WITH MIRRORS

Illusions
530 E. Chester St.
Long Beach, NY 11561

A new magazine devoted to movie special-effects and makeup. Miniatures, optical matte techniques, prop building. . . . I doubt if most of you share my obsession, but I could read about film tricks all day long. In fact, the only reason I turned to writing was because I didn't have the patience to build metal armatures for miniature stop-motion monsters. There are many other good maga-zines on film effects; I mention this because it's brand new. $2.50 sample; $8/four.

LEST WE FORGET

Stars of Lowbrow Cinema
PO Box 310, Cornell Station
Bronx, NY 10473

Very readable antifanzine grapples with questions like "What Makes a Lowbrow Star?" and offers articles like "Leading Ladies of Lowbrow" and "Third World Stars of Lowbrow Cinema." $2 each.

SLEAZE

AN UNBEARABLE VIEWING EXPERIENCE

Fresh Sounds Video
PO Box 36, Lawrence, KS 66044

Sells videos by "industrial" hell-music groups like SPK, Nocturnal Emissions, Temple of Psychick Youth, etc . . . many use autopsy films, newsfilm of violent death, and other grossly offensive "found" materials. Also some videos of Survival Research Lab's giant mechanical destructo-art pieces.

IT'S THE REAL THING

Pandemonium
Jack Stevenson, 171 Auburn St., #11
Cambridge, MA 02139

Dedicated to the gutters, the lowlife, America's underbelly: interviews with and/or raps on mass murderers like Ed "Chainsaw Massacre" Gein & Charlie Manson, along with such greats of disgusto-art as Burroughs, John Waters, and Charles Bukowski. $7 for the first issue of this Hercules of sickness. #2 ($9), The "Cult Films, Killers, and Attempted Assassinations Issue," will feature letters by John Gacy, John Hinckley, and Squeaky Fromme, plus interviews with Divine, Kenneth Anger, and George Kuchar.

But The Monkees Were The Heaviest

Pop Lust
Teenie Wompum Records
5259 Brooklyn Ave. NE
Seattle, WA 98105

A frenzied plunge into two-bit early-'60s pop-star mythology. Funny mutated cross between the punk and prehippie eras. So hilariously fanatical, and deliberately so, that it puts the whole scene in surreal perspective. Free . . . if they can find a copy.

Did Van Gogh Bleed For *His* Art??

Wrestling Observer
David Meltzer, PO Box 1228
Campbell, CA 95009

Keeps you up on the convoluted ins and outs of pro wrestling. Dead serious. It's like following a soap opera. But WRESTLING IS NOT FAKE. To say that the wrestlers are faking it would be akin to saying "Bob" Dobbs was just a piece of old clip art, and Jesus was just an unusually skilled preacher who accidentally got deified. And even if wrestling WERE fake, that would only make it the most noble of all art forms. These people *bleed* for their art. Does Christo bleed for his art?? Does Jasper Johns bleed for his art? Let's face it—this is the real thing. However, I'd recommend this newsletter only for rassling fanatics. $5/four.

Why Los Angeles Exists

Hollywood Book and Poster News
1706 Las Palmas
Hollywood, CA 90028

Catalog/newsletter from a store that specializes in film, TV, music, adult-film, and pro-wrestling memorabilia—posters, books, buttons, photos, T-shirts, anything. The newsletter has interviews with porn stars and comic-book artists—what a combo! Free with a big SASE.

GREAT BALLS O' GREASE

Kicks
Box 646 Cooper
Station
New York, NY
10003

Huge, funny 'zine that revels, or rather, wallows in the obscurer rhythm-'n'-blues world of the late '50s and early '60s . . . wacky and tacky. The sleaze of the low-rung rockers, movies, TV shows, pulp mystery novels, etc. Written entirely in the slang of the period! Extremely irregular. $3.50 for most recent sample.

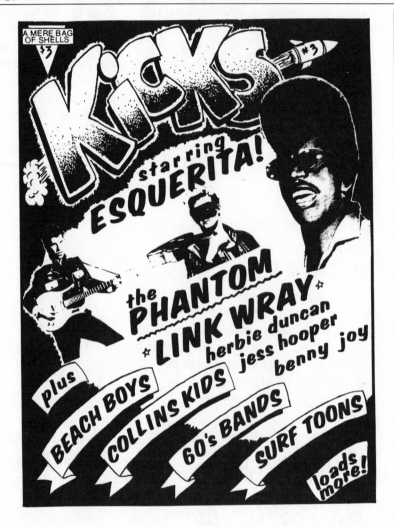

Thou Shalt Stab Thy Neighbor's Back

The Evening World
PO Box 5088, Nagel Station
St. Louis, MO 63115

This is nothing more than a weekly local tabloid of nasty gossip, tattling on "evildoers" in a poor St. Louis neighborhood. "Shame on LEWIS WASHINGTON of 645 Suchandsuch Street. Police arrested this black-hearted drunkard Thursday night in the cowardly act of viciously beating his poor wife and 3 children. You know he has been running around with LETISHA SHEPHERD who everyone knows to be a trollop. May he get 100 years. You can tell by his shifty eyes in the picture above that this no-good hooligan will never quit his wicked habits." That sort of thing, pages and pages of it. The finger-wagging, slightly literate editors and their victims are all black; this is the most appalling example imaginable of the kind of petty ethnic infighting that unwittingly subverts minority pride. Small towns are rife with back-stabbing like this, but rarely is it committed to print. Apparently the meanest, most self-righteous gossip on earth has inherited a printing press. I condemn it to this particular section in faint hopes that the culprits will realize just what kind of impression they're making. 3 months for $20.

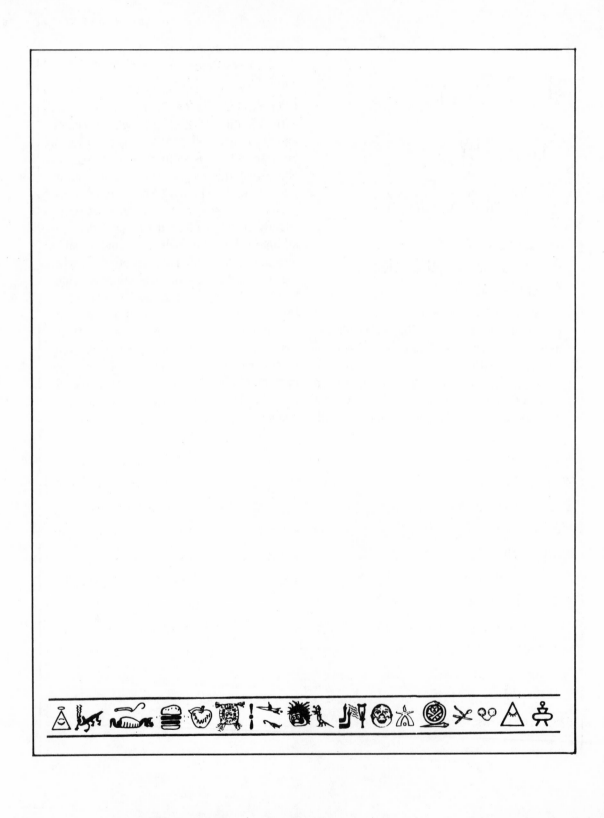

CHAPTER 17

THE AUDIOCASSETTE REVOLUTION

If you've been bored with the music you've been hearing lately, chances are it's all by bands who already have record companies behind them. The ones who don't yet, try much harder. The record companies have good reason for feeling threatened by a "cassette revolution." With home computers acting as rudimentary multitrack studios, and "dubbing decks" in every stereo store, anybody—no matter how technically incompetent or lacking in talent—can produce and sell their own music! Of course, this has resulted in a vast ocean of recorded sludge, but if you wade into it you can spot astoundingly original musicians bobbing up to the surface for a quick gulp of air or income.

First, a few of my favorite audio eccentrics and geniuses; then, the magazines that'll show you what else is going on.

DROWNING IN A SOCIETY OF SNOT

John Trubee and The Ugly Janitors of America
Space & Time Tapes
℅ John Trubee
11438 Killion St., #4,
North Hollywood, CA 91601

He'll be your new hero. Great twisted hell-jazz music behind Trubee's brutally honest jeremiads about the living hell of bad jobs, snotty mindless Normals, and societal dysfunction. Required listening for any would-be adventurer/genius trapped in menial survival jobs. Way too original, profane, and truthful to ever make it to normal radio. *Drowning in a Society of Snot, A Beazy Unit, The Last Dwarf Drops His Pants,* sixty-minute cassettes, $5 postpaid. Greatness comes in slimy packages.

A WINNING PERSONALITY

Zoogz Rift
Snout Records
19119 Victory Blvd., #16
Reseda, CA 91335

Just to give you a handle on this musical misfit, this giant among Elephant Men, I should invoke the name of Captain Beefheart. The surrealism is there, though Rift is definitely his own personality, and his songs are somewhat more musical, and ruder. A nasty man! And I don't blame him. Read between the lines for glimpses of hidden sensitivity . . . you won't find any. His self-distributed album, *Mutatus Mutandus,* is $8; sixty-minute cassettes, $10. Sample titles: *Amputees in Limbo; Music Sucks; Can You Smell My Genitals from Where You're Standing?* Catalog of pretty funny press reactions to this very human monster, $3. Zoogz now has two albums out on SST Records (See Negativland below for address), called *The Island of Living Puke* and *Looser Than Clams* (A best-of compilation—a great place to start). You can tell how hard he's striving for mainstream airplay—literally every song is rife with taboo words like *shit* and *fuck.* Sellout-proof!

RIP YOUR HEAD IN HALF WITH SOUND

Negativland
No address; their house just burned down! (See Ralph Records on page 271.)

This band ranks among the few *true* originals in modern music. They've invented their own high-tech genre, completely unlike anything else on vinyl. The "songs" are essentially collages of sound effects, orchestrated and edited with astonishing intricacy, weaving among each other to create incomparable semimusic. It's almost like "sound animation," the cuts happen so fast. In stereo headphones, this is one of the most spectacular audio experiences available on our otherwise drab planet. *A Big 10–4 Place,* their third album, is a great starter. It and the previous two are available for $7 from:

Ralph Records
109 Minna, Suite 391
San Francisco, CA 94105

I assume you already know all about this legendary outlet for The Residents, Snakefinger, Fred Frith, Mark Mothersbaugh, etc. If not, pray for a catalog before the world ends. Check out their bizzaro "folk music" sampler, *Potatoes.*

Negativland's relatively more musical new one, *Escape from Noise,* is $7 from:

SST Records
PO Box 1
Lawndale, CA 90260

SST also distributed those SCARY bands like Black Flag, Hüsker Dü, The Dicks, The Meat Puppets, Zoogz Rift, etc.

And yet a third distributor carries their ninety-minute tape, JAMCON 84, a compilation of their radio shows ($7):

Cause and Effect
PO Box 30383
Indianapolis, IN 46230

BEYOND YOUR PITIFUL HUMAN IMAGININGS

Mystery Tapes
Box 727, Station P, Toronto, Ontario
M5S 2Z1, Canada

Similar to Negativland, though not nearly as complex; the human mind can *almost* absorb this. Try to imagine music composed of tiny bits and pieces of dozens of "normal" records, all of it looped, overdubbed, slowed down, speeded up, phased, and RAMMED HOME. Granted, it's hard to dance to, but even harder to stop listening to. With all my heart, I PITY the saps who stay hung up in one or two traditional musical camps (like punk or reggae), never to know the indescribable psychedelia of such GODS as Mystery Tapes and Negativland. Mystery Tapes offers a $3 sampler cassette that will somehow keep you listening for hours, even though it's only twenty minutes long. Their other tapes run from $6 to $10 . . . ask for the cool catalog!

The Godfather Of Strange

Ken Nordine
Snail Records, 6106 N. Kenmore
Chicago, IL 60660

Nordine is the Charles Addams of radio, legendary among DJs for his black humor and golden throat, but too weird and original to be a household name yet. Help us change that, won't you? A one-time commercial announcer with an instantly recognizable voice, his straight jobs have supported these excursions into narrated madness. The tapes and records are collections of short spoken vignettes with sound effects and music; deliciously sardonic portraits of minds in turmoil. No human life is complete without regular exposure to Ken Nordine. Don't go to church or therapy; buy these tapes. *Triple Talk,* classic material from the *Word Jazz* radio series, is $10. Album *Stare with Your Ears* is $7 postpaid. Any two *Word Jazz* radio shows: $15.95. A new album called *Grandson of Word Jazz* is $10.

Ten Musical Careers In One Lifetime

R. Stevie Moore's Cassette Club
429 Valley
Upper Montclair, NY 07043

This one-man band and all-around musical prodigy has been called a cross between the Residents, the Beatles, and Frank Zappa. He literally cannot stop writing and recording songs; he has at least sixty albums and cassettes, all original and all very different. People will be ripping him off for decades to come, maybe centuries. Write for his ever-growing catalog. A best-of record, *What's The Point?,* is available for $6.50 from Wayside Music, PO Box 6517, Wheaton, MD 20906–0517.

A Mighty Symphony Of Selling

Daniel Stevens Crafts' *Soap Opera Suite & Snake Oil Symphony*
RRRecords, 151 Paige St.
Lowell, MA 01852

Crafts finds sound clips from a variety of ridiculously mundane sources, and edits them into mysterious collages of one-sentence clips. In this case, one side is terse statements from soap operas, the other is a slick mix of sales-motivation tapes. If you've never heard "found audio collage," CHECK IT OUT!! $6 for the cassette . . . ask for RRR's extensive catalog of many other unusual tapes and records—Fred Frith, Philip Glass, Half Japanese, Blackhouse, etc. . . . they also carry John Trubee and Negativland.

THE LAST SUPPER

WSNS (World Satanic Network System)
PO Box 116, London N19 5DZ
England

The ultimate picture-disc LP—live recordings of the last moments of The People's Temple in Jonestown, Guyana. Jim Jones on lead vocals. £16 for U.S.; £10 for U.K. . . . No U.S. dollars accepted. They also have a picture disc by Vagina Dentata Organ that comes with sterilized human bloodstains.

IT HURTS GOOD

The Wallmen *Eel Vibes From the Voodoo Kitchen* and *Slackadelics*
Dead Judy Records, 7711 Lisa Lane
Syracuse, NY 13212

Jethro Deluxe, Omar, and Lazlo Vegas play a variety of instruments and noisemakers as they explain the facts of life, producing something approaching music. Psychedelic leftovers from another dimension. From the growled vocals of "Kinda Wow KindaNow" to the gawdawful noise of "Camper," these guys will torture your ears and amuse your brain through careful programming of your foot gland. Beware of their venomous covers of famous rock songs, which will addle your taste for sure. The music consists of guitars, fuzz, eels, and disturbing clashes, with vocals somewhere between buzzsaw and snore. A few tracks: "Drag That Karma," "Slackless Torment," "Spank My Subconscioous," and "Armageddon Groceries." These tapes contain enough confusion to baffle any dupe of the Conspiracy. $3 for each tape album. ((Factsheet Five))

INEXPLICABLE

Function Disorder
Corpus Mucus Productions
475 Gate Five Rd., #212
Sausalito, CA 94965

Hard to verbalize about these experimental tape babies. I don't even know the right genre title. The combination of bubbling-under-water electronics and distorted vocals along with plenty of powerful noise makes for pretty interesting listening. Not off-putting at all. ((Factsheet Five))

FUKADELIC

The Swinging Love Corpses
DRUMMOND % Wilcox
338 Lakewood
Ballwin, MO 63011

The only Mystery Jazz/Acid Surfer music to be created a thousand miles from the nearest ocean. Takes up where Zappa (wisely) left off—nasty, nasty r&b&r songs equipped with Rey Hey's face-flaying guitar work and lyrical crooning by Philo and Sphinx Drummond, far outside the range of human taste. They create a new album on tape *every week,* so if you send $6 you might get whatever's most recent, no matter how badly recorded. I suggest that you *demand* the one mixed by Rey Hey with the songs, "Bad Mother Fucker," "Backside of Reality," "Dance With A Hard-On," "Total Fucking Bad Ass Bummer," and "The Day Sky King Died"; it's the best from the last of the psychedelic garage bands. $6/ninety-minute tape.

STUNKADELIC

The Fabulous Billygoons
Cleve Dunkan
℅ Toomey, 19 Court Rd.
Winthrop, MA 02152

The Billygoons are Boston's legendary Rude-A-Billy band of nasty boys and girls, whupping up on songs with titles like "Searching for the G-Spot of Your Love," "The Goons Are Drinking Again," and "Bite It" (a cover of an old Screamin' Jay Hawkins masterpiece). Gravel-throated crooning by Dr. Kruel combines with accomplished musicianship for an experience in lowered ideals, demolished expectations, negligent homicide, and more laffs-4-the-$ than you'll ever encounter again. $8 for the greatest party album this side of Uranus. Supplies are limited. Also the home of Iron Liver, the Goons' second-generation novelty band.

PUNK MUZAK

The Swinging Erudites
Cleve Dunkan
℅ Toomey, 19 Court Rd.
Winthrop, MA 02152

You know those cocktail-lounge bands you find, or avoid, in Holiday Inns? These guys sound like that, only they're doing *lounge versions* of songs like "Anarchy in the UK" by the Sex Pistols, "I Wanna Be Sedated" by the Ramones, or "Whole Lotta Love" by Led Zeppelin. Availability varies with the musicians' moods. Try sending $9 for a tape and you WON'T be disappointed.

THE SECOND GREATEST TAPE EDITOR ON EARTH

Puzzling Evidence
2140 Shattuck, Box 2189
Berkeley, CA 94704

If you send either, say, $8, or else something even Puzzling Evidence wouldn't believe, you *might* qualify for one of his tapes. Creator (and yet, paradoxically, *suppressor*) of a new genre of eardrum-slashing, fast-cut, "Bob"-killing tapes suitable only for those ready to move into the twenty-first century NOW. Might include parts of the radio show described below; might not. But it won't be like anything you OR Wanda hath dreamed possible. Just be ready.

THE SECOND GREATEST RADIO SHOW ON EARTH

More Than An Hour, Less Than A Show
Rex Research, Box 1258
Berkeley, CA 94704

$7 for each of twelve compilation tapes of the West Coast SubGenius radio ministry—1½ hours in the dead of night, during which anything can happen. You remember The Firesign Theater—how fast they were, how funny they could be when improvising. Well . . . IF you've been prepared by *many years* of Firesign addiction, you MIGHT be ready for this excursion into the mental bowels of hosts Hal Robins, Gary G'Broagfran, Puzzling Evidence, and Moebius Rex. And the sound effects . . . the infinite sound effects. DO YOU DARE??

BRING THEM OUT, THAT WE MAY "KNOW" THEM

Drs. 4 "Bob"
℅ Pitts/Gordon, #29 Broadmoor
Little Rock, AR 72204

Without question, the most worthwhile thing listed in this entire book. Oh, you *do* dare to question it? Okay, then, blow it off . . . see if I care. It's YOU that'll be missing the showboat to Salvation. I could say that Drs. 4 "Bob" consisted of excellent jazz-horror/country-western music combined with the most advanced surrealist revolutionary hell-ranting **ANYWHERE,** but that wouldn't mean anything to you unless you'd already heard at least a microsecond or two of this band. $6 gets you something your friends will admire you for discovering. You'll get laid several times just because of the rep you'll gain from being the first in your town to "know" Drs. 4 "Bob."

CHILDREN OF THE HYDRA'S TEETH

Occupant
Box 23061
Knoxville, TN 37933–1061

Can't promise anything about *what* you'll get; you may not even get a tape. But for $6 you'll get more than your usual soul's worth of expanded consciousness . . . tape, booklets . . . who knows? *Who can ever really know for sure??* Young *bulldada* prodigy Onan Canobite and the elusive bad boy "Mitch" are doing drastically twisted things with computer music; they can't stop creating long enough to isolate any one tape and promote it. The record companies would hate them.

DON'T FIRE UNTIL YOU HEAR THE WHITES OF THEIR EYES

ZBS Cassette Adventures
ZBS Foundation, RR#1, Box 1201
Fort Edward, NY 12828

I haven't heard a sample tape yet, but the choice of subject matter shows promise and certain technical aspects are of special note. They're audio adventures, much like radio plays but recorded in binaural sound—an amazing process that has inexplicably been ignored by most producers, even though it is to stereo what holograms are to 3-D photography. That is, you don't just hear sounds on left and right, moving back and forth, but also in front and back as well as above and below! Normal stereo can create an illusion of aural depth, but nowhere near as vividly. Yet binaural works with normal stereo playback systems. it's all in the innovative microphone design, which, like the human ear, is sensitive to subtle air pressure changes as well as normal sound waves. It's hard to imagine the difference without hearing it; while it's not so striking when applied to music, with environmental sounds the realism is positively shocking. The various ZBS cassette plays run from Stephen King and Ishmael Reed adaptations to satirical fantasy, sci-fi absurdity, and tongue-in-cheek mysteries. A 60 minute sampler is $6.50 postpaid; the catalog's free.

MORE THAN JUSTIFIED NEPOTISM

I *would* mention that the SubGenius **Media Barrage** tapes (ninety minutes, $8.50) and **Hour of Slack** radio compilations (sixty minutes, $5) actually surpass the greatness of all the above combined (largely because they're partially *composed* of the above), and that they're available from "BOB" at PO Box 140306, Dallas, TX 75214—but I can't, because that would constitute a conflict of interest. So, forget it. Who are *you*, that you deserve to hear even a *hint* of what's possible?? Some GOD??

EDGE AUDIO MAGAZINES

C.L.E.M.
Alex Douglas, PO Box 86010
N. Vancouver, BC
V7L 4J5, Canada

C.L.E.M. = The Contact List of Electronic Music—a sixty-page comprehensive listing (with capsule descriptions, addresses, and prices) of EVERYTHING related to electronic music of any kind. Publications, radio stations, organizations, and mountains of recordings, broken down by country of origin.

Updated roughly twice a year; $12 money order or $13 check gets you three.

The Fortnightly Report
Shel Kagan
Box 714
Bristol, RI 02809

Biweekly newsletter reviewing new noncorporate tapes and records for college and independent radio stations. Zeroes in on the uncategorizeable standouts. $15/year.

Sound Choice
PO Box 1251
Ojai, CA 93023

Probably the most extensive ongoing listings/reviews of alternative, noncommercial, and just plain homemade music. Eighty pages, several times a year. HIGHLY RECOMMENDED for **anyone** looking beyond the record bins. #6 also has a huge listing of offbeat (and beat-off) fanzine publishers. $12/six or $2.50 each.

OPtion
Sonic Options Network
2345 Westwood Blvd., #2
Los Angeles, CA 90064

A large bimonthly containing reviews and contact addresses for hundreds of independent record and tape artists. Also articles and interviews pertaining to the expanding borders of technology and music. Not limited to the worn-out clichés of "industrial" music and hardcore like so many. $3 each; $12/six.

Unsound
801 Twenty-second St.
San Francisco, CA 94107

Very similar to OPtion; slightly more limited in scope because it tries to be more "hip." Still an excellent review of the bands, radio stations, mad inventors, and unsung singers that the record companies are afraid to touch for fear of soiling their little pinkies. Good networking source for indies. Four/$12; $3 for sample.

Pollution Control Newsletter
1725 E. 115th St.
Cleveland, OH 44106

An ambitious and very helpful project that puts independent radio stations and bands in touch with each other. Helps distribute samples of new bands' materials to the stations that will play them. News, reviews, and articles of pressing interest to those eager to step around the monolithic rock-'n'-roll industry. Many practical suggestions. If you have just about given up hope for your band, try this. $1 for sample; six/$5.

Forced Exposure
719 Washington St., Apt. #172
Newtonville, MA 02160

One of the better magazines on hardcore punk and industrial music. The endless worship of basically identical bands and clone punk singers doesn't do much for me, but the extras, like sick poetry and depraved antisocial ranting, are hot. Why do the musicians who sing about individuality all look and talk so much alike? $2.50 each; four/$8.

Malice Fanzine
PO Box 241022
Memphis, TN 38124

Mainly reviews punk hardcore and industrial noise music. Ugly and hard to read, but good for keeping up with the nastier, meaner bands like The Crucifucks, The Cunts, Our Neighbors Suck, Scraping Foetus Off the Wheel, etc. $1 each.

Bloody Mess Publications
5523 Montello Dr.
Peoria, IL 61614

Large catalog specializing in rare live recordings, demo tapes, and bootlegs—hard to find items such as Tiny Tim demos from the '60s, or Alice Cooper guesting on Johnny Carson. Buys, sells, and trades all sorts of bizarre and interesting sounds. $3 for the updated list.

Smash Apathy *and* Ant Spoim
PO Box 1216
Fairlawn, NJ 07410

These hideously laid out hell-rock punk-fuck fanzines somehow manage to contain every overworked punkzine cliché, and still present a fair amount of worthwhile reviews and orignal collages/rants, mostly concerning hardcore punk music. Marred by political diatribes that are meant to be scathing but are instead unpardonably corny...yet another sign that punk, like its hippie and beatnik predecessor movements, is composed mostly of people ultimately concerned far more with fashion than any dedication to a cause. Try telling *them* that, though! *Smash Apathy* is $1 and *Ant Spoim* is 50¢. Cassette compilations of the music are also available at around $5 each.

BravEar
PO Box 3877
Berkeley, CA 94703

Reviews, rants, essays, and interviews concerning bands of major obscurity and/or hipness. Slick physical appearance; much of the writing is pretty self-consciously hip and smug, but some of you pathetic wheezers want that. $2 for sample.

Raunch-O-Rama Information Sheet
Brad Goins
PO Box 2432 Station A
Champaign, IL 61820

This small fanzine covers "raunchy music for the culturally aware." Brad distinguishes a lot of shades among what others might be satisfied to dismiss as just "industrial" or noise music. 25¢. ((Factsheet Five))

Cassette Mythos
Box 2391
Olympia, WA 98507

Ask for current info on this ambitious project—they're trying to round up all lone-wolf cassette-tape artists and release samples in a kind of audio magazine. Also, a giant book on the world of independent cassettes is in the works. $16 for four-tape subscription (sixty minutes each) on a quarterly basis. Excellent listings of the truly experimental tape manipulators.

Bitch
San Jose Face
Suite 164, 478 W. Hamilton Ave.
Campbell, CA 95008

The Women's Rock Magazine with Bite. Strictly about women rockers, but otherwise covering all ground from Heavy Metal to New Age. "Bitch to us, bitch with us, bitch at us —that's what we're here for." $3 for two samples; $15/year.

Firesignal
% Elayne Wechsler
PO Box 1609
Madison Square Station
New York, NY 10159

News about the activities of the complex, cerebral recorded-comedy troupe, The Firesign Theater. Three of them are back together and producing both albums and videos, if you hadn't heard. (In fact, I should mention their *Hot Shorts,* available for rental at many video outlets—they took various old adventure serials and redubbed all the dialogue and sound effects. The only "rude" Firesign work. Avoid **at all costs** the terrible let-down of *Eat or Be Eaten,* though—it just ain't the same without David Ossman. In fact, it's painfully stupid and amateurish, like some cheesy public-access video show by high school students.) Free for SASE.

Beautiful World
D. David
PO Box 1675
Old Chelsea Station
New York, NY 10011

Assume the Position, Spuds! This is a devolved newsletter for DEVO fans. $1.50 each.

A Few More Weird Audio Catalogs

—Outlets for the Out-of-the-Ordinary!

Paradox Music Mailorder
20445 Gramercy Place
PO Box 2896
Torrance, CA 90509

Hard-to-find albums, CDs, tapes, T-shirts and books.

Wayside Music
PO Box 6517
Wheaton, MD 20906–0517

Many overseas experimental groups, as well as American ones.

EXTRAS

You may want to ask for info from:

Insane Music Contact
Alain Neffe, 2 Grande Rue, B-6190
Trazegnies, Belgium

Sells compilation tapes of avant-garde music by dozens of bands worldwide.

The SubElecktrick Institute
475 Twenty-first Ave.
San Francisco, CA 94121

Modest selection of little-known but technically mind-blowing musical experimenters.

Widemouth Tapes
Box 382
Baltimore, MD 21203

Small catalog of extremely experimental tape-manipulation tapes by various artists including the great Saint tENTATIVELY, a cONVENIENCE.

The Starkman Concern
PO Box 875257
Los Angeles, CA 90087

Catalog of advanced electronic music tapes and records. Concentrates on esoteric computer music and audio collages.

Home Recording Rights Coalition
PO Box 33576
1145 Nineteenth St. NW
Washington, DC 20033

Fighting the new bills concerning royalty taxes on blank tape and tape decks, by which all consumers will be penalized for the losses suffered by immense record and video companies when people like me copy their releases instead of buying them. Also concerned with stymieing CBS's attempts to literally ruin the new digital audio tape technology with faulty copy-protection devices.

Reasons for Living
74 Beach St.
Jersey City, NJ 07307

Subtitled "A fanzine for gushing optimists," this is literally a series of testimonials by people whose lives were indeed saved by rock 'n' roll. $1. ((Factsheet Five))

THE NEW SICKNESS

G. G. Allin

Mr. G. G. Allin is definitely one of the most disgusting figures in rock today. He sings about rape, masturbation, bestiality, and less appealing subjects. His backing bands make gawdawful noises. His gigs feature profanity, onstage defecation, and visits to the hospital. Naturally, all this makes him rather popular in certain circles. Recently two 'zines showcasing his abilities have come out.

CONFLICT 43
($1 from Gerard Cosloy
62 Ave. C, #3
New York, NY 10009)

No-holds-barred review policy. (Your money gloatingly not refunded if you find a review you think sucks.) This issue features a full-length interview (and you can almost see the full length in the photo) with G.G. Covers all the expected topics like raping little girls, shooting up in the foot, sex with dogs, and other fun things to do on a Saturday night.

HATRED IN THE NATION
($2 from Bloody Mess
5523 Montello Dr.
Peoria, IL 61614)

This one is devoted entirely to G.G.'s career, 1978–1986. Bloody has toured with him, and this features explicit photos and personal reminiscences, as well as ephemera from past years. A vast collage of newspaper stories, record reviews, explicit sex, and other detritus. THE definitive story on "Public Animal Number 1." Definitely recommended for anyone fascinated by the darker recesses of punk. ((Factsheet Five))

RUDENESS AND THE WAR BETWEEN THE SEXES

"YOU MUST BE OVER EIGHTEEN"

A few of the following are "skin mags," "stroke books," whatever you want to call them. Why are they included in a list of weirdness, when they're available in Everytown's red-light peep-show district? Because, although many are even available at ordinary CONVENIENCE STORES, they're *just a tad bit* weirder than you might've supposed!! Most aren't full-X porn, but they're still plenty revealing—more of their readers' psychological makeup than of the model's physiques. I would particularly urge women who haven't previously paid porn any attention to check these out. You'll learn a lot, unless you decide to cling to the notion that only "perverts" read these. (Your boyfriend probably does.) Get off your high horse and join the fun!

Much of it's actually pretty tame—just drawings and text! If you want the true porn, just reply to a few ads in the back of any convenience store "men's manual." Indeed, some* would say that supermarket "women's magazines" like *Cosmopolitan* are the *real* pornography, for the way they depict women as vacu-formed *Normals*.

---

* "Some," specifically, being *SISTER KRYS*—one of the TOP SubGenius radio ranters. Upper New Jersey and NYC residents can tune her in on Monday nights on WFMU-FM, East Orange, NJ—that's *The Half Hour of Slack*—or in Dallas/Ft. Worth on KNON'S *Hour of Slack* (Sun. 9 P.M., 90.9FM).

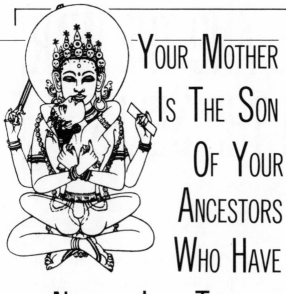

Your Mother Is The Son Of Your Ancestors Who Have Nipples Like Turtles!

Maledicta
331 S. Greenfield Ave.
Waukesha, WI 53186

Every foul epithet ever hurled by man, woman, beast, or thing, in any language, anywhere in the world, will sooner or later be covered, in depth, by these scholarly and erudite researchers. Expensive, but the historical material is incredible and CAN'T BE HAD ELSEWHERE. The cussing of a culture is its esophagus, down which you may peer to check its health. But you gotta be careful what it gags back up at you! Write for current subscription costs.

Overcomers

Aeon Press
PO Box 738, Seattle, WA 98111

Aeon—biannual journal of Magick, Tantra, Taoism, alternative medicine ... $5/copy.

Kalika: Quarterly journal of Tantric Art and Science (you know, kids—SEX, Indian-style!)—lists Tantric organizations and individuals. $2.50/copy. Also, reprints of Crowley's *Liber Aleph.*

Sinners Unite!

American Forum,
also TLC Int. Updater—The
Newsletter of Sex and Violence
Box 261, Dept. E
Staten Island, NY 10302

Quirky, unpredictable welter of clippings, opinion, ads for sex clubs ... a real mishmash. I challenge ANYBODY to figure out where these people are coming from. $13.95 a year for TLC Updater. Also carries *Get Kinky* and various "swingers'" amateur photo pubs—the photographic mating-calls of ordinary humans. Ask for a sample first!

THE INCREDIBLE FULK

Blowfly
13116 NW Seventh Ave.
Miami, FL 33168

The GOD of nasty Party Records . . . one of the raunchiest, most foulmouthed, stinkiest, nastiest, biggest-dicked sons-a-bitches that ever lived. Besides doing great XXX-rated disco music, this guy is also one hell of a surrealist. His multileveled filth-raps are straight from the Black Twilight Zone. Not "politically correct," though—but that's why it's SO GOOD! Titles like "Dance with a Hard-On" and "The Girl Likes to Fuck." BEYOND SEXISM. Pray to Blowfly for catalog of Blowfly records! The James Joyce of Bad Nigger Filth Talk. Buy these LPs or cassettes direct from the Master: $10 each postpaid. *Disco Blowfly* is a good starter.

In the same vein, watch the cutout racks this year in record stores for the many RUDY RAY MOORE party-record albums (on the dying Kent label), another Shakespeare of Black English and a regular MISTER BIG-DICK! *The Return of Dolomite* is his classic, though connoisseurs may dissent on that issue, pointing to Moore's earlier *This Pussy Belongs to Me* as his most sweeping accomplishment in ethno-linguistics. The only *sure* place to try would be *Jerry West's Oldies But Goldies* store, on S. Vermont in Los Angeles, which at last word procured all the excess stock from both now-defunct "X-rated Negro Party Record" labels, Kent and Laff!

NO WONDER THIS CULT IS SO SMALL

Shrine to Virginity
Gertrude Gutierrez
1569 Don Gaspar Ave.
Santa Fe, NM 87501

A lone crusader against sex, PERIOD! Some excerpts: "Sex-life breeds all sins, ALL EVILS AND ALL WARS . . . the fruit of sex-life is suffering and death. God does not recognize worldly education. God never told man how to increase and multiply but the devil did. Bishops and priests, too, tempt people to live sex-life just as the Devil tempted Adam and Eve. They are the Devil's agents—Married couples should try to live a virgin, chaste and undefiled way of life as a little child lives. Sexual marriage is pornography, and a grave sin." Boy, am I in trouble. Tell her you're tired of sinning, and you want—nay, NEED—ALL her writings. Asexual cloning is the only way to go. Even the cloacas of reptiles and amphibians must be BURNED. IF God had meant us to derive PLEASURE from base reproductive organs, He would've given us penes or vaginae, with erogenous zones.

AMERICAN CINEMA
AT ITS VERY BREAST

The Films of Russ Meyer on Videotape
RM Films International
PO Box 3748, Hollywood, CA 90078

Among established film directors with bodies of work behind them, my only real favorites are Federico Fellini, Frank Capra, and Russ Meyer—the unchallenged masters of, respectively, weird art, inspirational Hollywood mainstream, and crude lowbrow sleaze.* Capra's dead, so that makes Russ Meyer America's greatest living film artist in my book. His movies are too soft-core to succeed as pornography, but neither are they acceptable to intellectuals or Normals, so they aren't widely shown or even rented. I hadn't experienced them myself until sleaze archivist Cleve Dunkan started sending me video bootlegs of them, and I was born again in RUSS. However, the King of Busomania (his term) is now selling cherry copies of his masterworks on videotape. Unfortunately, Meyerian Enlightenment is by its very nature limited mostly to hetero males, and even then only the least socially intimidated ones ... those truly free, in other words, from that insidious superstition called "good taste."

For the mighty RUSS hath shown us the world as we secretly *wish* it could be, deep in our heart of hearts—despite what we may tell ourselves intellectually. With a few exceptions, his films are raunchy comedies in which all women possess gigantic breasts, no shame, and an insatiable lust to seduce all the men—who, in turn, are simple, decent-minded innocents more concerned with their jobs than the wild flings into which they are inevitably coerced. In short, *the exact opposite of real life.* The essential truths of Meyer's visionary philosophy (and, coincidentally, his skill as a comedy writer) are usually voiced through a verbosely droll narrator, whose hilariously overblown rants and fond commentary on small-town Americana serve to transform what would otherwise be dumb good-ol'-boy slapstick trash into transcendent, penetrating, *Holy* Dumb Good-Ol'-Boy Slapstick Trash. Russ Meyer movies may not be politically correct, they may appeal to the lowest and most juvenile macho sensibilities, they *certainly* have no socially redeeming values, but SCREW IT—they're some of the funniest god damn movies ever made. *And* they star Kitten Natividad, *one glimpse* of whose *perfect* butt is easily worth a hundred hours of verbal lashing by jealous feminist tongues. Of the comedies, good starters would be *Supervixens, Up!,* and *Beneath the Valley of the Ultravixens. Mudhoney* and *Faster, Pussycat ... Kill! Kill!* are typical of his lurid melodramas. If you can't afford the videos ($80 each), the catalog alone is well

---

* Ideally, the first SubGenius feature film should combine all three. All we need is that $40 million.

worth an SASE, since the dozens of capsule plot descriptions are very obviously written by Meyer himself in the same uncompromising style that grants the films their great and ageless Greatnesslessness.

THE KIND MEN LIKE . . . AND HOLD THE QUICHE!

Stinky and the Spuds
Billy Martin
PO Box 68, Garwood, NJ 07027

EP records that are truly offensive! You'll love 'em. One, "Do What I Say," is an anthem for chauvinist assholes: "You're my bitch and you'll do what I say!" Flip side is an equally nasty song against "Fat Children." Another EP features "Old Al Fish," an ode to a child-killer, and "Skeletons," a SCAAAARY song! $2 each.

MORE EXCUSES

Kalian
625 Post St., Suite 533
San Francisco, CA 94109

Sex-exploration magazine of Mystery Babylon. Not porno, just various extreme sexual libertarian viewpoints. Whoop tee doo. The average working-class peasant doesn't need written excuses—just a good country-western song on the jukebox, a bottle of beer, and something of the opposite or otherwise desired sex. YEEEE-haw! $1 each, or twelve for $12.

THE OTHER KIND OF "CHANNEL"

Hypatia Lee Fan Club
PO Box 1924
Indianapolis, IN 46206

You can buy the panties of this beautiful porn star. And she's "New Age," to boot! $8 for "Member"ship, but maybe you can woo her with sheer extremism of adoring verbiage. Tell her it's her *mind* you love.

PIMPS! NO, I MEAN MEN'S RIGHTS ADVOCATES

Arne Saknussemm's Guide to
International Brothels
Almasi Scholars
Box 9295, 537 Jones St.
San Francisco, CA 94102

Their description: "Helps international travelers BYPASS PORN-HATING FEMINISTS and their sexual bargaining tactics, palimony, divorces, paternity suits and lawyer's fees FOR DISEASE FREE FEMALES WHO WILL SHARE AN APARTMENT WITH A MAN, and establish an intimate personal, cultural and sexual relationship for a week or longer!!! ALL THE SEX AND COMPANIONSHIP YOU WANT WITHOUT THE NEED OF PUTTING ON AN 'ACT' AND GOING THROUGH A LOT OF 'COURTSHIP RITUALS.' ($19.95 per copy.)This is part of the "Patriarchal Network"; just send SASE for info on that, and you'll get some full-tilt rants that represent the most hardcore backlash against feminism I've ever seen outside of White Christian Patriot mags. But it isn't like the more shrewish feminoids weren't asking for it!

THE FUNNIEST TAPE IN THIS GALAXY

The Janor Device
PO Box 140306, Dallas, TX 75214

Sick cassette tape by a walking, talking psychotic . . . or is he the unsung beat poet of the '80s? **WHAT IS IT??** That's the question. WHAT made this tape? Ninety minutes of nonstop insane ranting, and I mean transcendentally insane, by this *thing* called Saint Janor Hypercleats (lead singer for *Doctors 4 "Bob"*). Some slick studio material, some live recordings from clubs(!), some recorded by Janor himself in his bathroom. Rids your home of unwanted guests and pests; kills all cockroaches within hearing distance. Best baaaad recording on planet Earth, anywhere, period. Probably over your head. $8.50 postpaid.

NO BOYS ALLOWED

Of A Like Mind
PO Box 6021, Madison, WI 53716

A big contact and philosophy tabloid that puts radical feminists and political lesbians in touch with each other—for those who detest all the other things mentioned in this section. Men, hold onto your scrotums when you read some of the scary and truly threatening rhetoric in this 'bloid! $2 for sample. ((T.S. Tellier))

FART ON MOM!

The Rats
PO Box 3000-780
Camarillo, CA 93011

Utterly juvenile fart/pee humor. Hand-scrawled; very sloppily put together. A superb shot-in-the-arm of the spirit of Youth. "Vermin Unite!" Freedom means being able to say, "I'm sorry . . . ASSHOLE!" Possibly more subversive than anything else here, just because it is so uncouth and, therefore, honest. Literally free; send SASE.

TOILET SUCK

Toilet Suck
Pete Warner, PO Box 16662
Jersey City, NJ 07306

"Armed and willing for the Pirate Jesus." Sickest humor of all . . . even lower and ruder than The Rats! (How can this be???) Uniquely repulsive use of clip-art graphics; one page is even splattered with fake sperm (Elmer's Glue). Brilliantly original, yet at first it looks like something that blew out the window of a mental home. A work of true genius. Where price would be indicated, all it says is "$." Send at least $2.

A BIT IMMODEST, PERHAPS

Pee Dog Comics #1
c/o Media Research
PO Box 140306, Dallas, TX 75214

Grade-school potty humor elevated to the level of—grade school potty humor. PURE. Picks up where the perverted comics of S. Clay Wilson leave off. This pocket-sized dirty book by "The Shit Generation" looks as if it was drawn by kids with serious anal fixations; it was actually done by two well-known underground artists who wish to remain anonymous. But let me put it this way—*Pee Wee's Playhouse* wouldn't be the same without them! Your Mom won't like it, but your kids sure will! A breakthrough in modern art. You

think I'm kidding? The original drawings for this sold for a fortune to collectors, $1.50; $3 gets you *Poop Dog #1* as well . . . a *satire* of Pee Dog.

DON'T DRINK THE YELLOW KOOL-AID

Mill Scaggs
PO Box 103, New York, NY 10276

Catalog of probably illegal bondage/urolagia videos. If you don't know what urolagia is, please don't send for this. Trying to masturbate to this would be a real challenge.

AND YOU GET A FREE CHASTITY BELT WITH EACH ORDER

Christian Dating Club
PO Box 27123
Golden Valley, MN 55427

A MUST-HAVE if you *ever* want to meet the kind of nice Christian date who can answer correctly questions like these: "You a virgin defined by RSV's Ezek.23:2 1?" "Is self-sodomizing masturbation a sin according to I Cor. 6:9–10?" "Will you ALWAYS dress very modestly with your date before marriage?" Don't get mis-mated with a nonbeliever! They have NO self-control. Gosh durn it, some of these filthy non-Christian women run around in short pants, right in front of men!! With their LEGS showing!!

REMEMBER THIS ADDRESS—YOU MAY NEED IT

Sex Over Forty
PO Box 1600
Chapel Hill, NC 27515-1600

Journal for folks who are "hard pressed" to "keep up" their sex lives as they age. Physicians' advice on such topics as preserving fragile erections, treatments for impotence, etc. At $5 for eight pages, chastity'd be cheaper! ((With Factsheet Five))

BATTERIES NOT INCLUDED

The Bedside Companion
Valentine Products, PO Box 5040
S. Norwalk, CT 06856

Big free catalog of sex devices, tapes, porn mags, etc. This is but one of hundreds just like it, but I'd be remiss not to mention at least one such. Shop-by-mail for enormous dildos with names like "The Wire Mule" and "The Black Mamba"! Vibrators of every imaginable shape—for those *hard to reach* spots! Jack-off machines. Pocket anuses. Cock rings in all colors, flavors. Foreskin-bearing dildos. Anal lube. Open-pud men's undies. "Pocket Puss." Spanish fly. Dildos with little faces on them! Dildos with little rubber lemurs clinging to them! (Honest!) Plus, of course, dozens of porn videos, including specialty subjects like lactating and pregnant women. Once you get on this mailing list, you'll get a big full-color catalog every other month. They must be doing pretty well! How come the Christian Dating Club can't afford full-color?? What does this *tell* you?

FOR THE LONELY SUBGENIUS, AND LESSER MUTANTS

Good Sex for Mutants Dating League
PO Box 7742
Salt Lake City, UT 84107

Their motto: "ALL THE WAY ON THE FIRST DATE." But not just anyone can join; you have to be WEIRD. But not necessarily *sexually* weird . . . it means just plain WEIRD weird—and *prove it* by filling out a long and very personal questionnaire. This national "ORGAN"ization (to cop punctuation from that anticircumcision society) matches weirdo with weirdo. Send $5 for a full set of application papers, and spill your heart out to "The Katlady!" She'll find you someone— maybe not with the same fetishes, but certainly with *equally embarrassing* obsessions!

THE GREATEST

Screw
Milky Way Productions, PO Box 432
Old Chelsea Station
New York, NY 10011

What a great loss to mankind, that *Screw* is known mainly to New Yorkers—unless you subscribe, which you should. This really belongs with the humor listings, except that it's so much funnier than anything else there, it'd make the others look bad. (In fact, I've decided to drop that whole listing from this book. They're all so hopelessly lame compared to *Screw* and *SubGenius.*) The blowjob shots peppering this tabloid insure sales; otherwise, this is far more than a stroke-mag. The editorial rants are more effectively antiauthoritarian than those in any political rag. I can't believe they haven't been shut down yet, what with all the porn collages in which they make it appear that, say, Ed Meese is "getting it" from Ronald Reagan. The news on sex discoveries and sex repression are presented in a pun-mangled style that is somehow better for gut yuks—unless you're UPTIGHT about it—than any "legit" humor book I can think of. Great regular features like "Smut from the Past," dependable "Consumers' Guides" to porn and live sex in every medium, and more. It's biweekly; you get to know the writers and the format, and after a few issues you'll be hooked. When somebody like Liberace dies of AIDS, *Screw* goes **nuts.** Call me politically incorrect! Then go fuck yourself! One year (twenty-six issues) is $23.50—a pittance for one of the noblest publications listed herein.

GUIDE TO DEGENERATE DENS OF DEGRADATION

Fat Black Broads/How Sluts Get Off/Nauseating Nookie

SCREW

Too Good To Ruin With "Explanations"

A Lewd Spectacle of Wanton
Depravity
Keckhaver, PO Box 5444
N. Little Rock, AR 72119

A cassette tape for $6. I won't say any more. Just DO IT.

El Estatua Del Carne!

Fotonovela Pimienta!
6360 NE Fourth Court
Miami, FL 33138

Most of you have probably seen various Mexican "fotonovelas," but only the more intrepid—and bilingual, and perverse—ever actually **study** one. If you're unfamiliar with the genre, they're photographic "comic books," generally of an extremely lurid nature, with worse dialogue than the dumbest monster movie. The stories aren't drawn, but staged with actors and printed as a series of stills. This particular stroker has all the elements that the fotonovela diehard expects: nudity with mutilation, bondage, sexual abuse, and TRUE LOVE. My favorite issue, Vol. 8 #39, takes place in a concentration camp run by haughty blond Nazi women. They torture and disfigure the brunette female inmates, have lots of sex, and get killed. The Spanish dialogue is so rudimentary that even someone like me, with three years of high school Spanish, can follow it. $1 each . . . ask for a recent sample.

I must admit that I had always assumed these magazines were printed in Mexico. Surprise, surprise!—they're made in Miami, and the writer and art director both have very Angloid names. No wonder these're so heavy on the blond Nazi gals! Born exploiters.

DEAR BUF
LETTERS FROM OUR LARD-LOVING FANS

Massive Mamas And Beefy, Bounteous Babes!!

Buf
G&S Pubs., 1472 Broadway
New York, NY 10036

"The Number One Magazine Devoted Solely to Plump and Heavy Women." WOW!! Someone finally caught on that many guys can better fantasize to stroke books featuring *accessible* looking women, as opposed to your airbrushed, pedestal-perching *Playboy*-style

"Miss Perfect." The women in these pictorials look like people you'd bump into at the supermarket. Each issue features two pleasingly plump "chubbies," as they call them, two really **fat** ones, and two outright obese and/or OLD ones. Lots of articles and fiction about the inestimable pleasures of them BIG gals . . . and imagine the letters column! $4.95 for single copies; $24/six . . . but these magazines can be found in convenience stores! "Roll 'em in flour and look for the wet spots." Personally, I think magazines like this are a good thing. Finally, ALL women can feel truly exploited!

LESSER-KNOWN JOYS OF MOTHERHOOD

Juggs, MM Pubs. Ltd.
155 Ave. of the Americas, Fifth Floor
New York, NY 10013

"The World's Dirtiest Tit-Mag." Well, it's not really the dirtiest, but it is one of the more available newsstand "beatin' bibles" to regularly present pictorials on the new porn fads of lactating and pregnant women. Apparently, many guys are thrilled by shots of milk squirting from breasts and nude models in the ninth month of pregnancy. This one also toys with the "Heavy Woman" fetish, but tries to stay within a "tasteful" range. *(!)* $3.75 each.

THERE WAS NO CLUE TO HER SPECIES, BUT I LOVED HER NONETHELESS

Bizarre Sex Comics
Kitchen Sink Press, #2 Swamp Rd.
Princeton, WI 54968

The name is accurate—this is a very well done series of undergrounds featuring sex-horror sagas by various artists. Hideous nameless alien beasts assault humans, and vice versa; for the dedicated alio-sexual, and anyone else who appreciates fine art disguised as sleazy "funny books." $2 each; ask for the Kitchen Sink catalog of other comic genres.

BORN TO PORN

Weird Smut
John Mozzer, PO Box 224
Brooklyn, NY 11218

Another sex-oriented underground comic, from a smaller publisher. No attempt at socially redeeming factors; no excuse. Caricatured human reproductive habits. One strip by the BAAAD SubGenius gal, St. EvE. $2.75 each.

THE SQUIRT'N SCIENCE

**Sexual Well-Being
Box 60332, Palo Alto, CA 94306**

A serious newsletter of articles on sexuality, done with "respectablity." (*SNORE*) Technical details on how erections happen, orgasm amplification, AIDS, birth control—the real stuff. Not funny. $3 each.

HE DOESN'T WANT TO COME RIGHT OUT AND SAY IT

**Victorian Vault
White Knight Prod., Box 656
Wautoma, WI 54982**

Photocopied 'zine "for the Connoisseur of the Victorian Underground, Victorian Dolls, Art, Music, Furniture & Photography. *Also focuses on the dark side of the Victorian period and explores taboos which exist today.*" (My italics.) $1 for recent sample of this mild pedophilia featuring pics from things like Barbie catalogs and Punky Brewster shows, and musings on slumber parties. Perhaps it means something that the same editor also puts out:

SWEET & SWISHY . . .

" . . . For the Long Hair Enthusiast—clip-pings, articles, photos of long haired girls." In other words, soft-core child porn for those who want to keep it strictly fantasy. (A wise move.) Also $1 each.

I have never even seen real child pornography, and don't want to. It's probably the one subject that would freak me out, ruin my day, and put me on a self-righteous moral soapbox. Just an old fuddy-duddy, I guess. But I still don't believe in capital punishment for these scum. I believe in *torture*.

FELLINI ON JUNK

**Deathtrip Films
R. Kern, PO Box 1322
New York, NY 10009**

I swore I'd steer clear of listing videos—that's another book—but R. Kern's unrelentingly hideous underground films have earned a place in ANY encyclopedia of the Great Unknown . . . videos as alien as *Eraserhead,* but cruder, funnier, and more emotional—short "art films" that make *Pink Flamingos* look like *Davey and Goliath.* David Lynch's *Blue Velvet* is a mere *tickle,* relative to Kern's full-frontal assaults. *The Right Side of My Brain* (starring, narrated, and co-written by my sweet, Lydia Lunch) is a riveting portrait of feminine sexual nihilism, simultaneously arousing and frightening. I *mean* that! Another, *Manhattan Love Suicides,* is a collection of very blackly humorous shorts about death, drugs, and obsessive sex among the denizens of NY slums. The average viewer would find these very hard to integrate into his or her worldview; they invoke a certain purity of **urge** that tends to be repressed in pretty much all political and cultural milieus. Honest to Gobbs, these are the most-copied films in my collection. (And at this point, you can probably imagine what my video collection is like!) Kern's latest is *Fingered*, also with Lydia Lunch, the new 'punk sex goddess.' Someone should give this guy a few million dollars, but in the meantime you can get Beta or VHS of the above films for $22.50 each. And if you DO have the few million, *I* could probably put it to even *sicker* use.

Don't Miss It!

A porn HINT: I dunno who's distributing it, but keep a Peeping Tom's eye open for the science-fiction porn film, *Café Flesh,* directed by "Rinse Dream"—the ONLY hard-X fukfilm that's also a classic piece of science fiction.

I Say, Nothing Pagan About Old Kennedy!

Triangle Magazine
Suite 102, Box 1912
1214 Wilmington Ave.
Salt Lake City, UT 84106

#8 has as the cover story, "GAYS AND WITCHCRAFT." Sort of a gay magazine and contact nexus. Rants and news of interest to gays, but from a slightly extraweird pagan/witchcraft angle. $6/year; 75¢ each.

Have Intercourse With A Beautiful Live *Thing*

Swinging Nymphos *and many others*
Modern Publications, Box 3636
Fort Pierce, FL 33448

Publishers of a large number of $7.50 "swingers' mags." For those of you who've somehow remained hopelessly naive, that means these are open sex catalogs. You send in your nude photo and a blurb describing just exactly what kinds of people you're willing to have what kind of sex with; they print the "ad" for a fee, and you start getting propositions by mail. Great source of amateur photos of perfectly average people with their clothes off, striking "sexy" poses that are sometimes hilarious. This particular publisher is included because they also offer specialty contacts for devotees of unusual sexual fetishes: soiled panties, S&M "slavery," humiliation-oriented "watersports," FOOT SEX, HAIR SEX(!), etc. Expensive as hell; send SASE for the nifty, photo-filled catalog. Finally, you've found your "niche"!

FOR THOSE WHO LIVE DANGEROUSLY

The Male Chauvinist Digest
TLC Int.
174 Ludlow St. (basement)
New York, NY 10002

A little homemade swinger's mag; the ads are the best part. Looking for "CAR SEX"?? Interracial Love? Orgy clubs? This is a dangerous field of endeavor, nowadays! Sample $1; $12/year.

IT'S OKAY BECAUSE IT'S "ART"

Yellow Silk
Box 6374, Albany, CA 94706

Artsy-smartsy erotic poetry. Occasionally heats up. $4.

MULTIPLE ORGASMS

PEPTALK Autumn 1986
PO Box 3912, Eugene, OR 97403

Quarterly newsletter of Polyfidelitous Educational Productions. As you might surmise from the name, they exist to promote polyfidelity, which is a form of closed group marriage. This issue has articles from a couple of cases that didn't work out as well as their more usual success stories, plus thoughts on home schooling and forming successful relationships. ((Factsheet Five))

PEPTALK for the polyfidelitous WINTER ISSUE 1986

CHOOSE ME! TOUCH ME! INFECT ME!

APA-EROS
Sylvia, PO Box 759
Veneta, OR 97487

An amateur press association 'zine devoted to sex and love in their many variations. Some people write about technique, others write erotica, others cross the line (or nearly so) into porno, as things are unedited. AIDS, VD, rape, touching, caring, and sharing have all been discussed. Several serialized stories have been running as well, portraying sexual Utopias. For all desires and orientations, and surprisingly uninhibited. SASE & state that you're over eighteen for sample. ((Factsheet Five))

optimism," and back issues of *Transition* magazine. Fashion tip: green eyeshadow is out this year. ((Remote Control))

REAL PROS

The National Organization of Gay and Lesbian Scientific and Technical Professionals
PO Box 39582
Los Angeles, CA 90039

What more do you need to know about these newsletters and pamphlets? $10/year. ((Factsheet Five))

BUDDING!! SO THAT'S HOW THEY REPRODUCE!

Confide
Box 56, Tappan, NY 10983

"For all-out help on gender problems." Information and counseling for the budding transsexual, specializing in hypnotherapy. Not to be confused with the Friends of Ed Wood, Jr. Society. Also carries the cassette *The Way of the Transsexual: Joanne's Story,* "a saga laced with suffering yet steeped in

MUSTA BEEN THE BEST TUCK-'N'-ROLL JOBS IN THE WORLD

Outcry!
Justice for Nazi Sex Experiment Victims, 6714 Selma Ave.
Hollywood, CA 90028

The little-known Nazi castration, sterilization, and especially sex-change operation victims finally have their voice. The author's theory is that the Nazis didn't really KILL three out of the six million, but changed the sex of many. These were sent to the U.S. after the war, *but were brainwashed first so that they'd never remember their original sex!!* One gets the impression that this is the most elaborate rationalization for uneasy homosexuals yet developed.

CHAPTER
19

GREAT CATALOGS

The greatest thing about them is that they're *free*. Most of them. If I don't mention a price, there isn't one.

WHAT YOU DON'T KNOW WON'T PUT YOU TOTALLY OUT OF COMMISSION . . . NORMALLY . . .

Loompanics
PO Box 1197
Port Townsend, WA 98368

"The Greatest Book Catalog In the World" —outlaw publishers who also sell outlaw books . . . including some by our military. "No more secrets, no more excuses, no more limits." A few of their categories: Underground economy. Tax avoidance. Fake IDs. Police science. Con games. Self-defense. Revenge. Guns. Bombs. Guerrilla warfare. Self-suffi- ciency. Alternate Energy. Life extension. Drugs. Heresy. Forbidden philosophies. Human pleasure. $2 for huge catalog that is a reading experience UNTO ITSELF. Opens doors you didn't want to know existed! Highly recommended. Like *A.M.O.K.*, below, this will scare the pants off some people, because it points out aspects of the world that just won't go away. Don't just buy the catalog—order the books before this company gets shut down. DATA is the latest commodity the authorities seek to regulate . . . .

HIP AND KOOL HORROR TRUTH

A.M.O.K.
PO Box 875112
Los Angeles, CA 90087

Very similar to Loompanics; not as extensive, but carries some books they don't. Somewhat more mystical/Discordian oriented; not as political. Similar categories: Secret societies. Situationists. Illuminati. UFOs. Surveillance. Satanism. Psychedelics. Magick. Surrealism. Quantum physics. Freaks. Murderers. Kitsch. Etc. The complete library of weirdness. $1.

A VERITABLE FONT OF UNHOLY LORE

William L. Moore Publications
4219 W. Olive St., Suite #247
Burbank, CA 91505

Vast catalog of rare, out-there books by and about UFO abductees, cover-ups, Fortean weirdness, and a zillion other "Cosmic Watergates." Good general source for many otherwise unavailable classics on cryptoscience and the paranormal.

PSSST . . . LOOKING FOR THE *REAL* NECRONOMICON??

Ben Abraham Books
97 Donnamora Crescent
Thornhill, Ontario L3T 4K6, Canada

Sells some very rare occult books—mystical tomes you can't find anywhere else. Atlantis, weird folklore, witchcraft, pagan religions, ancient civilizations . . . the really hard-to-find, "shunned manuscript" type things. Not like your "SAFE" books.

INVASION OF THE SAUCER MEN

SST Publications/DELVE Magazine
Gene Duplantier, 17 Shetland St.
Willowdale, Ontario, M2M 1X5
Canada

Great $1 catalog of UFO books; titles like *The Martian Alphabet, Secrets of the Popes, Hollow Earth at the End Time.* Many hard-to-find Hollow Earth books and contactee autobiographies here.

THEY'RE HEEEERE...

The Llewellyn New Times
PO Box 64383
St. Paul, MN 55164–0383

Big catalog of astrology and New Age books of all kinds... ALL kinds. Crystal power, Enochian magick, Tarot, you name it... also, many "subliminal tapes." A few articles too. Order a free catalog direct, by dialing 1-800-THE MOON. Buncha damn *lunatics!*

The Americas' Oldest Publisher of New Age Literature and Astrology

The Llewellyn NEW TIMES

Issue Number 843

October/November

$1.00

ON JANUARY 20, 1984, NEPTUNE ENTERED the sign of Capricorn. It will stay in this sign through 1998.

And during those fourteen years, it will determine America's destiny.

Sounds far-fetched? Consider...

American industry is being revolutionized by a new technology that threatens to eliminate many workers' jobs. The economy is foremost on everybody's mind... people are preoccupied with making money. Latin America is a hotbed of revolution, and the President has warned the Eastern powers to keep their hands off the West. Fundmentalist

Continued on page 4

That The Left And Right Hands Might Know What Each Other Does

Editorial Research Service
Laird Wilcox, Box 1832
Kansas City, MO 64141

Write for details on extensive bibliographies of books, mags, and monographs in various political extremes. Wilcox's *Master Bibliography* is *the* comprehensive source on such subjects as the American Right, the American Left, Political Psychology, Mass Movement Propaganda, Terrorism and Assassination, Espionage and Intelligence, Psychological Coercion, Disinformation, etc. ((With Remote Control))

All The "Nicer" Ones

Dustbooks
Box 100, Paradise, CA 95969

Sells catalogs of catalogs of small, independent magazine publishers and their catalogs. Not much weird stuff; mostly pompous "literary" garbage. Be ready to go wading.

New Age, Schmoo Age

Valley of the Sun
Metaphysical Catalog
Box 38, Malibu, CA 90265

Fairly typical, large New Age catalog. You'll probably end up on a zillion mailing lists for vitamins, weight-loss videos, motivational seminars, and assertiveness training. Wimpy to the max, but *comprehensively* so. Also from this address: *The Reincarnationist Newsletter*. If you vaguely remember being the High Priest(ess) of Atlantis, you'll want to send them lots of money. They'll certainly tell you just what you want to hear.

That's What They All Say . . .

Worldwide Curio House
Box 17095, Minneapolis, MN 55417

. . . But in this case, it may be true! "World's largest occult, witchcraft, voodoo supply house. 3 catalogs containing 7,000 curios, gifts, unusual items." Protective talismans, hundreds of miraculous good-luck charms (even Dungeons & Dragons figurines are sold as "Powerful Occult Symbols"), herbs, barks, berries, witch hats, Tiki god pendants, hex kits, signet rings with keen occult designs, "Double Fast Luck Spray," crystal balls, everything you need. They also carry goofy "gag novelties" like rubber eggs, magicians' supplies such as smoke powder, and eighteen zillion books on every imaginable form of juju. $2.

A funnier *looking* catalog, with neat pics, *may* still be available from Asturo Company, Box 495, North Miami Beach, FL 33160

FIRE TRAP

Paper Collectors'
Marketplace
470 Main St.
PO Box 127
Scandinavia,
WI 54977

You *subscribe* to this giant catalog ($12/12/yr.) of every kind of nostalgic cheesy printed junk—baseball cards, old dime novels & pulps, back-issue technical magazines, posters, ancient maps, photograph files, buttons...even more catalogs! Packed with classified ads from people buying and selling ephemera of every kind. $2/sample.

LAST STOP FOR 50,000 MILES

Roadside America
Fireside Books, Simon & Schuster
1230 Ave. of the Americas
New York, NY 10020

Well, this is a book, but it's also a catalog —a guide to the beautifully tasteless roadside tourist attractions of America. Written with fun-to-eat sarcasm, illustrated with photos that'll make your mouth water to go on a cross-country car ride in search of such holy spots as: Flintstone's Bedrock City. Forest Lawn Cemetery. Spongearama. Bratwurst Capital of the World. Prehistoric Forest Motel. Astro-Chimp Grave. Santa Land. Corn Palace. Chocolate World. Elvis-A-Rama. Dinosaur Land. $9.95 but write for postage/ordering info.

HEY, ALL YOU BUCKAROOS

Starland
PO Box 24937, Denver, CO 80222

Just a quick plug for these folks. They carry a lot of useless Star Trek and Macross

(Robotech) crap for the terminally juvenile. BUT, listen up monkey boy, they ALSO carry *Buckaroo Banzai* gear! Yeah! Team Banzai and Hong Kong Cavaliers T-shirts, ball caps, patches, posters, and even satin jackets. Everything you need to cross the Fifth Dimension in style. Free catalog. ((Remote Control))

ALL THIS, AND YET "THE BETTER MOUSETRAP" STILL ELUDES US!

Lor'D Industries, Ltd.
PO Box 14511
West Allis, WI 53214–0511

Chakra chargers, telepathy machines, psychic generators, aura stimulators, weird books, and strange electronics plans. Sort of a cross between *Popular Mechanics* and *Fate* magazine. Free catalog. ((Remote Control))

LEARNING THROUGH GROSS-OUT

Anatomical Chart Company
7124 North Clark Street
Chicago, IL 60626
(Toll free: 1-800-621-7500)

Biological supply catalogs are always good for laughs, what with their mummified split dogs and baby skeletons, but this enormous full-color catalog is a heavenly cesspool of goofy educational models and "practice kits" for medical students. From the gory to the obscene. Vinyl torso models for breast examination practice, V.D. detection, childbirth; fake accident body parts to sew back on; hideous cancerous giant smokers' mouths; deformed baby models. All this and more. No longer pleased by your inflatable love-mate? Headless but much more anatomically correct ones await you here. Unsurpassed clip-art potential. $2.95 for the catalog, *but possibly free to "doctors."*

THE AMATEUR SPLATTER FILMMAKER'S DREAM COME TRUE

Nightmares International Catalog
2615 Waugh Drive, Suite 255
Houston, TX 77006

This (and the Mike Evans catalog described below) should be enough to keep any overgrown monster fan kid licking his chops in orgasmic glee for hours. *Nightmares* sells GORE MOVIE MAKE-UP SUPPLIES! Not just your pitiful little fake scars and witch noses, but a huge line of ready-made prosthetic appliances and accessories that run the gamut of wound and horror effects. And at REALLY CHEAP PRICES to boot!! I could hardly believe it. As a child I would have traded my little brother—nay, my whole family—for something like this. Even if you have no interest in hideous make-up or accident simulation, the imaginative design and sheer variety of these gross-out tools is impressive. Just within the single category of "Things Imbedded in the Face" one finds ninja stars, space darts, giant screws, brain-eating snakes, razor blades, and even torn-off alien hands! Simply glue 'em on and you'll have Granny puking in seconds! Everything you need in the way of slit throats, bloody amputated arm stumps, enucleated eyeballs, torn-out tongues, pumping chest wounds, oozing brains, compound fractures, and even disemboweled guts—it's all right here, and shown in clear photos. Also carries a huge line of masks, monster hands, chopped-off body parts, rotting baby puppets, plastic murder weapons, squashed vermin, and rubber bricks, plus hard-to-find make-up supplies and how-to books. The catalog will fit inside a standard 10-inch SASE.

Now, World Takeover Is Within Your Grasp!!

Information Unlimited
Box 716
Amherst, NH 03031

Amazing Devices! Laser guns, high voltage plasma generators, ion generators and detectors, particle-beam weapon supplies, surveillance devices, geiger counters, stun guns and phasors, fireworks and pyrotechnics, and many how-to plans for even more sinister and useful gadgets. Don't be caught in a 1984/ Brave New World future society without it! *((Oops—too late—you already are!!))*

. . . And Some May Even Attempt To Rape The Catalog Itself!

Mike Evans Model Kits Catalog
Route 5, Box 120-I
Rockwall, TX 75087

Remember those Aurora plastic model kits of the Wolfman, the Mummy, etc.? We who, as kids, lived and breathed fantasy, spent many glorious hours assembling and customizing them, filling our rooms with the reek of glue and Testors Pla enamel paint. Only about a dozen monsters appeared in kit form, but we felt divinely blessed just to have those. These days you're lucky to find so much as a brontosaurus skeleton kit, if that. American kids want everything ready-made, now that the reading of instructions is a lost art. (Hot rod and aircraft models are still around, but only jocks care about those.) But in Japan—burdened with ample money and leisure time, yet without land or weapons to spend it on, hobbyists have been able to manufacture and sell obscure items far too specialized to be economically viable here. This Texan imports splendid plastic models that the most optimistic American monster buff would never have dared hope for: the cyclops from *7th Voyage of Sinbad;* The Thing (James Arness version, yet!); The Rhedosaurus from *Beast from 20,000 Fathoms;* the giant pickle from *It Conquered the World;* the *Mole People* uglies; Harryhausen's Ymir; characters from *This Island Earth, Aliens,* and even *Invasion of the Saucer Men!* Then there're the dinosaur kits, including obscure species like Gorgosaurus and Styracosaurus. Even the fictional animals of the book, *Life After Man,* can be had, not to mention a million outrageous Japanese creatures and spaceships. That's the good news. The bad news is that the models cost anywhere from $50 to $300! This catalog is photocopied (send SASE), but provides access to fantastic full-color Japanese catalogs; the very *idea* that these models *exist at all* might well drive some of you to *masturbate* over the pictures. . . .

Hoo-Doo Supplies

Ann Howard
200 West Sunrise Highway
Freeport, NY 11520

These voodoo/mojo catalogs will eerily appear in your mailbox *just when you need* her

Cleopatra Powder, Boss Fix Oil, Jinx-Removing Incense, Love Me Forever Luck Balls, and —scariest of all—Black Nail Polish! Complete with disclaimers printed in *supernaturally* tiny type. ((With Candi Strecker))

Lists Of List-Lists

Catalog of Mailing Lists
Hugo Dunhill Mailing Lists, Inc.
630 Third Ave., New York, NY 10017

A hundred zillion grillion godzillion addresses, categorized according to type of business/interest. Mostly industrial businesses; unfortunately, there're no "Eccentric Millionaire" or "Weird Fringe Group" categories. However, there are lists of *politicians,* from governors on down! Hmmmm . . .

A similar mailing-list supplier is:
Research Projects Corp.
Pomperaug Ave. (seriously!), Woodbury, CT 06798

1,001 Archaic Jokes

The Book Chest
300 E. Seventy-fifth St.
New York, NY 10021

Bookstore specializing in rare humor books; amazing scope and breadth of subject matter. Skimming the descriptions of archaic satires is most educational . . . and you'll wish you had the money for priceless obscurities such as *A Treatise on Dislocations and Fractures of the Joints,* or *The Frauds of Romish Monks and Priests, Set Forth In Eight Letters.* Someday, our hip contemporary literature will look equally ridiculous. I await that day with trepidation.

WEAR AN ATOM BOMB ON YOUR CHEST

Journal of Academic T-Shirts
Outer Products, Box 88
Lafayette Hill, PA 19444

A scholarly journal devoid of scholarly articles—just an awesome series of T-shirt slogans and images, mostly science-oriented, and all so strangely cool you'll be sure you can no longer live without them. And you can't, but fortunately these folks sell 'em. Examples: Frog Anatomy; The Quadratic Equation; Stegosaurus skeleton; radiation and biohazard hieroglyphs; brain cross-section; trilobite. And the shirts are only $6.60 each!

DIRECTORIES OF DIRECTORY DIRECTORIES

B. Klein Publications
Box 8503, Coral Springs, FL 33065

More infinite lists of address lists. "It's like having a full staff of researchers on your payroll—without the expense!" Huge books such as: *Guide to Directories; Mail Order Directory;* directories of museums ... college stores ... ethnologists ... Japanese new products ... solar tech suppliers ... on and on. ... MY GOD, how can you keep living without access to **all** information on **everything**??

Another such is *Directory Marketplace,* Todd Publications, 18 North Greenbrush Road, West Nyack, NY 10994

CAVALCADE OF THE HAS-BEENS

Christensen's Ultimate Movie, TV, & Rock Directory
Cardiff-by-the-Sea Publishing
Box 909
Cardiff-by-the-Sea, CA 92007

Addresses of 15,000 celebrities! Most of 'em are the "pink" Made-4-TV kind: the George Kennedies, Ernest Borgnines, James Franciscuses ... if you've ever even heard of them at all. Should be called *The Catalog of 14,000 Hopeful Nobodies and 1,000 Stars.* No one "hip" ... for instance, the "As" don't include Dan Aykroyd, yet they do list a David Ackroyd. Gee, THANKS!! But if you've always wanted to send hateful, inexplicable, disturbing letters to the lesser gods of the Normals, you know where to turn. Or pick one at random that you've never heard of, and start sending them gushy fan letters—then suddenly inform them that "their last work SUCKED" and from now on, you'll be telling everyone how BAD they are. Drive 'em out of show business—you'll be doing most of them a favor. $25, though.

A–Rooooo-Gah!!

Saurus
530 S. Fourth St.
Centerville, UT 84014

Dinosaur T-shirts, dinosaur fossils, dinosaur posters, dinosaur jigsaw puzzles, dinosaur coffee mugs, dinosaur models, glow-in-the-dark dinosaur skeleton kits. Basically, these people sell things having to do with dinosaurs. You know, Centerville sounds like a real nice place to raise your kids up.... Free catalog.
((Remote Control))

Grooonk!

Dinosaur Catalog
PO Box 546
Tallman, NY
10982

Plastic dino toys, of ALL makes...dino books, all age levels...posters of classic paleontological paintings...wooden Great Reptile skeleton kits...ceramic and pewter Thunder Lizards...actual flying full-scale robot Pterosaurs...and where else can you procure that incredibly stupid album, *Dinosaur Rock*?? Plus rubber stamps, calendars, stuffed "baby" thecodonts, serapod puzzles, T-shirts. When I'm rich, I'll possess it all.

CONTAINS DINOSAURS!

Psychic-Osis

Inner Space Enterprises
PO Box 1133
Magnolia Park Station
Burbank CA 91507

Guide to PSI (i.e., pertaining to the psychic) periodicals and tapes.

"I'm The Moon, Man!"

Robert Firester
Box 466
Port Washington, NY 11050

There were these "monster decals" that you used to put on your bike . . . Monsters saying things like, TAKE ME TO YOUR LEADER and KISS ME, BABY. They still exist! 50¢ for packet of twenty!

Deep

Reel 3-D Enterprises Catalog
PO Box 2368, Culver City, CA 90231

Every piece of equipment one could possibly need for 3-D photography in any of the existing formats, from Viewmasters to those eye-wrenching blue-red glasses. Slides, books, comics, projectors, viewers, etc. The art of 3-D has yet to be explored for its full psychedelia potential. Ever see a 3-D time exposure of someone swinging a lit Sparkler in the air at night? How about a simple 3-D accidental double-exposure? A bright horizon dawns YET for this mighty gimmick.

X-Ray Specs

The Fun House
PO Box 1225, Newark, NJ 07101

You know those ads that used to be in the back of comic books for all manner of stupid gags, magic tricks, novelties, etc.? Stinky-Gum, Fake "Live" Vomit, Sea Monkeys, Whoopie-Cushions . . . eighty pages of it, free.

Junkies

Johnson Smith's Things You Never Knew Existed
4514 Nineteenth Court E.
Bradenton, FL 34203–3794

Catalog of gimcracks 'n' geegaws like Mystery Kites, Joy Buzzers, LunaBalls, Ah-OO-Gah horns, monster and Reagan masks, giant bow ties, Bag o' Horrors, magic spy viewers, squirt toilets, talking cigars, electric pumping hearts, punk Mohawk wigs, Miracle "Punishment Cones," trick bras, etc.

PEE WEE'S HOME DECORATOR

Archie McPhee
Box 30852, Seattle, WA 98103

Great selection of kitschy toys and decor —lawn flamingos, fake rocks, duck hats, rubber dinosaurs, lobster-claw harmonicas, neat-o toys from the '50s, Japanese monsters . . . and good prices. One of the few remaining stockers of Potato Guns!! Huge free catalog . . . please do go to the trouble of asking for it. A postcard will suffice.

I HOPE *JAY WARD* GETS A CUT

Stanley Desantis Inc.
4250 Wilshire Blvd.
Los Angeles, CA 90010

A personal favorite. Specializing in T-shirts emblazoned with the images of Rocky and Bullwinkle, Boris and Natasha, George of the Jungle, Super Chicken, Tom Slick, Underdog, Dudley Do-Right, Snidely Whiplash, Peabody and Sherman, all the great cartoon characters. Catalog $1. ((Remote Control))

DESTROY ALL GIMMICKS

Monster Island Imports
241 King Street
Northampton, MA 01060

The place to shop if you're looking for giant six-foot inflatable Godzillas, little plastic articulated Godzillas or butane Godzilla cigarette lighters. On, no, there goes Tokyo. . . . Free information. ((Remote Control))

SO DAINTY AND SUBTLE

Ephemera Inc.
275 Capp St.
San Francisco, CA 94110

Buttons, buttons, buttons. My favorites are SMILE, YOU'RE ON SATELLITE SURVEILLANCE and OBSCENITY IS THE CRUTCH OF THE INARTICULATE MOTHERFUCKER. Free Catalog. ((Remote Control))

SLAM IT DOWN

Top Drawer Rubber Stamps
Box 38, Hancock, VT 05748

The name says it all. By far the most reasonably priced stamp company around and they carry *hundreds* of designs, including CHURCH OF THE SUBGENIUS stamps. Yeah! Lots of underground comix designs, too. Free catalog. ((Remote Control))

CAR-TOONS

Ed "Big Daddy" Roth
14245 San Feliciano Ave.
LaMirada, CA 90638

Remember those really gross T-shirts with RAT FINK and monster-piloted hotrods back in the late '60s–early '70s? "Big D" was the man responsible, and he's still turning them out. CHEVY'S EAT FORDS FOR BREAKFAST! A hefty $4 for the catalog ((Remote Control))

ANYTHING FOR A BUCK-TWO-EIGHTY

Tee Vee Stick-Ons
Box 43, LaSalle, IL 61301

This poor devil probably thought he had a new "Pet Rock" on his hands. Think again, pal! Vinyl mustaches, glasses, Groucho noses, and big ears that you stick on your TV, then wait for the newscaster or whoever to appear in suitable close-up, so that s/he's defaced by this CLEVER gag!!! Hyuk, hyuk!! Won't you feel "funny"! Originally $4.94 for the kit (HA!!), but I'll bet the guy is trying to GIVE 'em away by now, so try haggling. Just stupid enough to be amusing . . . maybe.

GODLY DUDS FOR HOLY DUDES AND DUDESSES

Almy Religious Wear Catalog
C.M. Almy & Son, Inc.
37 Purchase St.
Rye, NY 10580

Preacher 'n' priest fashions by mail. The finest in clerical wear: cassocks, robes, "surplices", "albs", clerical collars, rabats, "stoles", other garments whose names you never knew before, plus all the arcane doodads you need to hold a proper Communion. Seeing these mysterious and sacred garments described and pictured in classic Sears catalog fashion, complete with grinning fashion models (mostly male, of course), is a somewhat weirder experience than one might think. I always sort of assumed they got their clothes direct from God. Ask for free catalog (it's too big for an SASE), but preface your name with "Reverend."

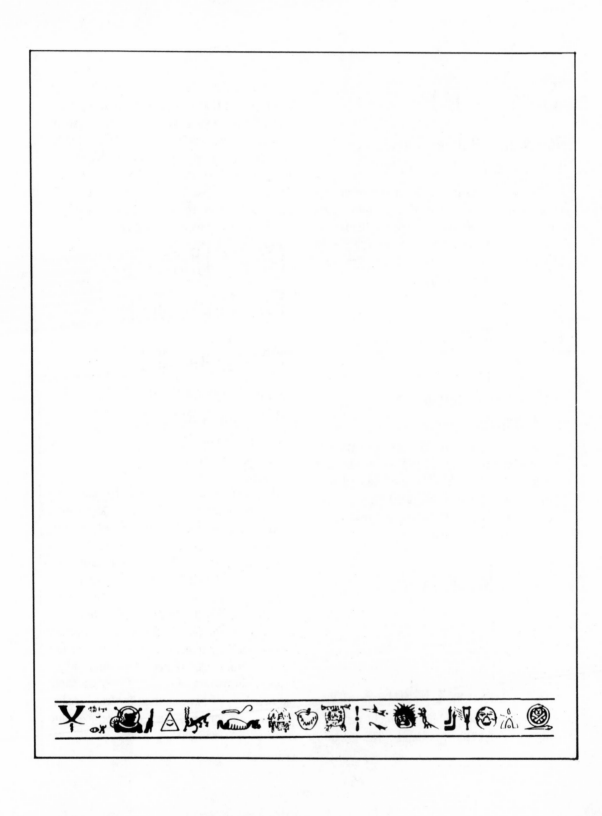

CHAPTER
20

THE GREAT KOOK-FINDERS

SOURCES FOR SOURCES FOR MORE OF EVERYTHING:

HESE ARE OUR **FRIENDS**—those whose listings I used and sometimes reprinted directly for this book. Unless you make all your acquaint-
ances buy copies of it, updated reprintings of *High Weirdness by Mail*
won't happen—in which case, the following will be your only "pushers" of
new kook lists.

MY HERO

The Amazing
Colossal
Mindblaster
Remote Control,
PO Box 3108
Scottsdale, AZ
85257-0060

NOT to be MISSED! The second-greatest magazine listed in these pages.* Truly hilarious "editorials," terrifying nonfiction about things you aren't supposed to know, and superb and inherently **sick** collages guaranteed to sever the optic nerve. AND KOOK LISTINGS!—the *right kind* of kook listings. MOUTH-WATERING! About forty of the funnier reviews in this book are taken DIRECT from the pages of *Mindblaster* (the ones tagged *"Remote Control"*)—I didn't edit a word, either, and that's saying a lot. (He's naturally every bit as sarcastic as I've strived to be.) Besides the "Amazing Mail" listings, #1 had material on spontaneous human combustion, false news rumors, 200 Ninja movie titles, and an intro to wiretapping in your spare time. #2 featured baroque conspiracy-theory updates, Joe Newman's perpetual-motion machine saga, the 1-800 phone numbers of all the Fundamentalist and military groups you hate and to whom you'd love to charge calls, original Robert Anton Wilson rants, and diseased book and movie reviews. Subscribe, and improve your sex life an hundredfold. Only $1.50 each, or $5 for four BIG issues! (That's $14,692 off the cover price! *Don't miss this deal!!*)

It Takes One To Know One!

Subjectivist League
Lou Minatti

1093 Broxton Ave., #567
Los Angeles, CA 90024

The SICKEST—but ONLY for the WORTHY, and that's no joke. Let them say it: "A research collective/think tank based in Los Angeles, with branch affiliates in San Diego and San Francisco. *The Subjectivist League* holds no meetings of a formal nature, has no logically definable platform of belief and presents no above-ground profile of such. Its reason for existence is the conservation of what its members term 'DISCREET INFORMATION,' meaning data normally thought unfit for mental consumption. Also engages in 'TELEPHONE RESEARCH' and maintains a recording library of its 'psychology experiments.'** Smaller minds term such activities 'prank calls.' The *League* maintains that they are a valuable data-gathering tool for uncovering the boundless gullibility of man. The *League* distributes recordings of teachings by members, affiliates, and other interested parties, released at the whims of their creators. Beyond these functions, *The Subjectivists League* exists to justify the personal tastes, prejudices, and quirks of its membership. These individuals constitute a small, alienated circle of 'cranks' who get so fucking sick of anyone and everyone that they feel the need to hide behind an organization logo in order to harass and defile at random."

* See *the Stark Fist*, below.

** These materials available to interested parties upon submission of written requests *and* photocopies/tapes/etc. of similar "discreet information."

NOBLE... ALMOST TOO NOBLE

Factsheet Five
Mike Gunderloy, 6 Arizona Ave.
Rensselaer, NY 12144

Every three months, almost seventy pages of reviews much like these—in fact, *including* some of these. Many of the small magazines and books covered in *Factsheet Five* are sci-fi fanzines, punkzines, anarchist newsletters, and dime-a-dozen amateur art and poetry magazines, but if you can hack your way through all that, there are plenty of great new cult and extremist listings to be found. Editor Mike Gunderloy has been faithfully cranking out this useful directory of outcasts for years ... a regular, dependable source for sources. Only problem is, he's too fair and objective. *That's* no way to sell magazines! I had to rewrite some of his listings for use in this book, making them sufficiently spiteful and vindictive to keep your jaded attention. I mention that fact mainly so that listees who hate this book won't blame him for opinions I inserted. He doesn't deserve Hell like I do. $2 each, four/$8.

ENOUGH TO DRIVE YOU...

Off the Deep End
Tim Cridland, PO Box 85874
Seattle, WA 98145-1874

Great semiquarterly collection of WEIRD-NESS, like a short version of this book ... but going into more depth on each abnormal. Tim's own description is best: *"Off the Deep End* is a revolver, with each chamber containing an ignored reality-tunnel bullet. The world continually snipes at you from every rooftop, TV set, magazine and glance from a passing stranger. *Off the Deep End* invites you to ignore the bullets of the status quo, let down your armor, place the revolver to your head and 'blow your mind.' " You can order some of the most famous Hollow-Earth and Mt. Shasta weirdness books from these fine folks, who also carry *The Principia Discordia*, Bible of the Erisians and Discordians, for $7. Sample *Off the Deep End* is $1.50; $2 for back issues or $5 for the next four.

off the deep end

#2 Winter 86/87

"The Spiritual Pilgrim Discovering Another World"

* ARTIFICAL GRAVITY*
HOLLOW EARTH*FREE ENERGY*
SEATTLE WINDSHIELD PITTING*
CENSORSHIP* AND OTHER FEATURES

OUR COMPETITION??

Join the Club
Turnbull & Willoughby
44 E. Superior St.
Chicago, IL 60611

A book by Todd Greenwood that should be out about the same time this one is. *An Eclectic Directory of America's Best Clubs to Belong To.* The author tells me he's concentrating on the funny and facetious clubs— not much of the tasteless kook coverage seen here. Thus, it'll cover much different ground. Dunno the prices; write for info or ask your local store.

NOT FOR THE FAINT-HEARTED

Murder Can Be Fun
Johnny Marr, PO Box 640111
San Francisco, Ca 94109

Published every few months "by Johnny Marr to document his deteriorating mental condition for future generations." Always has a nice page of kook and bizarro listings, followed by more in-depth psychotronics. #5 here has good poop on: Fatty Arbuckle's rape rap; *Strange Deaths in the Bible;* and hints on finding the most lurid old detective novels. Unspeakably hip. Only $1 each, except for the December '87 issue ($2), which is a 1988 calendar. Each date commemorates a famous evil deed or the birth of a psycho bad guy.

ALL??

There's a reference work that covers, supposedly, *all* American publishers ... although I'd be surprised if half the people I'm listing are in it. Most libraries should have it:
American Publishers
K.G. Saur, Inc., 175 Fifth Ave., New York, NY 10010

MURDER Can Be *fun*

Sylvia Likens

Do you really want to hurt me?

#2 ———————— 50¢

TIE ME SASQUATCH DOWN, SPORT

Philosophical Research Foundation
PO Box 570, Parkes. 2870
New South Wales, Australia

Plans to publish a comprehensive listing of all Australian weirdness, *Possibilities,* and another called *Methods of Growth.* Self-described as "...a surrealistic information center, producing directories in a wide number of subjects, specifically in weird religions, political deviations, futurism, etc." They welcome brags and blurbs from all fellow nut-groups. Write for current info.

Illustration: Rebecca Wilson

THE SMART PATROL

Funhouse
Lang Thompson
2111 University Blvd. E., Apt. 33
Tuscaloosa, AL 35404

Much smaller version of *Factsheet Five.* More oriented toward experimental audio, but still covers a lot of kookster ground. He has a pretty good eye for weirdos. You *have* to, living in Alabama. $1 each.

BENEFIT OF A DOUBT

Whole Earth Review
27 Gate Five Rd.
Sausalito, CA 94965

Has it ups and downs, the downside being wishy-washy New Aginess, but *Whole Earth* sometimes leaps into the high gear of usefulness to us Paradigmal Peeping Toms and sicko savants. #52 was a must-have masterpiece of bulldada: guest editor Ted Schultz devoted it entirely to fringe science, kooks, the paranormal, and skeptics. Goes into detail on all the books I wish I could've mentioned here. The *Whole Earth Review*s done in the past under Jay Kinney's editorship were also "chock" full (what the hell does "chock" mean??) of handy extremist news, and to this day it always has at least three or four indispensable maniac listings. Find it at health food stores. Single copies $4.50; $18/year.

By *May* Of 1998 You'll Be Willing To Sell Your KIDS For A Copy

The Stark Fist of Removal
SubGenius Foundation
PO Box 140306
Dallas, TX 75214

The only official newsletter of The Church of the SubGenius. One large section of this highly irregular and altogether *ultimate* journal for Abnormals, *Other Mutants,* is composed of listings like this. In fact, it *is these listings.* (Much of this book was excerpted from *Stark Fist* pages.) The rest of the magazine features indescribable art and text devoted to the Word of "Bob," much of it by people using sacred pseudonyms to protect themselves from The Conspiracy, the rest of it by yours truly. $3.50 per 100-+-page issue. It is beyond argument that *The Stark Fist of Removal* is the greatest and weirdest of all the thousands of publications listed here. What you call "life" is but a pitiful joke without it, a reasonless charade performed by broken puppets, a senseless ruse perpetrated by an insane God. Beware of cheap imitations! There are *plenty.*

No. 39 Vol. 17   Price $2.50

THE OFFICIAL NEWSLETTER OF THE CHURCH OF THE SUBGENIUS

FURTHER CONNECTIONS

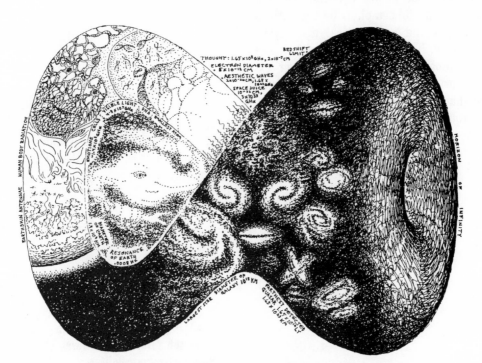

WAVES FOREST

LAST, BUT *NAY*, NOT LEAST!!

Further Connections
Waves Forest, PO Box 768
Monterey, CA 93940

One of the Robin Hoods of suppressed data. Anyone who seriously wants to look into the possibility that major scientific break-throughs ARE being hidden by THEM owe it

to themselves to send for his info, which includes listings and addresses for many fringe
research groups not covered in this book. Not
funny at all . . . horrifying, yes; outlandish-
sounding, HELL yes; but funny, no. Very per-
suasive, sobering, almost poetic essay/rants
with attached bibliographies on the various
technologies and metaphysical discoveries.
Be prepared, however, for some real shocks
to your programming. $4 should cover ex-
penses for the first mailing, which contains
more than 400 sources. A penny a source,
folks. You gonna pass it up? *Huh, boy?*

A *very* compressed and rearranged series
of excerpts from *Further Connections:*

When the map you're following is of some
imaginary land instead of where you really
are, of course you'll be mystified by what you
see around you.

. . .

Examining something from all available
angles yields a far more accurate picture of
it. Monitoring reports from sources with
widely differing outlooks provides a fuller
understanding of reality than adhering to
one type of source.

. . .

Formerly unconnected areas of knowledge are now reacting together with clues
from the forms and patterns of nature to
suggest new possibilities and wiser, gentler
methods of providing for human needs. The
emphasis here is on solutions that work by
moving with the basic forces instead of
struggling against them.

As the remaining connections are made,
the flow of information and energy will increase far beyond the present rate. This new
circuitry will help us to avoid the ecological
disasters widely predicted for the coming
years, and allow us instead to raise the quality and interest of life here higher than it
has ever been.

The mass media have largely succeeded in connecting exotic sciences with the lunatic fringe. While it's true there is considerable overlap, much information that could shed light on current mysteries is thereby neglected. The validity of information does not necessarily depend on the source's credentials; an underground publication might be mistaken eighty percent of the time, yet that remaining fifth turns out to be priceless. Useful knowledge can be found in very unlikely places, while respected news channels are dealing out mostly disinformation from official sources.

. . .

However, the jobs of thousands of government officials depend on no permanent solutions being found for the problems they are paid to work on.

. . .

Consider for a moment the economic upheaval that would result from broadly introducing fuelless crash-proof cars that float on cushion fields. The industries producing gasoline, tires, internal combustion engines, paved roads, and auto insurance policies would all become obsolete. With no more crash victims to patch up, a major source of income for the medical industry would be lost. Millions of workers would have to change jobs. Also, population groups are harder to manipulate when they can freely travel anywhere, and can take more control over their own lives.

. . .

Imagine you are among only a few hundred masters of a whole planet's resources, with five billion slaves surrounding you, many in bad shape because you've mishandled some resources, many others starting to wake up to the situation. In your attempts to strengthen your position you have seriously mistreated a lot of them, or hired others to do so, and you are slowly losing the struggle to keep the extent of your crimes and cruelties a secret.

If you were in such a position, would it feel safe to share with all citizens the advanced technologies developed in your top-secret "defense" labratories? Some of those discoveries could free mankind from dependence on your resource monopolies, and provide tools for a mass uprising and overthrow of your regimes.

. . .

It is important to appreciate the attitude of the "ruling class" toward the main body of mankind. They view themselves as a sort of royalty. They "own" the planet, and have no more reservations about exploiting the rest of humanity than they do about using any other natural resource on their property.

These people have been brought up to believe their special privileges are deserved because they are superior to the rest of us, and in some ways they are. They have shown far greater financial and political cleverness than most humans. To maintain their positions of control, most of them must operate at a much higher energy level than the sluggish masses; they must think and react faster. They have pulled off the most brilliant scams in the planet's history, and fooled nearly all of the people, all of the time.

. . .

When a man does something his fellows would strongly object to, and decides to keep the misdeed a secret, he mentally withdraws somewhat from the others, because now he has to watch himself to make sure he doesn't mention what he did. More misdeeds bring on further withdrawal. The intensity of the misdeeds and the secrecy surrounding them can increase to astonishing proportions.

It has actually reached the point where certain very powerful men, to ensure their personal safety and the perpetuation of their empires, plan to kill off two thirds of the world's population and overtly enslave the rest.

Since most of the general public just somehow don't feel right about genocide, the blatant exterminations of the '30s and '40s have been replaced by artificially induced wars, plagues, accidents, and "natural" disasters.

Earthquakes can be induced artificially by precise placement and timing of nuclear "tests." The shock waves spread out over the globe, then recombine at various harmonic intervals around the sphere to deliver a strong jolt at the desired location within forty-eight hours of the initial blast.

. . .

Under the Reagan administration, biological-warfare research spending increased 500 percent, primarily in the area of genetic engineering of new disease organisms. It is significant that the "discovery" of the AIDS virus was announced by Dr. Robert Gallo at the National Cancer Institute, which is on the grounds of Fort Detrick, Maryland—a primary U.S. Army biological warfare research facility. The AIDS epidemic emerged full-blown in the three U.S. cities with organized gay communities before appearing anywhere else, including Haiti or Africa, where it is supposed to have originated.

The ruling elite have no incentive to stop production of weapons and torture equipment, as long as their agents are allowed to stimulate markets for such things by creating (and funding) supposedly leftist terrorist groups, and overthrowing legitimate third world governments to install fascists

. . .

The governmental checks and balances provided in the U.S. Constitution were completely sidestepped by the formation of the CIA in the executive branch immediately following WWII, and stomped into the ground as more such agencies were added (DIA, DISC, DARPA, FEMA, etc). Few citizens are aware yet that the CIA was created by Nazi General Reinhard Gehlen, Hitler's chief of intelligence against the Russians. Gehlen was brought over to the U.S. right after the war with his entire staff, and given $200 million to continue the job for "our side." At the same time, hundreds of other top Nazis were imported (this was called "Project Paperclip") and given new identities and government positions. They formed the core of the new U.S. intelligence, defense, and aerospace establishments. Why do you suppose every CIA-engineered coup installs a Nazi-like dictatorship that suppresses, tortures, and murders the native populations?

But even though many government lies are exposed, many others have not yet come out. It is a common tactic to confess to small misdeeds to throw investigators off the trail of major crimes. Most people trying to reach the truth would prefer to pause at a safe plateau of group agreement along the way. However, the world situation has reached the point where learning what is really going on is far more important than maintaining confidence in governments, corporations, schools, and established media.

Or perhaps nations of sheep deserve to be fleeced, and then . . . ? Come on! It's time to stop pretending we don't know any better.

. . .

The major media are owned mostly by the same characters who own the energy conglomerates, so they should not be expected to publish alternatives to their monopolies. Citizens who are tired of being misled need to look into the scientific underground's information channels.

The U.S. Patent Office categorically denies patents to any invention that seems to involve "perpetual motion." Actually, the law of conservation of energy is not violated by such devices. They are merely tapping an officially unrecognized source.

· · ·

All through the 1950s, scientific journals carried stories of imminent breakthroughs in the field of gravity control. By the time of the JFK assassination such stories had vanished from the press, with no account ever given of what became of the electrogravitation research.

· · ·

The high-tech-feudalists keep secret as much as they can of this technology, and use a lot of it for their own purposes. They may disagree on many other things, but all share the need to keep their actions unknown to the public.

· · ·

Suppose "Star Wars" technology already existed, funded by appropriations obtained years ago under some other cover project. If a project really is top-secret, how else would funding for it be obtained, than by announcing the money was for something else? The cover project would have to sound believably advanced and expensive, but couldn't be anything still in the R & D stage.

· · ·

Furthermore, it is most unlikely that no contact has occurred between members of some space-going society and some earth government or quasi-government. It is even less likely that news of such a contact would be shared with the citizens under that government. How could political leaders maintain their status as senior authority figures if it were known that there are others far more intelligent and capable that citizens might turn to instead? The "king of the playground" loses his status and reverts to being just another child when the teachers show up.

Space is big, and hard to police. There is at least as much political, cultural, and moral diversity among space-going civilizations as there is on Earth. We do have more ethnic variety here than on many other planets with fairly homogeneous populations; as has often been pointed out, Earth is a sort of dumping ground for souls from many other locations, who are too brilliant, stupid, creative, domineering, imaginative, or criminal to fit into other societies without their noncomformity being disruptive.

Awareness is growing that one's own survival depends on that of the entire earth. Soon it will be broadly recognized that our well-being depends on the well-being of all life.

. . .

A rarely considered option is to simply forgive the ruling elite. Strike an agreement granting them complete amnesty, in exchange for a total end to the incarceration and abuse of all political prisoners, full disclosure of all information that has been concealed, and the diversion of the bulk of their fortunes into projects designed to improve conditions for all mankind, using all available technology. It might be worth it to them, not having to constantly be on guard against their victimized public, and each other. People do enjoy life more when they don't have to lie and worry about getting caught all the time.

Just acknowledge that they won the game they've been playing, where the goal was to concentrate control of the planet into as few hands as possible, by any means available. They got us, they proved they could pull it off and get away with it, so let's congratulate the winners like good sports and start a new game with a more interesting goal we can all get into, like making Earth a paradise for everybody.

—Waves Forest

SO LONG, SEEKERS!!

From here on out, friends, you're on your own . . . and who knows WHAT will be watching you, once some of these people start sending you mail, and counting you as one of their own? . . . Heh heh heh . . . EH-EH-EH . . . .

ABOUT THE AUTHOR

Rev. Ivan Stang is most infamous for his work in promoting The Church of the SubGenius.™ Functioning as Sacred Scribe Under "Bob" for that deservedly feared mind-control cult, he has produced *The Book of the SubGenius,* several issues of *The Stark Fist of Removal* magazine, almost two hundred radio programs, fifty nightclub "revivals," an award-winning feature-length SubGenius video, and a slew of pamphlets—all since 1980. He has also been a successful film editor, producer, and animator, whose credits include music videos for DEVO, the feature documentary *China Run,* countless commercials and industrials, and a series of PBS specials about Sioux art forms. His risque but darkly satirical films *Reproduction Cycle* and *The World of the Future* have been banned from television in dozens of countries, and even in the United States there is a law prohibiting mention of The Church of the SubGenius™ in any national television program or major news magazine. His nonfiction articles, however, have appeared in numerous major entertainment publications.

Stang is currently editing the next SubGenius tome, *Three Fisted Tales of "Bob"* (Fireside/Simon & Schuster—a collection of short stories by many top-ranking bizarro and cyberpunk authors), and producing his weekly radio show, *The Hour of Slack,* heard on KNON in Dallas and on several independent stations around the U.S. He still resides in Dallas, which, he claims, "has required the utmost patience, tenacity, and fighting skill." The neighborhood in which he lives boasts the highest incidence of violent crime in America.

More information on The Church of the SubGenius or Stang's forbidden film work is available from PO Box 140306, Dallas, TX 75214.